D1290064

VIRTUE

U ★ N ★ D ★ E ★ R

FIRE

Other Books by John Costello

★   ★   ★

The Battle for Concorde (with Terry Hughes, 1971)

D Day (with Warren Tate and Terry Hughes, 1974)

The Concorde Conspiracy (with Terry Hughes, 1976)

Jutland 1916 (with Terry Hughes, 1976)

The Battle of the Atlantic (with Terry Hughes, 1971)

The Pacific War (1981)

*"And I Was There": Pearl Harbor and Midway —
Breaking the Secrets (with Admiral Edwin T. Layton
and Captain Roger Pireau, 1985)*

JOHN COSTELLO

VIRTUE
U ★ N ★ D ★ E ★ R
FIRE

How World War II Changed Our
Social and Sexual Attitudes

Little, Brown and Company
BOSTON TORONTO

FIRST EDITION

*Permission to reprint copyright matrial is gratefully ac-
knowledged as follows:*

*Jocelyn Brooke, "A Soldier's Song," the estate of Jocelyn
Brooke.*

*Charles Causley, from "A Ballad for Katherine of Ara-
gon," The Woburn Press, London.*

*Extract from "Jane," Mirror Group Newspapers Ltd.,
London.*

*John Hammond Moore, "Over-sexed, Over-paid and Over
Here," University of Queensland Press.*

Alun Lewis, "All Day It Rained," from Raiders Dawn,
Allen & Unwin, London.

*"White Cliffs of Dover and "Lilli Marlene," EMI Mu-
sic Publishing Ltd, London.*

"Rosie the Riveter," Famous Chappell.

Photographs courtesy of the Office of War Information, the Women's Bureau, and from the pho-
tographic holdings of the National Archives,
Washington, D.C.

Library of Congress Cataloging-in-Publication Data

Costello, John.
  Virtue under fire.

  Bibliography: p.
    1. World War, 1939–1945 — Influence. 2. Sex (Psy-
chology) — History — 20th century. 3. Sexual ethics —
History — 20th century. I. Title.
  D810.S46C67 1985   306.7'09'044   85-16007
  ISBN 0-316-73968-5

DESIGNED BY JEANNE F. ABBOUD

*Published simultaneously in Canada
by Little, Brown & Company (Canada) Limited*

PRINTED IN THE UNITED STATES OF AMERICA

Contents

Acknowledgments

Why write a sexual history of World War II? The genesis of this project is rooted in a "war baby's" curiosity that his mother had "done her bit" with hoe and milk pail in the Land Army, while his father fought with the Royal Navy.

It was an idea that grew out of many personal interviews during a decade of writing about World War II. During the filming of a D-Day anniversary documentary, there were the French-women who still cherished romantic memories of their Allied liberators; veterans told of their amorous adventures; and there was the discovery from official documents of the contribution penicillin made to the success of the 1944 invasion. It was, however, while assembling material for *The Battle of the Atlantic* that official data and pictures graphically brought home the staggering contribution that the women of the United States and Britain made to the Allied victory.

The hundreds of former "Rosy the Riveters" who responded to a *New York Post* item on the Battle of the Atlantic book confirmed my belief that full story of the sexual impact of the war had yet to be told. As I discovered in my interview with one "Rosy" — Mrs. Anne D. Brown — her colorful recollections of wartime in the Brooklyn Navy Yard included personal romantic episodes.

It was Ken Nichols, whose own imminent arrival into the world retired his mother from wartime duty as a navy nurse, who crystallized the project. Now a senior official with the U.S. Commerce Department, he proposed that I write the "sexual history of the war" in the course of a Washington dinner party discussion about my research into the records of the wartime investigations of the morality of the women's military services. The idea appealed immediately to my agent, John Hawkins, and the proposal was submitted to my current publisher, then preparing *The Pacific War* for publication.

James Wade's enthusiasm for the subject was not shared by his publishing house, but the "war baby" he fathered was soon enthusiastically adopted by Little, Brown and Company. To Chris Coffin in Boston — as well as to Sonny Mehta and Simon Masters at Pan Books in London — I owe an enormous debt of gratitude for their confidence and support of what turned into an extended and complex project. From its infancy, the book emerged through disorderly adolescence into coherent maturity, during which their help was unstinting. A special contribution had been made by Teresa Sacco, whose own youthful wartime memories brought a unique addition to the final manuscript. To Tess and Chris, as well as Carol O'Brien at Collins, I am enormously grateful for the skilled editorial management that has brought the project to the printed page.

Virtue Under Fire would not have been possible without all the personal wartime accounts to which I have had access. So my principal acknowledgment is to all those men and women whose published and unpublished accounts are the documentary backbone of this book. Particular thanks are due to all the listed people who corresponded as a result of the cooperation of radio and television stations, newspapers, and magazines who broadcast my appeal on both sides of the Atlantic.

Grateful acknowledgment is made to the following for their response: "A Grandma"; Robert L. Abel; Dolly Ackerman; Jimmy Adams; R. Adams; W. Adams; Joy Adland; Agnes Allen; Jesse Allman; Eugene Anderson; Earl L. Archer Jr.; E. M. P. Arnold; V. Bannell; J. E. Barrington; H. U. Bell; Sarah Bell; Barbara

Bennet; J. Beverley-Smith; Joseph E. Biernacki; Gewn Bingham; Doris Bish; O. M. Blewitt; Ethel Botting; James A. Boyd; Elizabeth Bradbury; Betty M. Bryan; J. W. Bryant; Frederick T. Budde; C. A. Burke; Dorothy Callaghan; Philip Candiliere; R. Carpenter; James F. Champ; Knowlton A. Chandler; E. H. Churchill; Frank Clear; P. Climie; J. Collins; Evelyn Colyer; Wyn Costello; Patrick E. Creamer; E. T. Crees; D. M. Crompton; Carmine Cusmano; I. M. Cuthbert; Susan P. Daddo-Longlois; E. Davies; Ruby Davis; Lillian Davitt; Edward J. De Havilland; G. L. Dean; R. W. Dobie; Daphne Dodey; I. Dunn; Lucy M. Elliot; Jeremiah F. Enright; Alta M. Evans; Ruth Farnham; Richard L. Felman; A. Finch; Hilda Forrest; Zena Forster; Alden Francis; Terry Frier; John D. Fulgenzi; John O. Gallup; Arthur R. Gill; Hugh J. Greecham; E. C. Green; Myra Constance Griffin; V. Guzenda; S. Gwillim; Melvin E. Hawkes; Eileen Hayward; Joseph E. Hecht; Vicky Henton; Molly Higgs; Jean Howard; B. A. Humphrey; Stella Jarvis; Eileen Jones; Patricia Jordan; J. B. Keene; Jean M. Keitch; Helen Kerr-Green; V. E. King; Malcolm D. Kunes; M. Lauer; Joseph L. LeBlanc; Effie C. Lettle; Ben Levinson; Grace S. Love; W. Ludwig; M. McBride; Jean McCallan; Philip M. McGhee; William G. McGuire; A. A. McInnes; Norma Mann; Jean Marston; J. S. Martin; Laurence N. Mason; M. Mason; Jean Mason; M. A. Mason; E. Miles; Marietta L. Moellar; John D. Montgomery; L. Montgomery; Arthur Moore; Olive Morgan; Phyllis Moss; Geoffrey W. G. Munnery; Olive New; R. Oxley; Kathleen Parker; Anna Parkhurst; U. L. Patterson; J. Peek; Joyce Peters; B. Phillips; Christine Pitman; Harry Pozner; Barbara Prutton; Carlos Radcliffe; N. K. Radford; J. W. Ramsay; G. Reid; G. M. Reilly; Sir Frank Richardson; Irene Ritter; Beryl J. Robertson; Dennis A. Roland; Patience Saunders; D. Scharf; Lynn Scott-Southall; Donald Seebold; Michael Senko; Patricia A. Sexton; W. Shephard; Allan J. Simpson; M. Smalley; Babs Smith; Gerald F. Smith; I. F. Smith; Joyce Smith; Ruth King Spark; S. R. Sparks; Trixie B. Sparrow; D. Spencer; Ivy Stanier; Barbara S. Staton; D. Stephens; William Steward; Bernice Stoddard; Daureen H. Stover; O. G. Sutterly; Henry Swyers; Jean Tabor; Eve Taylor; Sherrie Thompson; Wilfred J. Toczko; Joan Tole; J. G. R. Trasker; Walter W. Tripp; R. C. Tynes; Thomas R. Upshaw; Anne Valery; M. V.V.; Nelson E. Walker; C. B. Ward;

L. Watson; M. E. Watts; E. D. White; M. Whyte; Phyllis D. Williams; Joan Williams; Thomas Henry Wood; Ruth F. Wright; Agnes Young.

In the United States I have been able to tap the extensive collections of books, magazines, and wartime memorabilia in the New York Public, the Library of Congress in Washington, and Columbia University Library. Without the friendly and efficient assistance of their staffs, this book would not have been possible. I am also grateful to the Public Records Office, Imperial War Museum, as well as the Cambridge University and British Libraries for the research facilities they provided.

Much of the original research in this work — as in my previous books — has been facilitated by the knowledgeable encouragement of the staff of the National Archives in Washington. Especial mention must be made of John Taylor and Edward Reese, who, along with Wilbert Mahoney, Terri Hammett, and William H. Lewis, make research in the Modern Military Section such a rewarding adventure. My thanks are also extended to Jerry Hess and Dr. Virginia Purdy for guiding me through the voluminous wartime files of the Labor Bureau, War Manpower Administration, and the Women's Bureau. Richard von Doerhnof and George Chaloux were instrumental in turning up fascinating documentation, and Jim Trimble provided expert assistance in locating photographs.

Over the four years that it has taken to research and assemble the material in this book, I have received logistical assistance, wise advice, and professional help from old friends and many new acquaintances who have all been unstinting in their support. Acknowledgment must be made, therefore, to the contributions made by: John Alston, Ed Anderson, Anthony Batten, Linda Aness, Betty Blackman, John Boileau, Larry Collins, Susan Costello, Irena Czaposa, Professor Christie Davies, Jonathan Copus, Robert Crowley, Captain Thomas Dyer, Admiral Sir Morgan Giles, Jim Gough, Dagmar Henne, Cherry Hughes, Terry Hughes, David Ireland, Gerald P. Jantzi, David Kagan, Professor Warren Kimball, Harald Ketzer, Admiral Edwin T. Layton, Gary Lazarus, Bruce Lee, Charles Lowdness, Jill Lowry, Jimmy Mack, Jim MacDougal, Barry Meanwell, Vic Meyers, Rob Michaels, John D. Montgomery, Diane Newman, Milo O'Sullivan, Mary Pett, Captain and Mrs. Roger Pineau, Colonel Harry Pozner, Harry Chapman Pincher, Murry Pollinger, Lawrence Pratt, General Sir Frank Richardson, Peter Rhodes, Karen Ross, David Rowley, Dr. A. L. Rowse, Gregory Saunders, Captain Raymond Schmidt, Robert L. Sherrod, Graham Sergeant, Professor Norman Stone, Chauncey W. Smith, Linda Wade, Tom Wallace, Nigel West, Robin Wight, Robert Wolf, Robert L. Young, and Hans Zellweger.

Alan Berube, who has spent many years interviewing and documenting the wartime homosexual experience, was most generous with advice and accounts. Orlando Figes, Brendan Lemon, and Andrew Lownie contributed valuable material and criticism during their spells as research assistants. My thanks are due once more to Diane and John Moore for their efficient collection of illustrations. To my trusty Morrow computer and its "Senior Partner" go all the customary accolades for typing and manuscript preparation made possible by the "magic" of Wordstar.

Last, but in no way least, I owe a considerable debt of gratitude to Anna Del Valle and William C. Bodie for their personal banking expertise which has underpinned the whole project.

John Costello
New York and London
December 1985

Introduction

> The mutual relations between the two sexes seems to us to be at least as important as the mutual relations of any two governments in the world.
>
> — THOMAS BABINGTON MACAULAY, HISTORIAN AND BRITISH SECRETARY OF STATE FOR WAR, 1840

I n books, films, documents, and especially in memory, World War II was the pivotal emotional experience in the lives of the men and women who lived and fought through the greatest conflict in human history. Individual testimony indicates that the answer to "What" people were fighting for had less to do with abstract notions of freedom or patriotism than with individual emotional values represented by sweethearts, wives, and families. Sex and sexuality in all its guises and complexities played an extensive role in the war experience. Whether it was pinups of Hollywood stars, well-thumbed pictures of "the girl back home," "Rosy the Riveter" or female pilots, war acquired an undeniable feminine aspect.

Virtue under Fire is an examination of the sexual aspect of World War II. In putting the experience in a social perspective, it does not set out to tackle the larger issue of why men and women did what they did, or how the social and psychological forces released by war worked dramatic historical changes. Forty years later the mechanism of these processes are still being hotly debated by academic historians and social scientists. This is, however, the first effort to document the sexual impact of mass warfare on twentieth-century American and British society. It is intended therefore as a set of signposts, rather than a roadmap, to the complex social topography that is the collective and often anomalous war-time experience of sex.

Inevitably because any discussion of sex involves moral issues, it is surrounded with social and religious taboos, which, by their nature, are controversial. Any account of the sexual aspect World War II is complicated by the conflict of conviction, the confusions of personal memory, and the imprecision of psychological interpretation. What the war did to individuals was arguably both beneficial as well as injurious to the social fabric, because it enhanced intimacy and the expression of love that liberated many people from traditional inhibitions. It is also possible to establish, from the broad cross section of documented record and individual recollection, that the war did make a very significant contribution to the economic liberation of women and the sexual liberation of both men and women. Even if this liberation was "for the duration only," the impact of "total war" on people's lives proved to be so pervasive that it became a powerful accelerator of the process of social change.

The trend toward liberalization of the moral attitudes and the coincident "liberation" of the female population was certainly speeded up by World War II. While this global conflict did not set the process in motion, the relaxation of moral restraints endemic in war has influenced sexual relationships and the relations between the sexes throughout human history. Apart from the impact on the Trojan War of the legendary Helen, it was the Carthaginian War that brought the first recorded success for women's liberation when the Roman Senate in 215 B.C. repealed the discriminatory Oppian tax law. This despite Cato the Elder's thunderous warning that "what women want is complete freedom — or, to put it bluntly, complete license."

The Hundred Years War in the fifteenth century saw Joan of Arc challenge the patriarchal authority of the Church when she led the French troops to victory over an English army at Orléans. She was condemned for daring to dress as a man "in violation of canon law, abominable to God and man." Four centuries later women were increasingly drawn into the active prosecution of wars after the Union recruited them to take over the clerical and factory jobs of the male conscripts in the American Civil War. World War I mobilized industrial and human resources on such a scale that Winston Churchill was moved to write: "All the horrors of the ages were brought together, and not only armies, but whole populations were thrust into the midst of them."

The sexual undercurrents stirred by World War I inspired Sigmund Freud to write his 1917 analysis of "Reflections on War and Death." He saw that the connection between violence and eroticism was evident in the collective tendency of a society in wartime is to throw off the repressions that civilization has imposed on the human sex drive. Wartime mobilization and regimentation replace the individual ego-ideal with the military bond and disciplined leadership necessary to carry out organized slaughter. Existing taboos were not cast aside completely, but in a society at war the mechanism of sexual suppression operates at a lower level. According to Freud the atavistic horde instinct essential to mass killing inevitably inflames the sex drive because the urge to kill and the urge to procreate are both subconsciously related as the extremes of the human experience.

"War aphrodisia," as it has been called, had been traditionally ascribed to men in battle. In "total war," however, a related hedonistic impulse reaches many other segments of society. The forces liberated by this process in World War I accelerated the process of social change by redefining the relationship between the sexes. Limited mobilization of the female population increased the opportunity for large numbers of women to find employment outside the home. Many who had been brought up in the Victorian tradition to look to a man as their supporter, breadwinner, and head of the family became "emancipated" when their men were conscripted for military service. The demands of the prewar suffragettes, ironically, became the patriotic duty of the female population in wartime as women donned military uniforms for the first time, and in larger numbers than ever before went out to work.

War service brought dramatic improvements in women's social and economic status and many were encouraged to expect equality in other areas as well. Enfranchisement was no longer the controversial political issue after the war that it had been in 1914. The female population in most Western countries, except France, received the right to vote. Women celebrated their new freedom after World War I with liberated fashions and liberal behavior.

They bobbed their hair, donned short skirts, smoked in public, and wore the heavy makeup that had formerly been the attribute of a harlot. The change in the postwar moral climate was evident not only in the sexually provocative fashions, but also in the hedonism encouraged by the optimistic economic climate of the twenties.

Nowhere was the new liberation more visible than in the United States, where a buoyant stock market, bootleg gin, and the racy novels of Scott Fitzgerald fueled the frenetic pace of a Jazz Age decadence. The emerging American movie industry packaged eroticism for the mass audience. It promoted the sex appeal of stars like Clara Bow, or the sultry masculinity of Rudolph Valentino; films such as *Alimony* promised "brilliant men, beautiful jazz babies, champagne baths, midnight revels, petting parties in the purple dawn, all ending in one terrifying climax that makes you gasp."

Across the Atlantic, Hollywood films had also rewritten the romantic dictionary, but Britain's postwar prosperity lasted only long enough to effect a mild moral thaw before the rigors of Depression restored some of the frigidity of the Victorian social climate. But some social changes could not be reversed. Government issue of contraceptives to protect troops from the wartime venereal disease epidemic had fostered a wider social acceptance of birth-control methods, although "mechanical devices" continued to be condemned by the Church as a sinful interference with God's command to procreate and as a wicked incentive to promiscuity.

Legislative reform had made family planning available. It was to become an economic necessity to many American and British couples during the Depression but did not extend to making available to the general public books that dealt with sex in plain language. Although James Joyce's literary masterpiece was banned in Britain, an enlightened New York judge had refused to proscribe publication of *Ulysses* in the United States, holding that obscenity must be tested by "its effect on a person with average sex instincts."

Just what constituted "average sexual instincts" remained a matter of private, rather than public, debate. "Sex" was still a word that most people preferred to avoid. On neither side of the Atlantic was sex education considered a suitable subject to be taught in school. The Depression also ensured that the thirties were a decade of moral, as well as economic, retrenchment. Divorce rates had plunged with collapse of the stock market. Significantly they reached a postwar low — 40 percent below the 1928 peak — in 1933, the year that the dole lines were longest. Weddings also fell as hard times caused many couples to put off marriage.

"Sex is one of the things Middletown has long been taught to fear," noted the authors of the classic social survey of Muncie, Indiana. Its citizens wanted to "keep the subject out of sight and out of mind as much as possible." The town newspaper advised that a "girl should never kiss a boy unless they are engaged," and the local librarian, when asked for books on sex education, snapped, "Not here!" The same attitude prevailed in Britain, where it was still not considered respectable for women to go to pubs unescorted and "halter-neck" bathing dresses were regarded as immodest by many church-going people. Prudery was still considered a public virtue, as the Ministry of Health learned when the British newspaper proprietors in 1937 refused to publish a series of advertisements that warned the public about the dangers of venereal disease.

Teenage girls might dream of a career outside the home, but only one in five single women in America and one in eight in Britain were in paid employment. The very idea of married women working out of choice, rather than necessity, was fiercely resisted by employers and frowned on by society. Those women who were at work were usually single, subject to discriminatory pay, and restricted in their choice of job by an unofficial code that determined what was suitable "woman's work."

The mobilization of the female population in the United States and Britain to fight a "total war" shattered resistance to the employment of married women and the old notions of "woman's work." Wartime enables the female population to gain rights that they would not be able to claim in peacetime, because "when the man is away the woman must play at being a man."

"Women's great progressive strides, though we wish it were otherwise, are invariably made in times of war," declared the chairman of America's Women's Bureau. "This is not so strange as it may first seem, because war is a teacher — stern and exciting."

The mobilization, disruption, and excitement of so many lives was not only a catalyst of social change, but it also sowed the seeds of a far-reaching shift in private and public sexual attitudes. "Moral taboos had not been banished, but their pride of place was gone," observed a former World War II soldier in the sixties. "The sex code by which this later generation lived was a permissive one, allowing chastity or promiscuity, frowning only on prudery and prurience."

To a far greater extent than World War I, the century's second global conflict was to prove the truth of the assertion made by A. L. Rowse, the Oxford historian: "There is a wide ranging association of war with sexuality, complex, intricate, intimate and at every level."

★ 〔1〕 ★

Making Love and War

> *O war is a casual mistress*
> *And the world is her double bed.*
> *She has few charms in her mechanised arms*
> *But you wake up and find yourself dead.*
>
> — CHARLES CAUSLEY, ROYAL NAVY

> We followed the fortunes of our menfolk across desert, the
> seas and the skies. As the war progressed we did not doubt
> that they would return. Bereavement was something that had
> to be accepted with a stiff upper lip.
>
> —BRITISH WAR BRIDE

"We were not really immoral, there was a war on," was how one British housewife explained her behavior during World War II. So pervasive was this attitude that it seemed sexual restraint had been suspended for the duration as the traditional license of the battlefield invaded the home front. "By most people's standards we were immoral," admitted an American soldier, "but we were young and could die tomorrow."

The urgency and excitement of wartime soon eroded moral restraints. Soldiers had always claimed the fear of death on the battlefield as an excuse for sexual license. "In a war one has to love, if only to re-assert that he's very much alive in the face of destruction," explained an American army sergeant. "Whoever has loved in wartime takes part in a passionate re-affirmation of his life."

The mass bombing raids on cities made life on many home fronts also appear as cheap and short as the front line. In Britain during the 1941 Blitz, sixty thousand civilians perished, a casualty level that far exceeded the combined armed force's total during the same period.

"It is difficult to write about relationships which occurred during that awful period without giving the impression that we were having it easy," explained a then newly married English woman from Birmingham. "Personal relationships were formed between men and women out of sheer loneliness and the need to be loved. I lived a mile away from the heavily bombed city of Newcastle, so I think you can say I was in the front line."

The population of the United States, while spared the terrible physical destruction of bombing, was nonetheless affected by a mobilization which generated the same hedonistic excitement in the population. Many war-brides were rushed into marriage by soldiers desperate for emotional security before they were posted overseas. This was evident from the attitude of one American girl who was talked into matrimony by her flyer boyfriend:

I don't love him. I've told him I don't love him. But he's an aviator and says I should marry him anyhow and give him a little happiness. He says he knows he'll be dead in a year, he hasn't any real chance of living through the war. But if he should still be alive when the war is over, and I still feel the same way, he says I can divorce him and it will be all right.

Not that everyone rushed into marriage. "There was never a shortage of young, healthy bucks," recalled an Illinois girl who admitted "having a ball" in Chicago. "We weren't as casual about sex as people are now. You held your breath and prayed. It was tough when you didn't want to get pregnant. . . . There wasn't anything foolproof except abstinence, and who needed that? I'd already tried that and didn't think much of it."

Separation, temporary or permanent, was a powerful incentive for many wartime love affairs. "It was here today and gone tomorrow, so I did not build up any longstanding relationships," recalled a woman who dated RAF fighter pilots. "The war encouraged flirtations, although not all were 'dirty weekends' because we girls were well aware of the stigma that went with pregnancy and being an unmarried mother."

Inevitably, chastity became an early casualty of war, as lovers were forced to abandon the traditional drawn-out period of courtship. The "weekend affair" snatched on a forty-eight-hour leave pass often substituted for a "honeymoon," which preceded many wartime weddings. But a formal ceremony, with as many trimmings as ration books permitted, was still regarded as de rigueur for solemnizing matrimony. Novelist Barbara Cartland recalled brightening many a WAAF bride's special day with wedding gowns borrowed from her many society friends:

Theirs was a quick rush wedding of wartime, the snatched honeymoon of sometimes only forty-eight hours, a happiness overshadowed by the inevitable separation from their husbands, a problematical future, with always the fear that they would be a widow almost before they were a wife. Yet they had their happiness; however quick, however fleeting, it was theirs. They were loved and beloved, and by this stage in the war love was about the only thing left unrationed.

The course of love during World War II seldom ran smoothly, even for those couples who accepted transient emotional relationships. The passion of affairs in wartime was heightened by the need to make the most of every hour and the sadness of frequent partings was intensified by the uncertainty of whether either partner would survive to meet again. Relationships were broken as fast as others began, for wartime excitement and boredom encouraged companionship. The war was a time of brutal savagery and infinite sympathy that matched peerless heroism with wrenching sadness. Amidst the upheaval that uprooted so many lives, loneliness was the universal wartime epidemic. Its cure for many was discovered in a changing approach to social — and sexual — relations as they adapted to a more dangerous, rigorous, and unorthodox lifestyle.

In the conflagration couples discovered a new intimacy in shared peril and passion. Love seemed to blossom with fresh vigor as men and women everywhere turned to each other for affirmation of life amid so much death and destruction. A young Polish sculpturess wrote of her ecstasy at finding herself in love with a Resistance fighter who was killed in the 1944 Warsaw uprising:

Life has suddenly taken on a special meaning. Has the world changed, or is it that I have changed? . . . How frightfully selfish we are. This sudden wave of personal happiness has managed to separate us completely from all the atrocities of the times in which we live.

Romantic liaisons were made and broken with a speed and improvisation characteristic of most wartime activities. "My war memories are some of horror, but also of an immense amount of good times," remembered one London girl: "It really was the happiest time of my life. People were friendly and we were all in it together."

The violence of total war subjected whole civilian populations to the extremes of violence and disruption. That this stimulated the urge to love and be loved, leading to a rapid increase in sexual activity, is evident in the sharp increase in wartime venereal disease and illegitimate birthrates. With the rise in juvenile sexual delinquency, the statistical barometer indicates the extent to which men, women, and adolescents were eventually to turn to sex as one of the few wartime pleasures available to all.

"The most wonderful days of my life," recalled a British woman. "Those days were dreams, every day exciting whether it was good or bad excitements," remembered another. "Despite the danger and the suffering, the war days were exciting days in many ways," was how one wartime housewife put it. "I had some wonderful, memorable and sometimes sad times, but I would not have missed my experiences during the war."

The rush and contrast of wartime emotions ignited many a romantic flame, but the frequent dislocations of people's lives often made it difficult to keep it burning. Jean Taber's was a typical wartime romance. It began in an Aldershot public house in the summer of 1942:

Carl was serving with the Canadian Army and I was seventeen and in the ATS [Auxilliary Territorial Service]. We spent the next two years meeting each other whenever we could get a pass because we were always being posted to different camps. We knew after a few months that we wanted to get married but had to wait for his application to be processed by the Canadian authorities. It came through just before D-Day. A wedding was out of the question then as I had not told my parents because I was afraid they would not want me to go and live in Canada. We managed to get a pass to see each other, and as military personnel were not supposed then to travel more than fifteen miles from their camps, I wore civilian clothes. It was the first time Carl had seen me in a dress. When we parted I knew that he was going into hell. I never thought I would see him again. I assumed the worst when I did not hear from him in France.

It was not until Christmas 1944 that I learnt he was still alive. The news came in letters from people who had heard Lord Haw Haw's German radio broadcasts when he read a message addressed to me which said: "I am a prisoner of war in Germany. Let all my folks know — all my love. I love you. Carl. 'You'll never know.' " I knew it really was my Canadian soldier because that was our "special" song. It was the best Christmas present I ever had. But it was not until the following May that I saw Carl again. I hardly recognized him. He was thin and ill and his teeth had been knocked out by a guard at his Stalag VIII B prison camp. But we decided that nothing was going to stop us marrying this time. We both went Absent Without Leave and arrived at my parents home at 11 A.M. on 4th June 1945. Carl was a complete stranger to my parents and they were shocked when we said we were getting married. We had five shillings between us, but we got a special licence at 1:30 P.M., and the local vicar promised to marry us the same afternoon.

I felt very lovely at the time, but now I realize I couldn't have done in my ATS uniform, with my hair tied up with a shoelace. We had no civilian clothes so it was a khaki wedding with carrot-tops and pinks from the garden as button-holes. We invited people from the local pub to a reception in the bar which consisted of spam sandwiches and a wedding cake "borrowed" from my nephew whose first birthday it happened to be that day.

My wedding very nearly didn't happen at all. As I was going out of the door to the church, two military policemen arrived to take us back to camp. But after we gave our word, they joined the party and allowed us to spend a few hours alone together that evening. Our "wedding night" was a disaster because of Carl's health — and a week later he was taken in handcuffs aboard the *Queen Mary* to return home. It was almost a year before we could get together again in Halifax, Nova Scotia, when I became Mrs. Taber for real!

Many wartime love affairs caused or were the result of emotionally shattering experiences. Martha was seventeen when her Viennese mother managed to get her on the last trainload of Jewish refugee children to reach England before war broke out in 1939:

My standards of morality went to the seven winds and I felt very dejected when I finally realized that my mother had been deported to the camps and I would probably never see her again. This prompted my search for love and affection. I had affairs, including a very serious one in 1943 with a Yugoslavian naval officer which left me expecting his baby. There was never any question of my marrying him since he was so much older. I was twenty-one and he was forty-nine, but he was a fantastically handsome man who looked just like my father. It was my great wartime romance. In the end I did not have the baby adopted and at the end of the war married a former German prisoner of war. It was a strange choice for a Jewish refugee girl, but he was one of the kindest people I met and not a Nazi, but a soldier who was only doing his duty and who did not want to be repatriated. Although he willingly adopted my son as his own, it was one of those things that happened in war. I suppose I never should have married him and it eventually broke up.

The emotional turbulence of war left a lasting impact on many marriages. In the past, wives had waved their husbands off to war on the assumption that strict fidelity on the part of men was incompatible with soldiering, but such was total war that even on the home front many wives were also confronted by new choices and opportunities. One English woman who confessed she had "enjoyed herself" conceded that the old dual standard of feminine fidelity was no longer acceptable to wives in World War II:

There was plenty of "sleeping around." In the services it was an accepted fact of war, although there were many innocent attachments with no sex involved. Even the most loving of husbands had, at the very least, friendships with other girls when they were away from their wives. Some marriages came to grief in such circumstances, but plenty survived, probably because the husband sensibly didn't tell his wife — and the wife may well have not realized.

"Personal relationships were formed between young men and women out of sheer loneliness and the need to be loved," as one British wife recalled of her own wartime affair. As a twenty-four-year-old mother of an eighteen-month-old child, "sheer terror" overtook her life after her husband had been called up into the RAF and she was left to face the bombing raids on Manchester. One night she had heard a German parachute landmine sweep over her roof and demolish nine houses in the next road as she huddled with her baby under the staircase. Like many British wives who fell in love with a yank, Mary is convinced that her wartime affair resulted from a brush with death:

We lived in a world of uncertainty, wondering if we were going to survive from day to day. My husband was away in the RAF as an air gunner and I'd conditioned myself to the fact that his lifespan was also limited and that our short, happy married life together was over. I lived in a vacuum of loneliness and fright as service in the army, navy and air force claimed five of our personal friends whom I mourned as if they were my own family. When 1942 came in with the hit-and-run air raids, I began to despair that the war was ever going to end. It was in this frame of mind that fate took a hand in my affairs.

The Yanks arrived and set up camps near Manchester bringing a wave of glamour, romance, and excitement that has never been experienced before or since. They were not welcomed by the British men, but to English girls they were wonderful. All I knew about Americans was what I'd seen on the films, but Fields Hotel, within walking distance from my home, became the meeting place where GIs danced under soft lights. Eating in secluded corners with their girlfriends, the GIs were able to forget the war for a few hours. There I was introduced to an American army captain. He was tall, with blond hair and blue eyes. I thought at the time what a marvelous German officer he would make on the films. I felt rather embarrassed at his flattering remarks about my long hair and attractive appearance. I felt even more embarrassed when we danced the American way, cheek-to-cheek. Outside in the blackout, Rick took my hand, clicked his heels together, and bowed to me, saying how much he'd enjoyed my company, then he walked down the path towards the waiting jeep. If I was expecting a goodnight kiss, I was surprised and a little disappointed. "And they say the English are a cold race," I thought and I didn't think I would see Rick again.

One weekend, as I prepared myself for another lonely sit-in, an unexpected phone call from Rick made my heart jump with pleasure. He came around about dusk in a jeep carrying a hold-all and bounced it on the kitchen table. "There," he said, "take a peek." It was full of tinned goods, butter, sugar, sweets, coffee, sheer nylons and makeup — not forgetting cartons of cigarettes. He had also thoughtfully brought two bucketfuls of coal.

So began another part of my life on the home front — I shared my extra food with my neighbors and friends. If they wondered where it all came from, they tactfully never asked. It took a couple of weeks before Rick got around to kissing me goodnight. He asked me a lot of questions about my husband and married life, which I had to admit was a very happy one. I did, however, write and tell my husband about Rick. He was delighted that I'd found someone to give me a break and that my captain seemed a really decent chap.

So with my mind free of guilt, I began to come alive again. It would be foolish of me to say that physical attraction never entered out lives; it did. For Rick, I knew it was love, but for me it was attraction and the need to hold on to someone. So it happened that we finally made love.

There was nothing cheap about our affair, and if Rick had my body, my heart was with my husband and somehow I didn't feel that I was doing anything wrong. Rick, a single man, had fallen in love with a happily married woman, but he knew it was hopeless as far as I was concerned. I loved my husband too much to consider leaving him. Yet he and I were together for two years during the final stages of the war until the evening when he was silent and withdrawn after he received orders to leave for Rome.

We said our good-byes at the garden gate on 31 May 1945. As I looked at Rick's sad face, I asked myself whether the good times were over because I had fallen in love and lost him. One last kiss and he was gone. Then my husband returned home and we tried to resume our old way of life.

This particular couple succeeded, where many marriages failed, in making a frank reconciliation of wartime infidelities. With her husband's blessing, she made a postwar visit to America, but when Rick embraced her on the New York dockside before she sailed for home she suddenly knew that her great affair was over. "How does one say good-bye to one so dear? Emotions shrink to a pinpoint and the impact hits you a few days later," she remembered. "I think we both knew that this was the final good-bye. As the *Queen Mary* moved off into the darkness, I stood on deck for what seemed like hours as New York disappeared from view. My war romance had reached its finale."

"It's very easy for some women to say 'I didn't let the war destroy my marriage,' " was the reaction of a war-bride. "I tried not to let it destroy mine, but it takes two to make a marriage and if a man's responsibilities are taken from him, he soon finds it easy to let 'out of sight be out of mind.' "

Wartime separation of husbands and wives made it inevitable that the institution of marriage took some hard knocks. Even if the war-bride had been left pregnant, the foundations of these relationships were often too fragile to sustain the emotional needs of either partner through years of separation under conditions of danger and loneliness. How well the bonds of a wartime marriage stood up to the strain of years of separation and sexual temptations depended more on mutual affection and respect than on a solemn nuptial oath. "Through all these troubled times, our love grew stronger," asserted a housewife from Bristol, who believed that "those six and a half years apart strengthened what we felt for one another."

Separation left wives in constant dread of news that their spouses had been killed in action. It added heavily to the burden of loneliness of wartime women. "Suspended thus between the joy of living and the thought of dying, there were moments when a sombre mood descended upon our little group," wrote a German girl before she heard her Luftwaffe fiancé had been shot down over France in 1940. "All of a sudden life collapsed into a heap. Then slowly I was invaded by the image of a very tall man with straight blond hair falling onto his forehead, who for all his charm and light-hearted bantering had always seemed perturbed by questions to which there were no answers."

"At first nothing made sense; that you were dead, that I was alive — I couldn't figure it out," a grief-struck young wife of an American flyer wrote. "When a boy like you dies there's always a tormenting 'why' left in the hearts of those who loved him."

The emotional trauma of bereavement left many war widows seeking refuge from a future the war made bleaker by clinging to the warm memories of the past. Other romances that began in the frenzy of wartime left couples waiting years for that longed-for wedding day.

When Lieutenant Donald F. Sebald arrived in Britain with an American Liberator squadron late in 1942, he first met and fell deeply in love with a WAAF nurse. "She was very pretty, very vivacious, and very married. Her husband was an infantry officer in the British army serving in Burma. Our relationship was very enjoyable, but she kept it purely platonic. (It did happen that way at times despite the war.)" Not until 1952, when he returned to England as a reporter on assignment, did he succeed in tracking down his wartime WAAF. He eventually married her after a further courtship. "Over the next five years I convinced her I was serious, honorable, and lacking the more heinous of the masculine vices."

For every wartime romance that reached a happy ending, many more fell victim to the turbulence of the times, like that of Susan. She was still in her teens when she joined the WAAF after her brother was killed in Sicily in 1943. Her love affair with a New Zealander in the RAF lasted until he was posted to the Middle East shortly after they had become engaged — then he jilted her:

The whole episode broke my heart, and in my desperation I had an affair with a young Polish sailor. He begged me to marry him after I was expecting a baby. But I could not bear to do anything of the sort, even though he warned me that such a decision might ruin my life.

Many British women, through loneliness and circumstance, broke with social convention in the wake of the "friendly invasion" of American troops in the year before D-Day. "Our own servicemen were set aside for the Americans, who appeared more glamorous in every way because of the movies and their generosity with money," recalled one British woman. "There were fights between them and our men over girls. I knew of two young wives that left and divorced chaps they seemed to have been devoted to."

The constancy of wives and sweethearts became a fixation for frontline soldiers as they anxiously awaited mail-call. For some, the army became a surrogate wife. Bill Mauldin, whose closely observed cartoons of frontline life epitomized the hopes, fears and earthy humor of the GI, put it this way:

There's the young guy who got married two weeks before shipping out, has been overseas for two years, and is desperately homesick. Some other guy will say to him: "You wanna go home? Hell, you found a home in the army. You got your first pair of shoes and your first square meal in the army. You're living a clean, healthy, outdoor life, and you want to go back and get henpecked?"

Yet, apart from a bullet or mortar shell, the receipt of a "Dear John" letter from home confessing infidelity or desertion was the worst blow that could hit an infantryman in an exposed foxhole. A group of GIs in North Africa had organized a "Brush-Off Club," whose admission qualification was to have been jilted. Most American girls interviewed in a December 1944 newspaper survey agreed that "to jilt a soldier is a serious offense"; but one of the more forthright interviewees insisted, "Those guys over there aren't just shy-eyed sheep in a jeep."

Soldiering in Italy especially exposed the Anglo-Saxon moral attitudes to the passions of Mediterranean women. "Thus love in America is divided into the classification of Having Sex and Getting Married," wrote one U.S. army sergeant of his experiences.

"Neither has much to do with love. It was Having Sex which began to strike us in Naples as being so cold-blooded."

Before going into action many soldiers experienced intense yearnings for the girl they had left behind. War thrust love and the emotional fiber of soldiers onto a razor-edge. "In fact women were always in their thoughts when they weren't actually in combat," wrote James Jones, one of the preeminent chroniclers of the raw life at the front. "When the presence of death or extinction was just around the corner or the next cloud, the comfort of women takes on great importance." Combat opened many men's eyes to love as the emotional lifeline that sustained them under fire.

Soldiers clung grimly to the battered photos of the girls they loved as battle talismans, and others keenly felt the lack of such tangible mementos of love. "I haven't got what you call a real girlfriend and on a night like this, it sure hurts," confessed one GI to his parents in a letter before he embarked for the D-Day invasion. "A guy sure gets lonely out here and should have somebody to want to come back to and share building a wonderful life together, hand in hand. And that means a girl you'd want to marry and have for the mother of your kids, and who would wait and pray for you on a night like this."

"It is my contention," reflected one GI, "that when a man loves a woman, she always remains a vivid memory." This particular staff sergeant's "sensual nymph, with brown eyes and red-black hair," had been a tap-dancer from Spokane, whose memory haunted him before he went into action. "Now that I may soon die on the battlefield nine years later, I realize more forcibly than ever that I am still in love with her."

"Our love will never die. It shall be part of your life and mine, that will live on, no matter what may happen," wrote an American fighter pilot to his wife before he took off on a dangerous mission over France in 1944 from which he never returned. "That love shall return to you some day, in some way, and you will perhaps not know it, but you will have a strange feeling of having known it before. . . . I love you more than anything in life. I have loved you always and it was only a matter of time until fate brought us together. A million kisses, darling, I'll see you again — sometime, somewhere."

* [2] *

Cinderella Legions

When the barrage opens up to greet the raiding Huns,
Don't forget the girls out there, the girls behind the guns,
When you hear the boom of fire, and see the sky alight
Remember they're on duty in the front line of the fight.

— ATS "GUNNERS" SONG

The position of women in the Services to-day is a significant
measure of changes both in status and public opinion which
have come about during recent years. History has many records of valour and endurance shown by individual women in
military operations. But these were heroines of romance, whose
activities were regarded as wholly remote from a woman's re-
cognised path.

— BRITISH PARLIAMENTARY COMMITTEE, 1942

At 11 A.M. on the fateful Sunday of 3 September 1939, it
was a female army auxiliary telegraphist who transmitted
the British government's formal declaration of war to the German Foreign Ministry in Berlin. Five years earlier, the Emergency Service formed by the Women's Legion had launched a
campaign that paved the way for the conscription of women into
uniformed service in a total war.

Long before Joan of Arc's military exploits had made her the
most celebrated female figure of medieval Europe, wars had inspired some women to disguise themselves as men to participate
in the quintessentially masculine world of soldiering. The American Revolutionary War made a heroine of Deborah Sampson,
who successfully disguised herself as a man to fight the British
Redcoats until she was unmasked because of her wounds. General George Washington unwittingly struck a blow for female, as

well as American, liberation when the Continental Army recruited hundreds of water carriers whose collective nom de guerre of Molly Pitcher was immortalized by Margaret Corbin's command of her husband's gun after he was killed during the battle at Fort Washington on 16 November 1776. Another celebrated female warrior of the eighteenth century was Anne Talbot, "a damsel that followed the drum," who as John Taylor served as both a foot soldier and sailor during the Napoleonic war.

The Crimean War in 1851 brought the first grudging recognition of women's military role when the single-minded determination of Florence Nightingale broke down the male prejudice against female nursing auxiliaries — but only after the public had been reassured that the men "never forgot the respect due to our sex and position." A decade later, during the American Civil War, an estimated thirty-two hundred women volunteered as nurses with the Union and Confederate armies despite fierce resistance by some military surgeons who objected to the very idea of "a delicate and refined woman assisting a rough soldier to the close stool, or supplying him with a bed-pan or adjusting the knots in a T-bandage."

Artillery warfare brought a vast increase in the numbers of wounded and established female nursing auxiliaries as an essential part of the military establishment. By 1914 British veteran volunteer nurses of the Boer War, the First Aid Nursing Yeomanry (known as FANYS), were the first women to cross to France to help run the ambulance and hospital services. By 1918, eleven thousand British women were serving long hours, often under arduous conditions, in the uniforms of Queen Alexandra's Imperial Military Nursing Service, the British Red Cross, and St. John's Ambulance Brigade. But throughout World War I, the army staff still resisted anything that smacked of "petticoat soldiering." Nevertheless, women's voluntary organizations supplied the kitchen staff for army canteens.

It was not, however, until 1917 that the War Office reluctantly conceded the army had a place for female auxiliaries, and there was considerable bureaucratic soul-searching among its senior officers whether breast pockets on women's uniforms would draw too much attention to the female anatomy and encourage public speculation about the lax morality of the corps. Primness won the day, and those girls who "did their bit" for King and Country in

the final year of the war paraded in jackets with no breast pockets and wearing khaki skirts that decently concealed female ankles.

The fourteen cooks and a waitress who crossed the Channel to
France early in 1917 were volunteers in Queen Mary's Army
Auxiliary Corps. A year later it had grown into a fifty-seven-
thousand-strong force of telephonists and drivers as well as canteen staff, a full-fledged military force that proudly marched in
the 1918 victory parades under the banner of the Women's Army
Auxiliary Corps. Although initially resistant to these females in
uniform performing anything other than traditional kitchen and
nursing duties, within months the army had been sufficiently impressed to assign women to administrative and communications
roles, releasing thereby an estimated twelve thousand more men
for the front line. The Women's Royal Navy Service had also been
formed, as had the Women's Royal Air Force, and by the end of
the war each had recruited five thousand females into their ranks.

The WAAC volunteers had stayed with the British army for
two years after the war to assist with the Allied occupation of
Germany, but by 1920 they had all been mustered out. The politicians paid their debts and expressed the national gratitude for
the service given by the female auxiliaries by extending the fran-
chise to women over thirty. Most of the veterans, who were in
their twenties, were therefore excluded from the promised re-
ward. Many women wanted to continue some military role, but
were shut out because the generals and admirals subscribed to
the popular myth that now the "war to end all wars" had been
fought, the nation would never have to mobilize again.

Some British women were more alert than their politicians to
the military threat of Hitler's rise to power, and in 1934 the World
War I female veterans in women's branches of the British Legion
began voluntarily organizing what they called the Voluntary
Emergency Service. The War Office and Air Ministry provided
encouragement and provided instructors for summer training
camps. In the aftermath of the national emergency precipitated
by the 1938 Czechoslovakian crisis, the government formally recognized their potential contribution now that war clouds were
gathering over the Continent by establishing the female volunteers as the Auxiliary Territorial Service. In the spring of 1939,
as the ATS began recruiting in earnest, the Admiralty revived

the WRNS, and the RAF formed its Women's Auxiliary Air Force. So when Germany invaded Poland in September, twenty thousand trained and drilled female auxiliaries stood ready to play their part in "manning" the nation's sea, land, and air defense systems.

An original volunteer member of this "very select group" of women who considered themselves already "at arms" when war broke out — even though King's Regulations strictly forbade the ATS from carrying guns — was ATS Private Oxley. While training she had endured summer downpours under canvas with "girl-guide-like" enthusiasm, although many units like hers were still without their battledress.

The first uniforms did not arrive until six months later, just one hour before our first ceremonial parade. We did not know which was whose, so we quickly used safety pins to make them fit. There was no time to clean the brass and we had to wear our shirts tucked into the most unbecoming, unfeminine KHAKI BLOOMERS which we called "The Biggest Bloomer of All Time." But we made that first parade, even though our feet bled after two hours of marching in the heavy shoes.

Women's khaki uniforms in World War II were equipped with the breast pockets that were considered too risqué in 1917, but they were designed by army supply tailors who made few concessions to the female figure and they proved uncomfortable and very unfeminine.

Amy volunteered for the Auxiliary Territorial Service in December 1941; she was dismayed by how shocked her parents, staunch Christians with the London City Missionary Society, were when she announced she had joined up. The ATS, as they were known, had a "bad reputation" because of the popular rumors of their loose behavior with the lads in the army. Amy, like thousands of other young British women who volunteered for military service during the Blitz, nonetheless defied her parents and gave up her well-paid job as a secretary. She was determined to hit back at Hitler for the death of her boyfriend at Dunkirk. Although she admitted to "being a bit of a rebel," Amy was totally unprepared, like most girls from sheltered homes, for her first taste of army life in drafty barracks on the edge of the Yorkshire Moors:

I can remember the shock we had when they came around with the drink?, washing-up water?? — no, army soup!! That really turned our stomachs. Was this because the camp was still being run by men, we wondered? We were awakened at 6 A.M. next day and lined up outside to be marched off to breakfast across the barrack square. We then had to go and fetch our uniforms. What confusion. The stores were once again manned by men! The first counter we walked past had a sergeant standing by sizing us up — literally. Small, medium, or large were the only categories and we received a kit bag full of goodies according to the size he had given. Then we went back to our barrack room to sort them. What a laugh! We first tried on everything as issued: bras, suspender belt — both in old-fashioned pink cotton and very coarse. Vests, khaki "silk" locknit knickers with long elasticated legs. We jokingly called them our "Man Catchers." The shirts came with separate collars and we also were issued with blue striped flanelette pyjamas. Then an orgy of swapping started in an endeavour to get a reasonable fit.

The first weeks of basic military training proved a far tougher ordeal for women than for men. In bleak, ill-heated barracks they shared the tearful miseries of homesickness and nursed feet swollen from marching and legs aching from drilling in heavy shoes. The army regarded discipline and drill as the prerequisite for all soldiers, regardless of their sex. Long sessions of physical education and games were considered the necessary antidote to "lecture-room staleness." What instructions the girls were given were on such subjects as how to survive a gas attack, social hygiene, security and service procedures — hardly subjects calculated to inspire the female imagination.

After a month of parade ground drill and lectures the women were considered sufficiently conditioned in service routine to be passed out as fit to serve on bases as clerical assistants and carrying out the traditional "woman's work" of cooking and telephonist duties. Those taking up specialized technical trades that soon included motor transport, welding, radar maintenance, or radio and electrical service, were sent on after their passing-out parade to special schools for a further course of training.

Officer candidates were selected from the ranks of a three-month training course — a policy that gave the ATS in particular a cohesion quite different from the class-bound caste of the regular British army. The ranks of the women's auxiliary services were to prove levelers of the traditional British social system, even if its officers were firmly middle class.

A WAAF officer candidate, a former journalist from the BBC, was to discover that she was ill-suited to the uniformed life:

There was a Cambridge girl, an elementary school teacher, an art student, two Harrods shop assistants, a child of eighteen fresh from finishing school and presentation at court, and an amusing collar-and-tie type who'd created records on the motor cycle, could take automobiles to pieces, and held a pilot's license. The general atmosphere inclined to heartiness, especially when the flyer was about.

To the surprise of most soldiers, many of their female comrades in arms found the endless drill a great stimulation — perhaps because it was one area of military life where women were on equal terms with the men. "I was very proud when chosen to be the marker in church parades," recalled one ATS corporal, "as the only female to walk out on the square with the men." Other recruits found the mind-numbing discipline made life unbearable, as barking army sergeant majors showed little understanding for the disoriented and apprehensive women who, as one recalled it, had "to be made into what you were not in a very short time." Yet the harsh disciplines of army life fostered close comradeship.

One officer recruit found the military to be a "cross between boarding school and prison" where orders were "given with an air of God, from burning cloud, and however impossible and preposterous, had to be carried out." This independent-minded WAAF engineered her discharge after bossy officers with "large bosom and behinds, in a tight uniform that made them look like overblown balloons," had ordered a particularly pointless exercise.

We were made to march over the innocent English countryside like young Prussians and when we got rather out of rhythm negotiating a twisting downhill, loose-stone bit of lane with hedges entwined with blackberry brambles overhanging just at the height of our faces, we were loudly abused by the Senior Section Leader and commanded to whistle "Hang Out the Washing on the Siegfried Line" to keep in step. The clockwork performance of this same SS leader was such as you simply daren't look at her face for fear of having hysterics.

But the majority of women recruits were sufficiently fired by patriotism and the determination to prove they could be as good soldiers as the next man. They drew their inspiration from the courage of the thirteen hundred army nurses who had endured the ordeal of Dunkirk alongside the men of the British Expeditionary Force in May 1940. A wounded soldier paid this tribute to their bravery under fire during the evacuation:

Out of that dreadful beach, with the sun pouring down on them, the German planes continually overhead and shells bursting all the time, they have worked without stopping for days past. If they have slept, they have done so on their feet, attacked by German planes and even tanks, with machine gun bullets whistling all round. I have seen them crawling into the open and dragging wounded men to shelter beneath sand dunes. I saw one party of them dressing wounded who were lying out in the open. A plane began bombing. They just lay down over their patients and continued bandaging. They have fetched food and water to assist the men. Angels is the only word you can use to describe them. I have seen some of them killed as they have gone about their work. We have asked them to go back to the rescue ships, but they have refused. Each of them has said, "We shall go when we have finished this job — there's plenty of time, so don't worry about us."

The same coolness under fire was displayed by the women of the ATS transport detachments and signal corps during the evacuation of the British Expeditionary from France. One unit of bilingual switchboard operators continued manning the army's Paris exchange until the final hours before the Germans marched into the French capital. The Fall of France marked the beginning of the Battle of Britain, when WAAF plotters joined with the female spotters of the Royal Observer Corps serving in lonely hilltop outposts to provide the vital links that enabled RAF Fighter Command to deploy its slender resources to meet the might of the Luftwaffe.

WAAF fighter controllers and plotters homed the pilots by radio onto the German bombers. "We were often too tired to eat after those shifts of plotting, where any mistake in the precise movement of the enemy would have meant disaster," was how one of them recalled the wild aerial dogfights that she tracked on the board from the messages flooding into her headphones.

These women were brought face to face with sudden death

when one of their circuits would go dead, indicating that another young fighter pilot had been "killed in action." Leading Aircraft Woman Ruth F. Martin summed up her emotions in a touching piece of wartime verse called "Hello 226 — This Is Flying Control, Do You Read Me?" dedicated to one of the RAF's Rhodesian squadrons:

We grew to know those boys so well as we spoke over the intercom,
Scanning the skies for their return, notching the landings, one by one.
Alas and many times alas, one or two failed to return, the hush in our
control tower, a silent tear, oh how our hearts did burn.

In August 1940 WAAF communications personnel found themselves in the firing line after Reichsmarshal Hermann Göring had ordered his Luftwaffe to turn the full weight of its assault on the RAF fighter bases. Many were to be decorated for bravery after they stayed at their posts to continue relaying vital information despite the falling bombs. After Corporal Joan Avis-Hearn's plotting hut was blown apart by a near miss, she continued to send reports, the first of which was: "The course of the enemy bombers is only too apparent to me because the bombs are almost dropping on my head."

The Luftwaffe's failure to secure air superiority for an invasion of Britain forced Göring to switch targets again, and in September the bombers were unleashed to attack Britain's cities. The ATS and WAAF units who helped man the balloon-barrage defenses now found themselves in the front line of the unrelenting German assault as they heaved on the ropes and strained to lift the 120-pound ballast blocks that controlled the whalelike silver blimps that were sent aloft to snag low-flying enemy dive-bombers.

"You can't hit back at 'em. You've just got to take it," was how one member of a balloon unit described downing a German plane:

"Christ," says one of our airmen. "He's going to machine gun us." "He isn't," says I. "He's going to hit the cable." And he did. He went smack into it. There was a crash and the cable went through the wing just like a grocer's wire goes through cheese. We celebrated our first Jerry with a nice cup of tea. Then of course we realised we'd have to put up another in place of *Annie*.

ATS units were assigned to plotting and maintenance roles on the radar units, searchlights, and anti-aircraft batteries that sprouted up in the winter of 1940–41 around major cities, ports, and military installations.

"We do not, as many people think, man the guns," explained a member of one of these batteries in a wartime press release:

The gun teams are all men, and always will be, for the simple reason that women have not the physical strength to load and unload the heavy shells. The part played by the ATS is to man the instruments which enable the guns to notify the battery of the approach of an aircraft, and to plot their position as they approach.

The British government still feared an adverse public reaction if it was known that women were too directly in action. "Anyway, a fit woman can fire a rifle better than an unhealthy man, and what could be more military than managing the ack-ack guns," acknowledged a senior bureaucrat. Official policy began to change after the commanding officer of the first mixed "ack-ack" battery reported unhesitatingly: "The girls cannot be beaten in action, and in my opinion they are definitely better than the men on the instruments. . . . and although they are not supposed to learn to use the rifle, they are as keen as anything to do so."

"In the beginning the idea of mixed units was viewed with great suspicion, but as time went on attitudes mellowed," recalled Joyce Peters, who was member of this first unit whose guns were set up near Richmond and which included "girls from leading public schools working well with ex-factory lasses to beat the Germans." She recalled that "we must have been worthy of note" because Churchill himself paid the unit a visit in January 1941 during an air raid. Suitably impressed, he conceded that to foster esprit de corps in the ATS, all such units could take the coveted title of "Gunners." Their "immense importance" was acknowledged with the prime minister's subsequent decision to step up female recruiting for "maintenance of a large number of batteries with the smallest number of men."

Early in 1941 a contingent of fifty-four ATS girls had completed secret training as operators of the giant searchlights used in conjunction with the anti-aircraft batteries to pinpoint enemy bombers. The dangers of becoming targets for German fighters did not deter women from volunteering for the "Searchlight Battalions," where they proved highly effective at differentiating enemy from friendly aircraft during the frenzied action of an enemy raid. According to official reports, "The standard reached was higher than most men." The female telephonists who transcribed the Morse code from the central gun control had to be particularly diligent because "if one miscounts the pips it means a wrong plot being made and perhaps a target being missed."

The ATS girls who wore the "Gunners" and "Searchlight" shoulder flashes were the elite of Britain's female forces, their morale sustained by plenty of action during the Blitz, which they cheerfully described as "hard work and great fun." Another member of a mixed ack-ack crew remembered the heady action of "rushing across the field in the early hours, dressing as we ran and falling face down in a cow pat. We plotted a hundred or more enemy aircraft, not smelling of violets. But luck was with us that morning because we brought down a German bomber."

"We had to stay at the site until it was in working order again, often all night, working by the light of a small torch," remembered a WAAF electrician of the nights when a "bombers' moon" heralded a certain German raid. Anne recalled the hectic drives between sites along twisting country lanes in a van affectionately known as a "Tilly." They were responsible for maintaining the radar on the batteries that were strung out between Bournemouth and Poole. "Conditions at those gunsites were often primitive, still all male, and many problems were caused to us girls as regards toilet facilities. Often we had to go 'picking blackberries.' " Steaming mugs of tea warmed up the bitter winter nights while they waited for the next wave of bombers and celebrated their victories with the final refrain of their battle song:

> When you hear the boom of fire, and see the sky alight,
> Remember the ATS on duty in the front line of the fight.

The ack-ack barrage, however, hindered rather than prevented most of the German bombers getting through to rain death and destruction on Britain's cities. During the "Baedekker Raids" in the spring of 1941, few centers of population of any size escaped the attention of the Luftwaffe. Then women in the Civil Defense Corps and the Women's Volunteer Service joined the action with those who had joined the fire services to defy the bombs, douse the conflagrations, and dig the injured from the rubble.

At the height of the Blitz, a sixteen-year-old girl dispatch rider on a bicycle in the Air Raid Precautions Service became the youngest female recipient of the George Medal. Many women auxiliaries were decorated for their bravery during the German air assault on the British home front. Wren Third Officer Pamela McGeorge was among those who received the British Empire Medal for the cool courage she had shown in delivering her dispatches to the commander-in-chief, running through a stick of bursting bombs after an explosion had blown her motorcycle from under her during a heavy raid on the Plymouth dockyard.

Yet when it came to recognizing the heroism of individual servicewomen, the traditional military chauvinism denied them the Victoria Cross, which was awarded only for acts of "conspicuous gallantry" in the face of the enemy (interpreted to mean on the field of battle). The George Cross, the civilian equivalent of the VC, was awarded to only four women during the whole war — including Corporal Joan Daphne Mary Pearson. She was a WAAF administrative officer who in May 1940 had saved the life of a crashed RAF pilot by shielding him with her body from a 120-pound bomb that exploded thirty yards away.

The contribution made by Britain's uniformed women had become so vital to the national defense that in April 1941 the government introduced parliamentary legislation to make female auxiliaries full military status as members of the armed forces of the Crown. A year later the problem of war manpower was to become so acute that Churchill's War Cabinet decided to make Britain the first country ever to order a general female conscription, which gave women the choice of enlisting in auxiliary services or the Women's Land Army, or accepting direction into government-approved jobs.

It was the Luftwaffe Blitz during the winter of 1941 that put British servicewomen on the home front into the firing line and earned them full military status; that year also brought the German invasion of the Soviet Union, which thrust women into military combat. The Russians had set a precedent during World War I when a woman officer in the Don Cossacks became celebrated as "Yellow Martha" because of her blond locks. British suffragette leader Mrs. Pankhurst had called it "the greatest event in the world's history" when she inspected a Russian female battalion in July 1917. But although some of them saw action, there was no official Russian policy of putting women into battle until it became a dire necessity during World War II.

In the six months following 21 July 1941, when Hitler unleashed Operation Barbarossa, three million Soviet soldiers had been taken prisoner. Leningrad had been circled in the steel grip of the Wehrmacht, and German tanks were pounding their way toward Moscow. Russian women had inevitably been caught up in military operations during the disastrous retreat, and millions had been mobilized into the industrial plants which had hurriedly been relocated east of the Urals. Thousands of Soviet wives and mothers volunteered to become transport drivers, others joined the air-raid militia, and many became nurses.

The Red Air Force was in desperate straits: most of its aircraft and pilots had been shot out of the sky by the Luftwaffe. Female aviators had already been called up to help train fresh pilots when the Soviet High Command, facing a crucial struggle for survival, decided in October 1941 to begin training women pilots for combat. Marina Raskova, Russia's Amelia Earhart and a Hero of the Soviet Union for her prewar record-breaking flights, broadcast an appeal on Radio Moscow for experienced women flyers to volunteer for action. Two thousand applications were received, and three air regiments of three squadrons of ten aircraft each were planned, in which all the personnel — pilots, bombardiers, navigators, fitters, and mechanics — would be female.

A thousand eager recruits arrived in Moscow to begin training in November 1941. As one of these volunteers recounted in *The Night Witches,* they were confronted by Major Raskova, "her blue eyes fiercely selective." She offered a last chance to withdraw after reminding each of them of the unprecedented demands and dangers they would face in aerial combat missions:

"The girls I do choose must understand beyond any doubt whatsoever that they will be fighting against men, and they must themselves fight like men. If you're chosen you may not be killed — you may be burned so your own mother would not recognize you. You may be blinded. You may lose a hand, a leg. You will lose your friends. You may be captured by the Germans. Do you really want to go through with this?"

Not a single girl withdrew, but they learned next day, when they reported to Moscow's Zhukovsky Academy to pick up their uniforms, that the Red Air Force was making no concessions to their femininity. "We didn't know whether to laugh or cry," recalled one of these recruits, as they picked through bundles of surplus boots, worn tunics, trousers, and coats. "Like all young girls we were pretty fashion conscious, even though there was a war on. Most of us had slim waists and, though we didn't expect uniforms tailored for us by a Paris couturier, we hoped that they had made some little concessions to the fact that we were a different shape from most soldiers." After working all night cutting and stitching, the potential fighter and bomber crews left for their training base at Engles on the Volga, feeling like "clowns at the Moscow State Circus. God knows what the Germans would have thought."

The Germans would discover to their cost that women at the controls of a warplane were every bit as deadly as men. Many of these fiercely determined women had lost their homes and families in the enemy advance, and their fighting spirit was roused by a burning desire for revenge. A unique camaraderie grew up between them, recalled a survivor, with "surprisingly little bitchiness of the sort you might expect when girls are flung together like that."

The girls learned to become real soldiers through the experiences they had in combat. That was the real character builder. I know discipline is important in any military force. But really there was never any serious problem of that sort in the girls' regiments. There was so much mutual respect that people just tended to get on with the job without having to be ordered. Of course you need people in command and we had that. But a group of really motivated females does not, I think, need quite the same sort of rigid discipline that men do.

After the melting snows of the spring of 1942 led the Germans to resume the fierce offensive that threatened to rout the Red Army, training was completed and the female aircrews were assigned to their regiments — a third to fighters and the remainder to bombers. They were determined to fight and kill like men, yet as one of them recalled, "none of us wanted to act like men or look like men when we left our aircraft." Repeatedly they found it necessary to "remind ourselves all the time that we were girls." Many of the female aircrew clung to their femininity by defying regulations to cut their hair short. They dyed their white silk un-derhelmets pastel shades and put on light makeup and pale lip-stick before taking off for combat. Their fighter and bomber planes also had to be modified for feminine physiques that could not reach rudder pedals without special blocks, and seat cushions had to be raised to allow women to have all-round vision in the cockpit. Just manipulating the cumbersome and obsolescent YAK bombers often required the combined leverage of both pilot and copilot to yank back the control stick at takeoff.

When it came to actual combat, most of the female pilots lost their initial fear in the intense concentration and exhilaration de-manded by battle. One pilot admitted "retching as I taxied out for take-off. I felt like switching off and getting out. . . . But it was strange — the moment the aircraft left the ground and I raised that undercarriage, all my nerves disappeared." Another recalled, "There really wasn't much to think about" the first time she took off for combat and flew straight into a stream of enemy bombers:

I flicked the guard off the gun button and pushed the nose straight down. I started firing right away and, keeping the power full on, just charged straight through the middle of the formation. It was terrify-ing. I passed very close to one of them as I dived through, then I pulled the stick back and zoomed up above them again, and did the same thing again.

One of the Russian women bombardiers recalls her "fantastic sense of achievement" in making her first raid on the German advance headquarters at Voroshilograd. The YAK PO–2 bi-planes crewed by the women of the 588th Night Bomber Regi-ment were so antiquated they could not have survived daytime raids. Even at night their noisy engines had to be cut and the bombing run made in a shallow gliding dive so as not to alert the German mobile flak batteries. This technique required cool nerve and teamwork between the pilots and their bombardiers:

I could clearly see the buildings and I knew that if I hit the target, Luba, behind me, would be able to aim at my fires that I started. The Ger-mans hadn't seen me coming because of the gliding approach, but now the searchlights came on and the flak started coming up. I realized, as I got more experienced, that this was indeed light opposition, but on that first night it seemed pretty terrifying to me. I didn't want to spoil my aim so I just flew straight on through the explosions until I was right over the target. The airplane bucked in the blast from some explosions, but we kept on flying. Then I yanked the release wire and dived away from the searchlights and steered for home. I saw flames coming from one of the buildings and thought that Luba would have a beacon to aim at.

When two of their bombers failed to return from that first mission, the excitement that they were "really going to show the men what we were made of" was submerged in a general grief at the death of these crews. But battle-reaction soon hardened the girls to dangers of combat and cemented the comradeship in the bombing group. Flying up to ten sorties a night back and forth across the front lines during the desperate, climactic months of the battles around Stalingrad in the autumn of 1943, the Russian women earned the respect of the Germans for their courage and skill; they were dubbed "the night witches."

The Soviet women's contribution to their country's all-out battle for survival was heavily embellished by Stalin's propaganda machine, with the intention of both rallying the Russian people and persuading his British and American allies to open a Second Front in Europe. A celebrated woman sniper, who had reportedly shot no fewer than 309 German soldiers while fighting with the Red Army on the Dneiper front, was sent on a well-publicized tour of the United States. Throughout the summer of 1943 American newspapers and magazines featured heroic exploits of other Soviet military heroines that gave the impression that women and men were fighting alongside one another all along the Eastern Front.

The reality was less spectacular, if no less heroic, for those individual women were not officially in frontline Red Army units but were guerrillas operating behind the German lines. Nor, as the testimony of some of the veteran female pilots reveals, had the Soviet military come to terms with the female warriors in its midst.

"We were to have equality in every possible sense, though in reality we had to struggle for that in some cases when we got to the front," recalled one of the woman pilots. None of them faced a greater initial resistance then a stunning blonde with gray eyes and winning smile, named Lily Litvak. The commanding officer of the unit near Stalingrad to which she was initially posted in August 1943 refused to let her fly with his men and ordered her to seek an immediate transfer. But Lieutenant Litvak turned her considerable charm to advantage with the plea she made for just one chance to prove her combat skill. The skeptical Red Air Force commander could not resist, and Lily was given a plane to show what she could do. After a dogfight in which she skillfully out-maneuvered a German to share the "kill" of a Messerschmitt 109, Lieutenant Litvak removed all doubts about a woman's ability in combat. She was welcomed to a permanent place in the squadron.

Her male comrades, however, were probably behind a practical joke during one mission that terrified Lily's female wingmate when she discovered a mouse while on patrol ten thousand feet above the river Don. "I know it sounds crazy — a fighter pilot frightened by a mouse — but I'd always had this fear of mice," Olga Yemshokova recalled years later. "And particularly now it was sitting on my lap looking up at me, in that tiny cockpit." She admitted she "could feel her flesh creeping" as she opened the cockpit and flung the little furry creature out into the slipstream.

During the next ten months Lily Litvak bore a charmed life as she outflew and outfought German pilots over the Eastern Front to become a Soviet fighter "ace" as well as a focus of romantic rivalry among the men who flew with her. But Lily left no one in doubt that she had fallen in love with the handsome Lieutenant Alexi Salomaten, with whom she had flown in her first combat mission. Such personal relationships were strictly discouraged in the mixed Red Air Force regiments. Women were deliberately quartered at a distant part of the airfield, even if this meant they had to live in converted cowsheds. But no regulations could prevent emotional attachments.

"Lily told me that it was agony up there sometimes when Alexi was being attacked. But of course it gave each of them an incentive to fight really well," remembered her mechanic Ina Pasportnikova. "Far from their love for each other affecting their concentration, I think it helped. Lily had always shown the sort of aggression you need to be a good fighter pilot. But her love for Alexi was the thing that turned her into a killer."

Lily Litvak survived a burst of German cannon fire that caused serious leg wounds, leaving her with a limp and sharpening her killer instinct. This hardened into an driving obsession after her lover Salomaten died in a crash. Shortly afterward she claimed her tenth victim, a famous German "ace." He had the misfortune of surviving to be confronted by the pilot who had ended his career. The Luftwaffe hero refused to believe he had been outfought by a woman until Lily coldly explained the maneuvers in the action that had brought him down. "The German's whole attitude, even his physical appearance, changed," reported an eyewitness to the confrontation. "He was forced to concede in the end that no one except the pilot who had beaten him could possibly have known, move by move, exactly how the fight had gone. There was no question of saluting the victor. He could not meet her eye. To have been shot down by a woman was more than he could bear."

Only two more victories remained for the legendary "Rose of Stalingrad." Lieutenant Litvak was herself shot down and failed to bail out when her fighter, decorated with its white rose emblems, invited a mass attack by a swarm of German Me-109s. Her final letter to her mother in Moscow provided a chilling insight into the psychological strain that a woman fighter faced at World War II's sharpest end. "Battle life has swallowed me completely. I can't seem to think of anything but the fighting," was the epitaph left by Lily Litvak in a final letter home. Combat hardened feminine sensibilities.

Galia Boordina also felt the brutalizing effect of killing as she took part in the titanic aerial actions of 1943 over the Kursk battlefield in which some four thousand aircraft were locked in one of the fiercest air-to-air combat of the whole war:

The sky was so full of aircraft in such a small area of airspace that it was terrifying. German and Soviet fighters were whirling and diving everywhere. You would be involved in a fight with another aircraft and a couple of dogfights would be taking place in between yours, it seemed. The risks of collision were enormous — even with your own side. It was a complete melee, and most of the aircraft were flying at very high speed. I broke out of the fight briefly to gain height and look for a target. I dived down and pulled up underneath a Messerschmitt 109 and raked it with machine gun and cannon fire. It fell away immediately, burning. I had shot down other Germans before that — a bomber and a transport — but that was my first fighter. I didn't feel any pity for the man I killed. When it's kill or be killed, you don't feel that sort of thing. I preferred not to see the faces of an enemy. Once when I was attacking a bomber I got close enough to see the features of a gunner, and I remembered that it was other human beings we were firing our guns at.

Women also played an important role in the Red Army. There was female conscription — although not to combat regiments. But so total was the conflict in the Soviet Union that women who played a leading role in army communications, transport regiments, and medical duties often found themselves swept up in frontline action. This was the case for assistant surgeon Pavlova who assumed command of a convoy of food and medical supplies when it was attacked by the Germans. With a detachment of Red Army soldiers, she led them in surprise attack that wiped out a German infantry regiment.

Some women engaged in combat in the Soviet armored regiments that had suffered such high casualties during the German assault. Female truck and tractor drivers were recruited from the collective farms for duty behind the front, test-driving and delivering tanks. It was therefore a short step to the 1943 decision to alleviate the acute shortages of trained male tank drivers by calling on these experienced women to volunteer for frontline duty. In the final year of the war, some of them were being promoted to commanders.

The most celebrated of these female "tankers" was Sergeant Maria Oktyabr'skaya a resilient Ukranian who was thirty-nine years old when her husband was killed in 1941. She volunteered as a driver behind the battlefront and saw her first combat in October 1943 as the driver of T-34 tank on the Vitbesk sector of the front when she knocked out a German antitank gun by crushing it under her machine's tracks. A year of almost continuous combat was ended when, navigating her tank through a minefield, she was blown up. Mortally wounded, Oktyabr'skaya was hauled out of the burning tank, and after her death was elevated into a national hero by being posthumously awarded the Order of Lenin.

The final six months of the war brought thousands of British female soldiers over to Europe. Behind the advancing front they manned the anti-aircraft batteries that defended liberated Brussels from German bombers. Those women who were killed in the 1945 raids brought to nearly four hundred the ATS casualties during World War II. British female servicewomen had been operating behind the front lines ever since 1940, when transport and signal detachments had been sent to France. Their performance had so impressed the service chiefs that by 1941 the first contingent of the ATS volunteers was on its way to the Middle East, where they helped keep communications and supplies flowing to the front during the North African campaign that defeated Rommel. A pioneer Wren unit was also posted overseas to Singapore in the summer of 1941 to assist with the wireless and telegraphic duties. They were evacuated to India before the Japanese invasion, and many of them were to become part of the uniformed female staff at Lord Mountbatten's South-East Asia Command.

In England as well as at the overseas headquarters, servicewomen played a vital role in securing the Allies' triumph of wartime codebreaking. Britain's intelligence nerve center was the so-called Government Code and Cipher School at Bletchley Park. Here, under conditions of great secrecy and security, hundreds of Wrens, WAAF, and ATS telegraphic staff fed the primitive computers with the intercepted enemy code messages that had been picked up by the listening stations. Many of these relied on carefully trained ears, which scanned the radio waves around the clock, tuning into the coded Morse transmissions which were the raw material of the Allied victory in the secret war.

The invasion of Europe in June 1944 was not only the biggest Allied military operation of World War II, but it depended on thousands of women, from the highly skilled photo-reconnaissance interpreters to the plotters and communications staff. Wren Chief Officer Dorothy Faith Parker made a special contribution to the successful landing of a million Allied troops. As Assistant Staff Officer for Escorts, she was instrumental in ensuring the smooth function of the assault and was the only woman to witness the actual Channel crossing from the bridge of a destroyer.

Even if they did not see frontline action like their Russian allies, British servicewomen established a proud wartime record alongside their menfolk. When eighteen-year-old Princess Elizabeth joined the ATS Transport Corps in 1943, it marked a symbolic endorsement that female military service was now socially acceptable. For the future queen, in common with thousands of British girls who joined up, it was a powerful, liberating experience to be thrust into what had always been an exclusively male military environment. A typical female veteran felt that the most important influence was that she "grew up," her one reservation was that "being in the WAAF may have been good for me. But living amongst men for five years made me think like one. It made me much more sociable, but in those days one would probably have said 'more common.' "

Service in the armed forces inevitably cost women a loss of traditional femininity. But while many saw it as another demonstration of the legitimacy of their claim to equality with men, many more British women were left in doubt about how to translate their experience into political and economic benefits in what was still a very patriarchal society. It was this indecision that persuaded the majority to return with cheerful resignation to postwar duty with home and family. In Britain to a greater extent than the United States, the liberation that many women had found in wearing military uniforms was seen as time out for the duration.

Even in the Soviet Union, where sexual inequality was supposedly swept away with the class system in the Revolution, veteran female warriors were left with doubts. "Sometimes, on a dark night, the wind tugging at my hair," reflected Nadia Popova, one of the decorated Soviet wartime pilots, "I stare into the blackness and I close my eyes and I imagine myself once more a young girl, up there in my little bomber. And I ask myself, Nadia — how did you do it?"

★ [3] ★

"You're in the Army Now, Miss Jones!"

Women made, in my opinion, the best soldiers in the war.

— GENERAL IRA C. EAKER, USAAF, 1945

We want to help make the world free — and get a thrill out of doing it.

— WAC PRIVATE, 1943

The military services are so conspicuously a man's world that the appearance of women therein was startling. Women who joined to do a job found themselves objects of great curiosity. Suddenly they were representatives of "womanhood." . . . The surprise of men at the accomplishment of women was not flattering, but it was fun.

— CAPTAIN MILDRED MACAFFEE HORTON, U.S. WAVES

Long before the Japanese attack on Pearl Harbor, the fascination of Americans with the role that women were playing in the war in Europe was evident from popular magazines like *Life* and *Saturday Evening Post,* which found Russian female fighters and British girls in tin helmets operating searchlights, dousing blitzed buildings, and marching with snappy precision irresistible subjects for photo spreads and articles. Yet surprisingly, for a nation where women already played a more prominent role than in any European society, it was to take nearly five months of intensive public debate and lobbying by the administration on Capitol Hill before the House of Representatives and Senate passed the bill that allowed American women to serve their country in uniform.

A similar uneasiness over the establishment of a female militia had surfaced in World War I. In 1917 the secretary of war had refused a petition from the New York Women's Self Defense League Auxiliary to be sent to France after diligently drilling at the 66th Street Armory with puttees and rifles. With the same finality he rejected a proposal from the chiefs of staff for congressional approval of a women's army auxiliary that would parade in "soft brown" uniforms — "no furs shall be worn" — because "the action provided for in this bill is not only unwise, but exceedingly ill-advised."

The War Department held firm to its policy even after receiving repeated requests from the commander in chief of the American Expeditionary Force in France for five thousand female auxiliaries. General John ("Black Jack") Pershing had been so impressed with the WAAC telephonists that he had arranged to "borrow" a hundred for his headquarters, but the contingent of American volunteer civilian telegraphists that he was sent never matched the efficiency of the British army auxiliaries because they were not subject to military discipline.

The Navy Department, however, had already enlisted 12,500 women clerical assistants as "Yeoman F" — popularly known as "yeomanettes" — bypassing the need for obtaining the necessary congressional approval by the ingenious device of assigning them as crew members to abandoned navy tugs. The Marine Corps had also appointed three hundred "marinettes" and the original estimate that three women could replace two marines engaged in clerical duties, proved to be a ration that was reversed in actual practice.

The American generals proved to have a far greater aversion to women in uniform than the admirals, and not until 1917 were female civilians permitted to be employed in military camps, and then only under "careful supervision" to prevent "moral injury either to themselves or to the soldiers." Proposals for a women's auxiliary were still being shuffled around the War Department when the end of the war enabled the secretary of war to shelve the controversial plans. The yeomanettes and marinettes left off their uniforms and were rehired back at their old jobs.

During the interwar years, the U.S. army's plans for a female auxiliary service were intermittently dusted off and revised by ranking officers who did not share the traditional antipathy to the idea of women in uniform. But it was not until Hitler went to war on the other side of the Atlantic that the patriotic fervor of women's organization in the United States once again became a voice that dimly penetrated the offices of the War Department.

The indefinite extension of the Selective Service Act for men that followed President Roosevelt's declaration of a National Emergency in 1941 prompted groups like the Women's Self Defense League to enroll seventeen thousand members "who can do anything helpful to replace a man in the event of war." From Los Angeles to Pittsburgh and Washington to Toledo, the War Department was bombarded with pleas from similar groups "to include women in the national defense plan in some capacity." In May 1941 Congresswoman Edith Nourse Rogers, who had herself served in France as one of Pershing's civilian auxiliaries in World War I, launched a bill in the House that would establish a twenty-five-thousand-strong noncombatant Women's Auxiliary Army Corps.

The majority of the U.S. army staff were still nursing their World War I distaste for anything that smacked of a "petticoat army." With little encouragement from the War Department, the Rogers bill quickly sank under the weight of male congressional opposition. Only in the crisis weeks of November 1941, when it became clear in Washington that the United States was sliding toward war with Germany and Japan, did the army change its tune. An aide to the U.S. army chief of staff, who had been one of the few supporters of the idea of a female auxiliary, remembered how "General Marshall shook his finger at me and said, 'I want a woman's corps right away and I don't want any excuses!' At that, I displayed considerable energy."

More energy and considerably greater initiative was to be shown by a handful of enterprising American women who set out to enlist in the British armed forces as soon as the Japanese attack on 7 December 1941 had plunged the United States into the global war. One of them was Maria Elizabeth Ferguson, who showed her bravery soon after sailing from New York when her ship, the ill-fated *Avila Star,* was torpedoed in a U-boat attack. The nineteen-year-old girl was awarded the British Empire Medal for "magnificent" courage during the grueling twenty-one days that she spent in an open boat nursing twenty-seven male survivors, eleven of whom perished in the three-week ordeal before rescue finally came. Another who risked the U-boat-infested Atlantic and reached the shores of England safely early in 1942 was Emily Chapin, a secretary and spare-time pilot from New Jersey who joined the select band of women flyers in Britain's Air Transport Auxiliary ferrying fighters and bombers to RAF bases.

American women wearing British uniforms were already helping to defeat Hitler while Congress debated the pros and cons of authorizing the U.S. army to set up its own female auxiliary. Congresswoman Rogers had by now won official War Department and White House backing for a relatively small female auxiliary force of twenty-five thousand, but the arguments continued to delay the passage of her bill through Congress. In Britain, however, there was little opposition at the end of April 1942 when Parliament approved the conscription of all able-bodied women between the ages of nineteen and twenty-five not already in essential work. The only exceptions were mothers of children under twelve.

Like the British government, military authorities in the United States insisted women must never be allowed actually to fire guns or engage in combat. Opponents of the bill for establishing a female army auxiliary argued that this violated the historic right of men to fight in defense of their womenfolk and homes. If women were once allowed to bear arms and female generals conduct battles, it would undermine the central male rationale for war. The traditionally conservative military mind subconsciously resisted the idea of women in uniform because it directly challenged an exclusive male preserve.

"I think it is a reflection upon the courageous manhood of the country to pass a law inviting women to join the armed forces in order to win a battle," thundered one member of the House of Representatives. "Take the women into the armed service, who will then do the cooking, the washing, the mending, the humble homey tasks to which every woman has devoted herself? Think of the humiliation! What has become of the manhood of America?"

The belief that women in uniform were an insult to the collective machismo of the American male was a theme repeated in many of the letters that flooded in from soldiers already locked in battle with the Japanese enemy in the Pacific. Typical of them was the GI who protested that "we would throw away our own self-respect — our right to pledge in earnestness to 'Love, Honor, and Protect' the girls we want to marry when we get back."

That this was not a view shared by the majority of women was evident from the even greater volume of mail that the War Department received from wives and relations of draftees, who begged to be given the chance to serve their country in uniform. At last, on 14 May 1942, the WAAC Bill for establishing the Women's Auxiliary Army Corps was squeezed out of the Senate by an insubstantial margin of just eleven votes. The navy, which had calculatedly resisted all efforts to win its support for a joint bill, had already initiated its own separate legislative authority — but only after Mrs. Roosevelt had interceded with the president to obtain the secretary's support. The navy bill was passed by Congress ten weeks later for a women's auxiliary, which would become known as the WAVES, a contrived acronym for "Women Appointed for Voluntary Emergency Service" that was soon jokingly interpreted as "Women Are Very Essential Sometimes."

The navy bill also authorized a women's reserve for the marines, in which its commandant, in the best tradition of the corps, refused to make any sexual distinction between male or females — they were all called "marines." The members of the corps out in the Pacific took a somewhat more jaundiced view of this egalitarianism. "Female Marines? They'll be sending us dogs next!" spat one hardened old Leatherneck. The U.S. coast guard, which had also come under direct navy control on the outbreak of the war, decided to call its female corps the SPARS, a contraction of its motto " 'Semper Paratus,' Always Prepared."

The final passage of the WAAC Bill had been assisted by the increasing sense of national emergency fostered by Allied defeat and reverses on every global battlefront. In the week before the crucial Senate vote, Japan had stormed the Philippine fortress island of Corregidor, the British army in Burma was retreating toward the frontier of India, and the Japanese fleet was threatening Australia from the Coral Sea. German panzer divisions in Russia were pounding their way toward Stalingrad and advancing unchecked in the Crimea. In North Africa, Rommel's Afrika Korps appeared poised to drive through Egypt and on to the Middle East. With fewer than two million American men under arms, the female auxiliaries offered the opportunity for a quick increase in the frontline strength of the army if the nightmare of final Axis victory in Russia, the Mediterranean, and Far East became a reality.

Even as Mrs. Oveta Culp Hobby was being sworn in by General Marshall as the first WAAC and the new corps' "director," the War Department doubled its intended strength to fifty thousand. This presented a formidable task for the wife of the former Texas governor, an ex-newspaper executive and thirty-seven-year-old mother of two who was chosen for the post that she had helped to bring into being from her work in the War Department liaison office. Mrs. Hobby was short in stature but long on legal training and had been in Washington long enough to have learned how to cut through bureaucratic tangles with a determination that earned her the nickname "Spark-Plugs."

At her first press conference questions focused on such burning issues as whether WAACs would be permitted to wear makeup, if they would be allowed to date enlisted men, and what would happen to them if they became pregnant. The next day her careful answers were sensationalized under headlines such as "Doughgirl Generalissimo" and "Petticoat Army," which suggested that opposition to the whole idea of women auxiliaries was not yet dead. The press proved unable or unwilling to resist the temptation of running pictures under such captions as "Whackies," "Powder Magazines," and "Fort Lipstick." One columnist compared the WAACs with "the naked Amazons . . . and the queer damozels of the Isle of Lesbos." Another demanded with ill-concealed prejudice: "Give the rejected 4F men a chance to be in the Army and give the girls a chance to be mothers."

The U.S. army's determination to make no concessions to "feminine vanity and civilian frippery" soon resulted in a wrangle over women's uniforms. Director Hobby argued for a stylish martial cut patterned on uniforms of regular soldiers. Army brass, determined to put as much distance as possible between men and women, argued for blue uniforms — and only conceded to olive drab because the use of existing army cloth was an economy measure. The final design was a committee compromise; the skimped, unpleated skirt with belted jacket and the kepi-style cap had none of the smartness or practicality the navy achieved with no acrimony by commissioning its ensemble from the New York fashion house of Mainbocher, the couturier patronized by the Duchess of Windsor and Hollywood stars.

The U.S. army was also to deny its female auxiliary the coveted eagle badge, and WAAC officers wore a hybrid in their caps that some said was a buzzard. Director Hobby rejected the proposed "Busy Bee" shoulder insignia because it looked like a "bug." The head of Pallas Athene, the Greek goddess of wisdom, was finally deemed appropriate.

"It will be no picnic for glamour girls" was how the camp commandant welcomed the press, inquisitive to look over Fort Des Moines, in the heart of Iowa, where the first four hundred white and forty black WAAC recruits, selected from thirty thousand applicants, were due to arrive for basic training in August 1942. Female reporters were shocked by the spartan conditions of an old cavalry barracks, which lacked partitioned showers and toilets. The first intake of WAACs, however, were most perturbed by the disconcerting mud-brown slips and foundation garments.

"You're in the Army Now, Miss Jones," was the popular adaptation of the previous year's hit song about the rigors facing male recruits. Women knew they were entering hostile territory when they faced the wolf-whistles of the draftees at the army recruiting offices. "The recruiting station was the dirtiest place I ever saw," complained one recruit. "It was in the post office next to the men's toilets," recalled another, and many would-be WAACs had second thoughts, particularly one girl at whom a captain bawled out, "Are you one of them Wackies?"

Much of this ill-concealed resentment by male enlistees was because the women could choose whether to volunteer for military service, whereas the men were drafted. The female intake was also of a much higher standard. Nine out of ten were college graduates and the others were chosen because they had made successful civilian careers before they had stepped forward to serve their country "for the duration plus six months."

"You have just made the change from peacetime pursuits to wartime tasks — from the individualism of civilian life to the anonymity of military life," said Director Hobby addressing the first intake. "You have taken off silk and put on khaki. All for essentially the same reason — you have a debt and a date. A debt to democracy, a date with destiny." These inspiring words were perhaps the reason that none of the new WAACs had need of the smelling salts proffered awkwardly by an embarrassed male medical orderly as the girls received their inoculation shots.

Most women were already earmarked for the first officer class and most surprised their male instructors — just as the British ATS had done — by their aptitude and affection for precision drill routines. "They learn more in a day than my squads of men used to learn in a week," a sergeant confessed. But on the eve of the parade three weeks later, when they were due to muster out as full-fledged WAACs, it was found that their young male instructors had given the highest marks to the youngest and prettiest WAACs. Since the average age of the female intake was significantly higher than that of the men who trained them, the younger women had been unfairly upgraded by ex-college soldiers of nineteen, to whom any woman over thirty was already an antique. Yet the mature judgment and stability of the adult women volunteers was soon to prove one of the corps' most valuable assets.

U.S. Army Chief of Staff General Marshall, a fervent supporter of employing women to release men for active duty, encouraged the War Department to increase the planned strength of the WAACs after initial surveys showed that women might eventually replace two out of three men in clerical and administrative jobs, in motor transport, and the supply corps as well as in radio communications. The only duties now considered "improper for women" were those that might expose them to enemy fire — or supervisory positions in which they could decide which men went into combat!

Accordingly, it was decided that by recruiting 1.5 million women, an equivalent number of men could be released for frontline duty. On paper, a woman's auxiliary on this scale translated into a hundred infantry divisions at the front. This was on the bold assumption that the WAACs could recruit nearly 10 percent of the estimated 13 million American women of service age. Director Hobby appealed for caution, since her advisers were strongly of the opinion that even reaching the new targeted strength (150,000) for the corps in little over two years would not be practical without British-style conscription.

Soundings taken on Capitol Hill, however, quickly revealed that the chances of getting Congress to pass a female draft act were nil. Moreover, as American production geared up, the War Manpower Directorate argued that industry must be given priority for recruiting able-bodied women, who, they insisted, would make a more effective contribution to the so-called Victory Plan in the shipyards and factories rather than by unproductive drilling in military uniform.

The services could not offer the same economic incentives as the production line, and a powerful disincentive to military service was what WAVE director Mildred MacAffee Horton termed "a threat to their individuality." Moreover, since the WAACs like the WAVES were volunteers, nothing could be done to keep those women who grew unhappy with military routine and discipline. After a year, military service had lost much of its glamour for many of the original enlistees. Desertion and AWOL rates began rising sharply after two sisters established a unique military precedent ordering their own discharge by cable to their commanding officer:

HAVE BEEN IN WAACS 3½ MONTHS. NOW AT HOME ON EMERGENCY FURLOUGH. HAVE NO INTENTION TO RETURN. CANNOT TAKE BEING IN CORPS. NERVOUS WRECK AND WILL LOSE OUR MIND IF NOT RELEASED. MA NEEDS US BOTH AT HOME AND CANNOT UNDER ANY CIRCUMSTANCES STAY. PLEASE TAKE IMMEDIATE ACTION AND REPLY.

New recruits vented their frustrations in songs that nevertheless expressed a "grin and bear it" determination, such as one of the many choruses that became popular at the Des Moines training camp in 1943:

> *Hats and shoes and skirts don't fit,*
> *Your girdle bunches when you sit,*
> *Come on, rookie, you can't quit —*
> *Just heave a sigh, and be G.I.*

To check desertions while boosting the prestige and flagging recruiting drive, the War Department asked Congress to pass legislation changing the status of the corps from an auxiliary to an integral part of the U.S. army — a step the British government had taken a year earlier with the ATS. After months of renewed political wrangling over the desirability of having women in uniform at all, the WAC (Womens Army Corps) was given its birth by a stroke of President Roosevelt's pen on 1 July 1943.

Women who elected to stay in the corps could now enjoy full military status, insurance, and pension rights. But they were also to be subject to army discipline — and through the summer almost half the strength of some WAAC units melted away as those women who decided not to sign on for a more military career opted for honorable discharge. "Feel I can do more good in war industry" . . . "Cannot accustom myself to military life" . . . "Unable to concentrate since my husband reported missing" were among the reasons given by some of the fifteen thousand who left by the September deadline. "Overstatements and unfulfillable promises by recruiting officers" were other contributory factors according to an official analysis, which suggested that the main cause was "the public attitude that the war is all but won."

The Women's Army Corps, as it was now designated, consisted of less than fifty thousand and hopes were abandoned of a rapid further half-million increase in 1943 that would have avoided the necessity of extending the 1943 draft to fathers of young families. With the army planners now calling for two million more men in anticipation of opening the Second Front in Europe in 1944, General Marshall reluctantly passed to the White House the order extending Selective Service.

Army life had become tarnished. Too many young women had suffered from homesickness during basic training, there was mounting public concern at the press coverage given to charges of immorality among servicewomen, and better pay without military discipline was offered by the war industries. A company commander claimed also that male soldiers were becoming increasingly resentful and disparaging of the WACs "now every man assumed that their uniforms gave him the right to insult them." Surveys confirmed that 40 percent of servicemen gave negative answers to the question "If you had a sister 21 years old or older, would you like to see her join the WAC or not?"

An ill-judged recruiting campaign on the theme "Release a Man for Combat" had implied that if wives and girlfriends enlisted and replaced men, they might be sending their own or someone else's loved one to risk death at the battlefront. The WAC recruiting was never fully to recover from the negative aspects of this ad-

vertising or the brash posters that followed. These oversold the
glamour of military life with the cheery hype of slogans proclaiming "We're the Luckiest Girls in the World — And We Know
It!" . . . "I Joined to Serve My Country, And I'm Having the
Time of My Life" . . . "I Felt Pretty Important When That Tai-
lor Fitted My Swank New Uniform to Me." These were greeted
with derision by new recruits, and veteran WACs angrily protested the harm that would be done by painting such an overrosy
and false image of the corps.

The campaign to restore the appeal of the WAC reached its
nadir in Cleveland in the summer of 1943 where an all-out advertising and recruiting drive culminating in the personal canvass of 73,000 families produced only 168 recruits. At that abys-
mal rate, enlistment officials calculated that there were not enough
families in the United States to enable the corps to reach even its
modest hundred thousand target strength. The army therefore
decided, against the advice of Mrs. Hobby — who now ranked as
a full colonel — to drop educational requirements from high
school graduation, which until then had been the minimum WAC
and WAVES requirement. Lowering of standards of female enlistment did not markedly increase the inflow of recruits, while it
gave the unfortunate public impression that the WAC was desperately scraping the bottom of the barrel.

Nine days after her induction one new WAC claimed to be the
Duchess of Windsor; another woman had joined up after her
parents removed her from an asylum. Drunkards and prostitutes
who had evaded screening procedures did irreparable damage
to the reputation of some units. "Well I thought it would get her
off our hands," said one police chief who later admitted concealing a woman's criminal record.

At Colonel Hobby's insistence, standards were raised again at
the end of 1943 as recruiting began to improve. Although the
corps was never to achieve its intended strength, it did reach a
wartime peak of just over a hundred thousand. At some bases
potential recruits were scared away by army psychiatrists. One
insisted on testing the emotional balance of potential enlistees by
asking the girls to strip before asking: "How often during the past
month have you had intercourse with a soldier or sailor?"

The WAC's contribution to the American war effort was

nevertheless significant, not just because it released the equivalent of seven army divisions of men for active duty, but because women often proved more effective at certain administrative and communications duties, especially on radio intercept stations, which required long hours of concentration listening to Morse transmission on headphones.

Inevitably, some commanding officers regarded WACs as merely substitute clerical staff, but others encouraged women to apply their talents to a variety of military tasks. The precedent was set by General Eisenhower, who had been impressed by the part British servicewomen were playing in their country's war effort during his mission to London with General Marshall in the spring of 1942.

When Eisenhower was appointed commander in chief of the Allied landings in North Africa in the fall of that year, he made female auxiliaries an integral part of his campaign headquarters. The first five officers were handpicked WAACs, who reached Algiers only five days after the first American invasion troops had waded ashore. Their arrival was an occasion of high drama rather than military smartness, although Eisenhower had sent his top aide to provide a welcome.

Five very bedraggled and grimy WAACs wearing borrowed men's trousers stepped onto the dockside from a Royal Navy destroyer that had fished them out of the Atlantic after a U-boat had torpedoed their transport. A month later the first company of WAAC enlistees arrived less dramatically in what a newspaper correspondent called "the first American women's expeditionary force in history." These WAACs had their baptism in soldiering behind the lines by being trucked daily between headquarters and the convent where they were housed.

WAC strength in North Africa had increased to nearly two thousand within a year, which saw the Sicilian and Italian campaigns. An advance contingent had joined the Fifth Army headquarters on the mainland by November 1943, moving with General Mark Clark's headquarters staff, bivouacking in the rough terrain twenty miles behind the front line. In Italy, despite initial reservations, the WACs appeared to thrive on the hardships and danger.

One American WAC corporal wrote to her mother from Italy,

"I greatly doubt that I shall ever be inspired to put such whole-hearted energy and effort into anything which my life after the war will demand of me."

In Britain during the build up and planning of the D-Day operations, Eisenhower's headquarters were populated with WACs who, along with their British women counterparts from the navy, army, and air force, took on a considerable measure of the administrative and communication burden for the largest amphibious operations in military history. General Ira Eaker singled out the contribution that women had made to the crucial pre-invasion bombing campaign: "They were the best photo-interpreters . . . keener and more intelligent than men in this line of work."

Among the first of the Allied women to set foot on the Normandy beach head was a Frances Sandstrom, a flight nurse from the 9th U.S. Army troop carrier base whose transport aircraft flew in to pick up the critically wounded only nine days after D-Day:

We were the first plane to land on the first steel-mat strip put down by our advance engineers. They had just finished the job when our C-47 came in. Wrecked gliders were scattered all over the countryside. The troops were fighting only three miles away, and we could hear land-mines exploding all around us. I was told to stay in the plane, since all German snipers had not been cleared and were taking occasional shots at the landing mat. The loading teams brought my patients aboard. Many of them were badly wounded. They were dirty, right out of foxholes. Many of them were suffering, but I heard not one murmur of complaint from any of them. It was hot and dusty, but they were calm and asked for nothing except water. Each time I gave a man a drink he smiled, or tried to, and thanked me as if I had done something very heroic and wonderful.

Three weeks later, the first permanent contingent of U.S. army nurses in steel helmets and combat fatigues arrived on 10 July. As they splashed ashore from a landing craft, they were greeted by wildly cheering GIs. The military nurses were soon followed by a volunteer WAC unit, which was attached to the forward communication echelon, and by October there were over three thousand American female soldiers in France carrying the myriad communications and clerical duties that a modern army even in the field trails behind it. The WACs took no part in fighting, but they were often close enough to the front to hear the battles and endure sporadic attempts by the Luftwaffe to break through the mighty umbrella that the Allied forces maintained over northern France.

The WACs shared the deprivations of frontline troops, living in tents and cellars, bathing from their helmets, and wearing standard combat jackets and trousers. Even behind the battlefield some of the more enterprising managed the occasional hairdo, and, as a reporter who kept up with them recorded, this involved a great deal of improvisation:

Beauty parlors in Normandy had become war casualties along with the pillboxes and enemy strongholds. We set up operations in our tents. There was no privacy from passing cows, nurses, doctors, GIs or German prisoners. Such is the price of vanity. My hair troubles were something the French understood. The French women fought the invasion with fashion. They wore with a flair hats they knew German women would copy, but which were not becoming. "If French women had not remained chic, Les Boches would have known they had broken their spirit," one of them said.

The reports that appeared in the American press brought a rush of would-be recruits in the final months of the war from women wanting to join the adventure overseas. When Germany surrendered in 1945, there were eight thousand WACs on the Continent. This was the largest contingent in any foreign theater, although it was still only half the sixteen thousand that Eisenhower had originally planned. The Supreme Commander Allied Force Europe was to hand America's female soldiers a heartfelt tribute: "During the time I have had the WACs under my command they have met every test and task assigned to them. . . . Their contributions in efficiency, skill, spirit, and determination are immeasurable."

On the other side of the world, General Douglas MacArthur was unstinting in his praise of their fortitude when he termed the WACs in the Pacific theater "my best soldiers" — confiding that his WACs worked harder than men, complained less, and were better disciplined. This did not prevent some of his subordinate commanders from reporting that women had no business in the Southwest Pacific because the "hardships, isolation and privation of jungle theaters are jobs for men."

The WACs who were shipped out to join MacArthur's advance

headquarters staff during the New Guinea campaign in 1943 faced not only the perils of the jungle, but the humiliation of having to be locked up in barbed-wire compounds and given armed escorts because of the fear that GIs, many of whom had not seen a western woman for a year and a half, would lose control. Single-couple dates were strictly forbidden and those WACs assigned to mail censorship became demoralized because much of what the men wrote home to wives and girlfriends was so sexually graphic.

On Hollandia, during the final stages of General MacArthur's New Guinea campaign, the local regulation required all WACs to wear trousers, not just as protection against mosquitoes but against the men of the naval construction battalion. The women in the army air force devised a way to circumvent regulations until, as one of the Seabees recalled, their sister soldiers extracted an uncomfortable revenge:

At the big Seabee dances, the WACs would appear in their inevitable pants. Then the few flying WACs would come sashaying in, also wearing pants, but carrying overnight valises. The flying WACs would step into the "head" and appear shortly thereafter "sans pants" and sans valises. They'd be wearing trim skirts and the wolf lines would form on the right. Of course the pants-wearing WACs weren't going to take it long. After the dance one night, when the flying WACs went back to the head to change their pants, they found that liberal quantities of beer had been poured into their valises: their clothes were saturated! After that the flying WACs never dared shed their pants at the dance hall. Everybody kept her pants on.

The underlying prejudice in the military flared up again during the final weeks of the war when *Yank,* the semiofficial magazine of the U.S. armed forces, published a scornful letter from a Sergeant Bob Bowie belittling the contribution that uniformed women had made to winning the war:

Why we GIs over here in the Pacific have to read such tripe and drivel about WACs beats me. Who the hell cares about these dimpled GIs who are supposed to be soldiers? All I have ever heard of them doing is peeling spuds, clerking in the office, driving a truck or a tractor or puttering around in the photo lab. Yet all the stories written about our dears tell how overworked they are. I correspond regularly with a close friend of mine who is a WAC, and all she ever writes about is the dances, picnics, swimming parties and bars she has attended. Are these Janes in the Army for the same reason that we are, or just to see how many dates they can get? We would like them a hell of a lot better, and respect them more, if they did their part in some defense plant, or at home, where they belong. So please let up on the cock and bull and feminine propaganda. Its sickening to read about some doll who has made the supreme sacrifice of giving up her lace-trimmed undies for ODs.

The counterbarrage of protest from outraged servicewomen which crashed onto editors' desks included a well-aimed salvo at male prejudice by Private Jane Nugent:

Thanks for the bouquets, boys. Go right on sticking the knife in our backs. . . . When it's all over we'll go back to our lace-trimmed undies and to the kind of men who used their anger on something besides the WACs!

As one official U.S. army historian wrote: "Perhaps the greatest achievement of the WACs was their triumph over the prejudices of the male military mind. The half-amused, half-scornful attitude of some officers in responsible positions was not justified by the performance of the WACs."

Women questioned by wartime surveys, however, did not see themselves as the shock troops in a war of liberation. Yet a large number of women did join the auxiliary services on both sides of the Atlantic to escape the traditional limitations imposed on them by civilian life. This was revealed by a 1943 survey conducted by the U.S. army among a cross section of typical WACs. The in-depth interviews discovered that over 40 percent of the female enlistees were motivated by a desire to escape from unhappy homes, or boring jobs or to search for adventure; 25 percent wanted to improve their economic or social status — and less than 20 percent were genuinely motivated by patriotism. Typical of the majority consensus for change were such comments as "I was sick and tired of that typewriter, I couldn't stand it any more" . . . "I wasn't getting anywhere" . . . "We wanted to help make the world free and get a thrill out of doing it" . . . "I never realized what women could do" . . . "I guess it is like the soldiers — after so much routine you want to get out and fight" . . .

"I wanted to see something of the world before the War ended"
. . . "I think the Army needs me and I need the Army."

Military service had a powerful liberating effect on many
American women, which was summed-up by one WAAC who told
the researchers, "I feel competent for the first time and independent. It is a good feeling to be able to take care of yourself."

"Nothing could be more conducive to the emergence of the individual girl, for the first time separated from the setting with
which she is normally identified. Wealth, social position, ances-
try, professional experience — all vanished upon entrance into the
service; and everyone started again to become identified as a
person in this new relationship," asserted Captain Mildred
MacAffe Horton. The former president of Wellesley College,
Horton had run the women's arm of the U.S. navy throughout
the war. She was therefore in a better position than most to judge
the personal and collective impact that uniformed service had
when she observed in 1946 that: "If military service individual-
ized women, it also made them more conspicuously women than
they had been before."

Whether women's newfound identity and purpose would produce an immediate wave of postwar feminine liberation was
doubted by Captain Horton, who made this prescient forecast:

It is my impression that women are not likely to demand rights for
themselves as veterans on the score of meriting a nation's gratitude. By
and large, they know they risked relatively little, compared to their
combatant brothers. Their changed estimate of themselves may make
problems for themselves and their communities, but I prophesy that they
will be the problems of individuals rather than of women veterans as a
group.

★ [4] ★

The Khaki Issue

Vague and discreditable allegations about the conduct of women in the Forces have caused considerable distress and anxiety not only to friends and relations at home but to men fighting overseas.

— BRITISH PARLIAMENTARY REPORT, 1942

Men have for centuries used slander against morals as a weapon to keep women out of public life.

— U.S. WAC OFFICER

"She'll be wearing khaki issue when she comes" was the ribald wartime version of the old American favorite "She'll Be Coming Round the Mountain." Loaded with lasciviousness, it was a favorite ditty with which British soldiers had welcomed the first ATS units in the early years of World War II. Soon the playful joking about the novelty of the female auxiliary was to be replaced by a groundswell of male resentment in which servicemen spread tales about the alleged promiscuity of the ATS. This was no laughing matter for the thousands of women in army uniform who had to endure accusations about their immorality from servicemen and public throughout the war.

"Virtue has no gossip value," as one British member of Parliament rightly observed, and the wartime climate of censorship and secrecy was fertile ground for rumors. The women in the army and air force, but not the navy, were considered fair game. The ATS attracted the disparaging epithet "Officer's Groundsheets" and the WAAF were referred to as "Pilot's Cockpits" in coarse humor. "I don't think air force men went out with WAAFs particularly. In fact, just the opposite," observed one RAF flight ser-

geant. "They tended to shy away from women in their own uniform and go for women in the Wrens and Land Army." The
Wrens escaped such vulgar labels. This may have been because
its ranks were drawn from middle-class girls or, as wartime Royal
Navy officer Nicholas Montserrat observed, "There seems to be
a special affection in the Navy for Wrens — by which I mean that
they are looked on, not as fair game, but as part of the Service
and thus to be protected and preserved from outsiders."

"There was the attitude about girls in uniform, that they were
easy, but they weren't any different from other girls," insisted one
WAAF, who admitted that she used to change into civilian clothes
at wartime dances to stop men from getting too fresh with her.
Women who joined the services quickly learned to ignore the wolf-
whistles and frequent sexual overtures from soldiers. One sixteen-year-old girl who had added a year and a half to her age to
qualify for the WAAF took seriously the adage "forewarned is
forearmed" when attending her army camp cinema:

An airman got very fresh and several of us younger girls had armed
ourselves with hatpins for protection because we could hide them in the
lapels of our uniforms. I had occasion to use mine. The lights came on
when the airman screamed and clutched his bottom. Everyone stared
at me. After that I was known as "the pin-up girl."

Learning to defend themselves against the unwelcome attentions of soldiers was not part of the formal basic training course,
but it was a lesson that most women learned when they joined
up and grew up rapidly. One new WAAF recruit recalled her
embarrassment at "doing physical education on the beach at
Morecombe in large navy blue knickers in the middle of winter
while RAF rookies cheered us on." Another Scottish ATS woman
recalls nearly fainting when she was detailed to assist a quartermaster rekitting male troops: "He just gave me a brief talk and
showed me how to fill in the clothing forms. But when the soldiers came in and he ordered, 'Easy and drop 'em!' I was quite
shocked as I'd never seen a man without trousers before."

Confronting the naked reality of masculine army life matured
many young women in a manner that, in retrospect, they found
more amusing than shocking.

The incident I recall was after one regular monthly medical inspection which took place in a long Nissen Hut with changing benches along one wall. We women were allowed to change in the privacy of the doctor's office, but on one occasion we emerged straight into a line of men, absolutely starkers. We fled, but were ragged about it afterwards. In those days we were fairly innocent, the word *sex* hadn't entered our vocabulary.

Sex-education lectures were embarrassing and frequently delivered by unsympathetic army doctors, who were also responsible for the regulation medical inspections, which, according to one ATS recruit, did more to frighten than inform:

We were examined for venereal infections when we joined the army, and every month at the medical inspection. Great moral emphasis was laid on not having affairs with men, which sort of filtered through — although nobody paid much attention. Yet at the same time girls in the army became obsessed with the whole VD thing during the war, as it was drummed into you so much. Most of us had never heard of VD or knew what it was, but like many others I developed symptoms out of pure psychosomatic terror.

Medical examinations were not only perfunctory, but were performed by orderlies with little or no gynecological training, according to one ATS private, who vividly recalled the morning PT parade was abandoned when a member of her unit gave birth: "There were men present, but we were even more surprised because, although she looked pregnant, girls who had come with her swore that she had always been that size."

Wartime censorship prevented such incidents appearing in the British press, but by the second year of the war the government's monitoring survey reported increasing public concern about allegations of immorality in the ATS. One woman in York believed there was a local "maternity home for ATS babies." Another told her doctor, "I'd like to join the ATS. He said, 'Don't you dare!' " Mothers said they "would not recommend any girl joining," and one girl confided, "Oh, I could not join the ATS. All my friends would think I was one of 'those.' "

Such views were so widespread that the conclusion was that "morality of the ATS is attacked universally, but this condemnation appears to originate almost wholly with members of the

Forces . . . inspired by the men's preoccupation with their own or comrades' lack of morals." The survey found that the ATS was generally considered to be an "unglamourous" service, the legion of Cinderellas, domestic workers of low degree among whom one expected, and got, "a low degree of immorality."

Wild rumors about an epidemic of pregnancy and VD rates in the auxiliary services in 1941 generated a flood of protests from worried parents, churchmen preached against wartime morals from the pulpit, and questions were tabled in Parliament. So vociferous had the outcry become that, at the height of the Blitz, Churchill's cabinet, which was concerned about their intended plans for female conscription, announced on 2 December 1941 that a parliamentary committee would investigate "amenities and welfare conditions in the three women's services."

The investigating commission was set up under the chairmanship of the distinguished lawyer Miss Violet Markham, and its leading spokesman became Dr. Shirley Summerskill, the forthright Labour member and founder of the Women's Home Defence Unit. While the Luftwaffe did their best to bomb Britain to its knees during winter of 1941, the Markham Committee braved the disruptions of the railway system to tour 123 military camps and interview thousands of servicewomen. After six months of exhaustive investigations, their report unanimously advised Parliament that there was "no justification for the vague, but sweeping charges of immorality which have disturbed public opinion . . . one or two cases which, in the course of gossip, have been multiplied many times over."

The Markham Report was, however, critical of the quality of officer training ("too much time is devoted to factual instruction"), accommodation ("visits to the latrines may mean mackintoshes and gum boots"), and army food ("Sausages and mash and roly poly pudding may be excellent in themselves but unsuitable for anyone suffering from a sick headache"). Lectures in general, and sex education in particular should be improved "not because the sex morals of the Forces are more precarious than those of civilians but because life in the Forces . . . presents new educational opportunities."

When it came to the sensitive issue of "khaki morality," the report acknowledged the "emotional stresses due to the war which lead to extramarital relationships," but pointed out that the disciplines of service life were "corrective rather than an incitement to bad conduct." This was confirmed by the statistics that showed that both illegitimacy and VD rates for the ATS and other women's services were lower than, and in some cases half that of, the comparable age and sex group in the civilian population.

"In civilian life cases of immorality are spread over a wide area," the Markham Committee noted, while "in the Services they occur in small compact communities and are at once concentrated and conspicuous." Nor was there any evidence to indicate that Nazi sympathizers were trying to undermine the national war effort by rumor-mongering; rather, the report put the blame on male resentment:

The British, though they fight when called upon to do so with unfaltering courage and determination, are not a military race. They cherish a deep-rooted prejudice against uniforms; consequently a woman in uniform may rouse a special sense of hostility, conscious or subconscious, among certain people who would never give two thoughts to her conduct as a private citizen. The woman in uniform becomes an easy target for gossip and careless talk. To be seen drinking a glass of beer in a public house is to provide a text for fluent remarks about the low standards of the Services. Further, though the service rendered to their country by women is generally recognized, there are exceptions and critics within and without the Forces. Strictures in particular, from soldiers, sailors and airmen, small minority though they be, carry weight out of proportion to their numbers, and may be repeated often with exaggerations, since no story loses in the telling.

The British parliamentary commission noted that similar "mischievous and false" sexual obliquy had been generated when women donned uniform in World War I. The government commission that had then been sent over to France in 1918 to investigate "wild and fantastic tales" of immorality in the female auxiliaries had also concluded that "a vast superstructure of slander had been raised on a small foundation of fact."

The overseas postings of women in uniform had evoked the same response in the German army. In 1942 the Wehrmacht issued a directive that "female army assistants" were to be protected from "enemy propaganda." It appealed to the traditional "chivalry" of "every German soldier to defend the honor of these girls. If a German soldier humorously refers to the women as

'Blitzmadchen'— blitzgirls — there is nothing wrong with that; but if offensive remarks are passed, it is hoped that a more respectful comrade will object strongly."

It is not without significance that each side blamed the other for the assaults on the virtue of their female auxiliaries, but chivalry had become another early casualty of total war, and the Wehrmacht command, like the British army, soon discovered that most of the slander was spread from within their own ranks. Despite initial hopes by the WAAC and WAVES directors that GIs, in the best of American tradition, would be more respectful of the female auxiliaries, the same sexual smears circulated. By 1943 "The Slander Campaign," as the phenomenon was labeled by the administration directorate, was in full swing.

In the United States the anti-Roosevelt press played on the public impression of widespread promiscuity in the auxiliaries by inflating stories to headline proportions as in the classic *Washington Times-Herald* headline "STORK PAYS VISIT TO WAAC NINE DAYS AFTER ENLISTMENT." Army newssheets as well as civilian newspapers delighted in cartoons that made fun of women in uniform. Khaki brassieres, empty or otherwise, were a constant source of comic inspiration to cartoonists who paid little attention to making fun of male undergarments of the same military color.

Crank letters condemning the sinfulness of women in uniform were ammunition for radio evangelists, who railed against army medical inspections that supposedly paraded lines of nude females. Temperance campaigners denounced the increase in wartime drunkenness that encouraged promiscuity between the ranks on mixed military bases, although statistics showed that WAACs contracted venereal infection at a fraction of the male soldiers' rate and their pregnancies in the corps were a fifth the level of a comparable group of female civilians.

Rumor and speculation about sexual activity in the female army spread rapidly across the United States during the spring of 1943. From New York it was rumored that shiploads of pregnant WAACs were being sent back from England and North Africa under armed guard to prevent them jumping overboard rather than disgracing their families. At Camp Lee, Virginia, soldiers believed that anyone seen dating a WAAC had to report for medical treatment. At Hampton Roads, a major port of embarkation, GIs going overseas were convinced that 90 percent of the WAACs were prostitutes and that 49 percent of the corps were discharged for pregnancy. In Florida there were stories that WAACs openly solicited soldiers, and that physicians examining female recruits had been ordered to reject all virgins. There was even a bizarre report from the foxholes of New Guinea that GIs were thumbing through copies of an army sex-hygiene pamphlet illustrated with pornographic photos of WAAC girls.

In June 1943 the slander campaign reached a peak after the *Washington Times-Herald* leaked a sensational story that Mrs. Roosevelt and "the New Deal Ladies" were behind a supersecret agreement that "contraceptives and prophylactic equipment will be furnished to members of the WAAC." It referred to a pamphlet that the War Department described as a "wholesome manual" on sex hygiene intended for briefing WAAC officers. The booklet in fact dealt with the various aspects of personal feminine hygiene with a modesty calculated not to upset "a girl unaccustomed to attributing precise meanings to words." The sensitive issue of contraception was sidestepped by stressing the need for continence.

The War Department, unwisely as it turned out, decided that it was beneath official dignity to release the inoffensive pamphlet. Nor were official denials forthcoming rapidly enough to destroy the damaging nationwide press story that suggested the army was condoning and encouraging promiscuity among its troops by issuing free contraceptives to female, as well as male, soldiers. "Long distance calls from parents began to come in, telling the girls to come home," reported a WAAC camp commander. "The younger girls all came in crying, asking if this disgrace was what they had been asked to join the army for." One WAAC sergeant "went home on leave to tell my family it wasn't true."

When I went through the streets, I held up my head because I imagined everybody was talking about me, but when I was at last inside our front door, I couldn't say a word to them, I was so humiliated — I just burst out crying, and my people ran and put their arms around me and cried with me.

The WAAC director, normally a most composed woman, broke down at an emergency staff meeting where it was decided to launch an official counterattack. The president himself went on record to condemn what he called this "deliberate newspaper job," which he blamed on "orders from the top" of the anti-administration *Chicago Tribune* without actually naming his old foe Colonel McCormick. Mrs. Roosevelt believed that Hitler and home-grown Nazis might be behind a sinister plot, because "Americans fall for Axis-inspired propaganda like children." Secretary of War Henry Stimson also saw a Nazi plot, because any drop in WAAC recruiting would "interfere with the increase in the combat strength of our Army." Congresswoman Edith Nourse Rogers, the "midwife" of the WAAC bill, agreed that "nothing would please Hitler more" and that "loose talk concerning our women in the armed services cannot be less-than-Nazi-inspired."

A nationwide investigation was ordered. But the combined resources of military intelligence in cooperation with the FBI was unable to bring to light the slightest shred of evidence to suggest the Germans were involved. The unpalatable truth was that rumors of WAAC immorality were not spread by Nazi sympathizers but were the product of "Army personnel, Navy personnel, Coast Guard personnel, business men, women, factory workers and others. Most . . . have completely American backgrounds." Motivation was believed to be supplied by "male military personnel who are sometimes inclined to resent usurpation of their long established monopoly" and "soldiers who had never dated WAACs" or who had "trouble getting dates." The investigators discovered that gossip was relayed by "officers' wives over bridge tables" and "local girls and women who resent having the WAACs around," and encouraged by men "who cannot get used to women being in any place except the home."

The U.S. army study concluded, as the British parliamentary commission had also discovered, that the biggest perpetrators of slander were servicemen themselves. This was confirmed by reports from military censors that V-mail letters from GIs were spiced with such disparaging references as: "You join the WAVES or WAC and you are automatically a prostitute in my opinion" . . . "I told my Sis if she ever joined I would put her out of the house, and I really mean it. So if you ever join, I will be finished with you too.". . . "Get a damn divorce. I don't want no damn

WAC for a wife.". . . "The service is no place for a woman. A woman's place is in the home." . . . "About joining the WACs the answer is still NO. If they really need service women let them draft some of the pigs that are running loose around town."

In the summer of 1943 the War Department launched a major counteroffensive to restore the image of the WAAC to coincide with its elevation to full military status as the WAC (Women's Army Corps) that September. Statistics were released to show that women in uniform were more moral and cleaner living than the men, and a planeload of prominent religious leaders and politicians took off on a tour of major WAAC training bases. Their joint press statement reported that "parents concerned about the moral and spiritual welfare of their daughters can be reassured." But no amount of publicity about the number of servicewomen who dutifully attended mass, or statements by congressional committees that "no self-respecting patriotic American would indulge in such a cowardly, contemptible, despicable course" could undo all the harm.

"Men have for centuries used slander against morals as a weapon to keep women out of public life," a WAC liaison officer observed, noting how successful the old technique had proved again when the WAC directorate resigned themselves to the fact that they would never reach their ambitious recruiting target of over a million.

The slander campaign had a much more drastic effect on American enlistment because it was voluntary. Significantly, the parliamentary committee which investigated the same charges in Britain while agreeing that the gossip about the moral standards of the female auxiliaries was wildly exaggerated, nonetheless conceded that "a certain bravado in much talk that takes place between young people about sex questions" might have encouraged many stories because "standards of sexual behavior have changed greatly in the last generation and some people to-day conduct their lives on principles remote from those termed Victorian."

The frank recollections of one British ATS corporal suggest that this wartime sexual "bravado" was by no means restricted to male barrackroom life:

While in mixed company women were submissive and accepted the role men expected them to play, in our barracks we were something completely different. We played dangerously and talked dirty. Men were an alien element, yet everything that we women desired. Getting enough sex was all part of the dare that the war represented for us women, because it allowed us to express our liberty and rebelliousness from the male-set archetypes of loving wife and mother that they had always tried to tie us to. This naturally brought women together, and, apart from the prim or religious ones — of which there were quite a few — it enabled women to talk together about men.

The Markham Report had also cautioned about using wartime pregnancies as a measure of the level of promiscuity among women since the "use of contraceptives of recent years has spread through all classes of society and sexual intercourse may be common without pregnancy resulting." Male service personnel, moreover, were issued with free condoms while servicewomen were not. Such was the stigma against getting PWP — "Pregnant Without Permission" — that it was perhaps assumed that servicewomen would ensure their partner took the necessary precautions. But despite the ready availability of contraceptives, some girls were not always willing — or informed enough — to insist on this. In WAAF barracks a ditty about "Sleeping Out Passes" (SOP) was sung to the popular wartime tune of "Jealousy":

> 'Twas all over my SOP,
> That settled how my fate was to be,
> For he was an officer in the RAF
> And I was a poor little innocent WAAF.

> He gave all his kisses to me,
> And now all too late I can see,
> I'll have to tell mother,
> There's goin' to be another,
> 'Twas all over my SOP.

Pregnancy was grounds for automatic discharge from the women's services in both Britain and the United States, although with no financial penalties or dishonorable stigma, regardless of marital status. After female conscription was introduced in England, some girls found that having a baby was their only escape route from compulsory military service. "You could get two months' pregnancy allowance," explained one former member of the ATS, so "many women would get pregnant deliberately to get out and then go and have a back-street abortion. The risk was well worth taking for those who had had enough of the army life, because you could not be called up again."

British regulations required expectant mothers to resign by the fifth month, and while unmarried mothers were prohibited from reenlisting, married women were eligible to be reinstated if their child was cared for. The U.S. army adopted the same practice, and while neither country penalized women getting pregnant, both military establishments concentrated a great deal of effort on preaching continence to their servicewomen because of fears about the public reaction to VD.

A secret conference on the sensitive subject of the "Prevention of Venereal Disease in Female Personnel" was held in Washington in July 1942, a month before the first women were inducted. It accepted that both the army and navy were ill prepared with instructional films and pamphlets suitable for women. A survey quoted Dr. J. E. Moore of Johns Hopkins University. This showed that while only a quarter of unmarried men were continent, 25 percent regularly engaged in sexual intercourse, and the other 50 percent did so "sporadically," the equivalent proportions for unmarried women were 40 percent continent, 5 percent promiscuous, and 55 percent having sexual experience from time to time.

"The 40 percent are taken care of, the 5 percent can never be helped particularly," agreed the chairman of the National Research Council's committee on venereal disease, who pointed out that they could not "evade our duty" to give proper prophylactic advice to half the female intake who might reasonably be expected to be sexually active. The committee therefore concurred in taking a positive approach advocated by the report of observers who had been sent to England to learn how the ATS dealt with problems of social hygiene.

The British Royal Army Medical Corps had been reluctant to release any statistics to the American observers on either VD or pregnancy rates in personnel — perhaps to conceal that there had been a rise in the ATS rates that year. But what the American fact-finding team discovered gave them cause for concern. Sex-education lectures were "entirely inadequate" because they "skate around sex and briefly mention syphilis and gonorrhea as venereal diseases." Checking the spread of these "social diseases" had been complicated by the overseas postings of many British servicemen and thousands of Free French, Polish, and other exiled soldiers who had taken refuge in England. Such foreign troops were especially attractive to Britain's lonely women and it was generally recognized that "lack of VD control in the Women's Services has created a problem of major proportions."

A visit to the main VD treatment center at the British army's Shenley military hospital by an American venereologist had revealed that an anticipated maximum of six beds a night for treating female VD cases had been expanded to fifty. The weekly trainload of female VD cases were "completely ostracized" by the staff, who appeared to believe that part of the treatment was to deal with the women as "moral lepers." This contributed to psychiatric problems and attempts to hide infections while girls sought unauthorized treatment at their own bases through friendly medical orderlies who had access to the new sulfonanilamide therapeutics: "If the boyfriend is infected and received treatment he tells her to take the drug too."

When the committee's recommendations reached Director Hobby, she rejected the idea of making contraceptive advice and prophylactic stations available for female as well as male soldiers, seeing this as potentially explosive. As a result of protests to General Marshall, the U.S. army surgeon general laid down that social hygiene lectures "should be presented in a dignified and wholly acceptable manner, in line with the common practice in outstanding colleges for women in this country." It was clearly not the army's wish, or role, "to promote social reform in time of war."

Mrs. Hobby remained unshaken in her conviction that considering "the character of the women who will likely be accepted in the WAAC, it is anticipated that venereal disease and pregnancy will not offer a problem of major importance." While the director was prepared to believe that the etiquette of a ladies' seminary could somehow be made compatible with army life, other advisers cautioned against "efforts to impose boarding school types of discipline on adult female personnel of the WAAC." But Mrs. Hobby was firmly convinced that "taboos and punitive measures do have a deterrent effect on large numbers of people" and that

to provide contraceptive and prophylactic advice would "reflect
an attitude toward sexual promiscuity that, whatever the practice, is not held by the majority of Americans. The Army, I repeat, is no place to propagandize new social attitudes."

It was inevitable, though, that life away from home in these
circumstances would generate its own nexus of sexual liberation
for WAACs. This had already been the effect that army life had
on the girls in Britain's ATS according to one of its recruits, who
frankly admitted that her sex life began when she joined the army
at eighteen:

Quite apart from the free barrack-room talk about sex, there was a universal language that we all picked up from the graffiti on toilet walls.
We discovered that the men for sure used this as a way of communication with each other about the women in our camp. They would write
"Try Shirley, she's easy" and so on. It was particularly useful to those
who were in transit and needed a quick information as to who was a
good lay so that they could get one before moving on. But we women
would use it also. This graffiti was a useful guide for the new recruits;
toilet information was a useful "sexual noticeboard" through which girls
could tell each other anonymously what they had learnt. This was one
of the ways in which the army really did help educate us about sex, yet
because of the competition there was never really any way to be sure
how many men anybody really had or with whom — except for the virgins and nymphos — because everyone was eager to be having as much
sex as possible.

Soldiers who recovered at military hospitals in World War II
considered their duty to flirt outrageously with the nurses in the
hopes of obtaining very personal comfort. A GI wrote of an army
nurse from the U.S. military hospital in Casablanca with particular affection:

She told us to call her Butch. She was from Dorchester and she was the
biggest gal I'd ever seen. When she bent over to take my temperature,
I thought from her wide breasts and budding belly that a witty and
motherly cow was ministering to me. We loved the lieutenant for her
laugh that was cynical and rich. She specialized in making the appendix
patients laugh until they all but burst their stitches. There was a smell
of cologne and soap about her. One night she had a baby on the stairs

of the nurses' quarters. The colonel had to deliver her himself, it was the first time he'd practiced obstetrics in thirty years. He was so mad at her for waking him out of a sound sleep that he shipped her and her baby back from Casablanca to the States.

The military nursing services inevitably, therefore, acquired a reputation for turning a blind eye to sexual permissiveness. The currency of their immorality was often exaggerated by envious enlisted men who saw officers monopolizing the company of nurses.

The nurses themselves became hardened to the gossip, particularly in the Pacific hospitals where they learned to cope with sex-starved patients and the rigorous life. As Second Lieutenant Elizabeth Itzen summed it up in verse she titled "Personal Report":

> My life consists of bully beef,
> Soggy clothes and wiggly teeth,
> Gunshot wounds and jungle rot,
> And days that are so bloomin' hot
> That even hell compared to this
> Would seem a simple life of bliss.

Because nurses had been a uniformed army auxiliary since the turn of the century, the War Department in Washington was less concerned with their alleged immorality overseas than with countering the bad publicity their sisters in uniform were attracting in the United States. In 1943 a tighter control was ordered by the WAC directorate on overnight passes after an investigation of misconduct following complaints from hotels near army camps that women enlistees were checking into rooms with soldiers. Occupants of some of the rooms were "not fully dressed."

Such cases might adversely reflect on the reputation of the corps, but controlling the lives of female soldiers offduty was very problematical, the more so after women were granted equal military status in 1943. The judge advocate general's office pointed out in a review of a similar hotel incident in July:

The women who make up the WAC are, therefore, to be treated as enlisted and commissioned personnel of the Army rather than inmates of some well-chaperoned young ladies' seminary. . . . While it might be readily surmised that this young woman and young man, after a certain amount of convivial imbibing, might have withdrawn to a bedroom of the suite to indulge in more intimate relationships and while it might be conjectured that two people of opposite sexes that were discovered to be alone in a bedroom with the articles that were discovered to be present were there for other purposes than to repeat their "pater nosters," yet the law requires more conclusive proof of an evil act before it will sustain a conviction.

Homosexual activity was not considered the same disgrace when practiced by women in uniform as it was with men. Although it posed the same inherent threat to military discipline, it did not attract the same penalties, a reflection of the dual standard applied by civilian laws. Queen Victoria's refusal to believe that such women existed excluded lesbians from the harsh criminal penalties of Britain's Sexual Offences Act, and while the so-called sodomy statutes applied to "all persons" without distinction, they had never been successfully invoked against any American woman.

The WAAC selection boards attempted to screen out the women with homosexual tendencies, who, it had been anticipated, would be attracted to the segregated army life for other than patriotic motives. Since the percentage of the female population with exclusive homosexual tendencies was found by the Kinsey research to be only a fifth of the estimated 10 percent incidence of male homosexuality, it was not surprising that it did not pose the same problem for the military authorities. The identification of homosexuality in the female services was complicated because demonstrations of physical affection were considered socially acceptable among women. Army psychologists also advised that the development of close comradeship was an important element in the building of esprit de corps. Nevertheless, the "potential problem which may be expected when a large number of people of the same sex are in constant association" was tactfully dealt with in the sex hygiene course pamphlet prepared in 1943. "Homosexuality is of interest to you as WAAC officers, only so far as its manifestations undermine the efficiency of the individuals concerned and the stability of the group." Officers were specifically cautioned to avoid "hunting and speculating" of every close attachment that developed between enlisted women.

"Every person is born with a bisexual nature," the pamphlet

cautioned, urging officers to be "generous in your outlook" when it came to dealing with "fine and generous friendships." Distinction was to be made between the "active homosexual," who should be "discharged as promptly as possible," and the female soldier "who has gravitated toward homosexual practices" because of the new close association with women, loneliness, or "hero worship." This type "can be influenced away from homosexuality by sympathetic guidance." Transfers, shifting barracks, and the advice of the post surgeon were recommended remedies.

Officers were cautioned against "playing a game of hide and seek, particularly with those more confirmed in the practice," and only if it became necessary to protect enlistees from an "active homosexual" was she to be discharged. Courts-martial were to be a last resort because of the difficulty of proving an offense had been committed against army regulations. The guidelines warned that "any officer bringing an unjust or unprovable charge against a woman in this regard will be severely reprimanded."

Women homosexuals, therefore, enjoyed more tolerance and protection in the United States wartime services than did their male counterparts. The difficulty of obtaining enough evidence to warrant any courts-martial allowed the official U.S. army historian to affirm "the problem of homosexuality occurred so rarely in the WAC." Not so rarely, judging from the threat of a public scandal that early in 1944 forced the army to take action against a group of lesbians at one of the largest WAC establishments in the eastern United States.

The WAC command initiated a full-scale investigation at its Georgia training camp after the secretary of war received a letter "to inform you of some of the things at Ft. Oglethorpe that are a disgrace to the U.S. Army." The complaint came from the mother of a twenty-year-old WAC from Wisconsin, "who I know was clean of heart and mind when she joined up. . . . It is no wonder women are afraid to enlist. It is full of homosexuals and sex maniacs.

"Unless this vice is cleaned out I am going to reveal that scandal to the world," wrote the mother, giving the names of a lieutenant and sergeant among "many other practicing this terrible vice" with her daughter. She explained how the shocking discovery had been made from "disgusting" letters that had recently arrived for her daughter who was on sick leave suffering from measles. Since the WACs had still not recovered from bad press the previous year in the "Slander Campaign," it did not take Colonel Hobby long before she acted to prevent headlines being made of love letters on USO notepaper.

The lieutenant who emerged as the ringleader of the lesbian circle at Fort Oglethorpe was a worldly, divorced lawyer in her early thirties. In an off-the-record session she successfully traded a general court-martial for a dishonorable discharge. She admitted "her guilt and assumed the entire blame and responsibility." The camp commandant indicated in her testimony that most WAC officers preferred to turn a blind eye to the lesbianism issue.

In talking about any of these subjects: sex, venereal disease, homosexuality . . . these are grown women supposedly. Most of them have at least heard dirty jokes about it. . . . I think we have had very few cases of overt homosexuality, of emotional basis. I think we have gotten most of them.

A leading male psychiatrist in the U.S. army confirmed the official view that, as far as female troops were concerned, homosexuality was not considered a major threat to good military order in the WACs:

I think it is a sort of mutual masturbation, if you ask me. I think it is very frank and haven't said it publicly, but I think they are away from home; they are somewhat lonely; they are away from their mothers, sisters, and so on, and I think it amounts to practically that. I don't think it is anything that they can't be, with any guidance, gotten out of. I would treat the matter exactly as we treat, for example, venereal disease. We have finally dragged the general subject of venereal disease out into the open to fight it rather than burrowing under ground.

The WAC directorate, however, was certainly not going to let the Fort Oglethorpe incident come out into the open, and so an officer was sent to Wisconsin to assure the corporal's worried mother that a full investigation had indeed "cleaned out" the culprits. The mother then agreed she "would never say anything that would harm the Army. . . . I wrote it when I was angry and should have waited, but it hurt me so badly, I have never had anything hit me like that." This allowed the investigation to wrap up its report on a reassuring note that while "homosexual addicts have gained admittance to the WAC," Fort Oglethorpe was not "full of homosexuals and sex maniacs." The lieutenant and the sergeant were permitted to resign, and the enlisted women involved in lesbian entanglements were transferred to alternate bases and the whole affair was confined to a confidential administrative file that remained stamped "Top Secret" for nearly forty years.

Among the many lesbians who were never discovered and who found both sexual opportunity and a surprising degree of tolerance in the WACs during World War II was a West Coast writer who recorded her astonishment at the welcome she received the first day she arrived at her basic training camp:

As I walked in with my suitcase, I heard a woman from one of the barracks windows saying, "Good God, Elizabeth, hear comes another one!" Everybody was going with someone or had a crush on someone. Always the straight women I ran into tended to ignore us, tended to say, "Who cares? It leaves all the men for us."

A WAVE recruit from Iowa recalls how she discovered her own sexual preference after joining up:

I was sitting in the barracks in Florida with this one woman I admired greatly. We were sitting next to each other with our feet propped up on the table, and she started stroking my leg, and I thought, "Wow! What's all this?" Eventually we got in bed together. She said that she had never related to a woman before. We didn't talk about what we were doing; we just did it and felt good about it. I just thought, "Well, this is the way it's going to be forever."

It may be presumed that the close confines of their barracks enabled many women both to observe and discover homosexual attractions in themselves. While most did not become lesbians as a result of their wartime encounters, many acquired a tolerance of and understanding for such tendencies in others that contributed to a relaxation of their prejudices in later postwar life.

★ [5] ★

Plaster Saints

A soldier's the sort
For rape and slaughter
Not fit to escort a patriot's daughter

— SERGEANT GRANT A. SANDERS, UNITED STATES ARMY

The Army does not officially condone profanity; unofficially, it knows it can do little to stop it. The society of soldiers is not polite. It is a society of men, frequently unwashed, who have been dedicated to the rugged task of killing other men, and whose training has emphasized that a certain reversion to the primitive is not undesirable.

— *U.S. INFANTRY JOURNAL,* 1943

The making of the "civilian" soldier during World War II involved a dramatic personal transformation for a large cross section of the male population. According to the *U.S. Infantry Journal,* war was to be compared with the "tussle over a mate" between animals of the same species, or their aggressive defense of their young and habitat:

Men, being two-legged animals, may fight for any and all of these reasons. But because they have minds capable of being moved by abstract ideas such as honor, glory, freedom, sympathy, justice and patriotism, men fight also for what they believe to be right.

Despite the *Journal*'s printed denial that it was "not the mouthpiece of the War Department," there was an unmistakably "official" ring to the simplistic sophistry in its articles. "Psychology for the Fighting Man," for example, stressed that civilians could be transformed into effective fighters by a diet that was high in disciplined subordination and red meat — to ensure plenty of thiamin, the so-called morale vitamin.

The "unquenchable spirit" needed by an army in the field, however, came not from the daily intake of vitamin B_1 or the patriotic "rush to arms at news of the enemy's evil designs or brutalities." Neither food nor patriotism was enough to make an enlisted man endure the physical privations of soldiering and accept the possibility of self-sacrifice. The mass citizen armies demanded by total war had to be produced by a rapid and brutal conditioning process designed to overcome the individual instinct for self-preservation, to make the new soldier capable of killing or dying on command.

Men in the armed forces learned that although they might be called upon to give their lives to defend civilized society, they were expected to abandon its most cherished principles for the duration. The transformation in attitude this demanded was vividly summed up by American author James Jones, who himself went through the process to become a GI:

He must make a compact with himself or with Fate that he is lost. Only then can he function as he ought to function under fire. He knows and accepts beforehand that he's dead, although he may still be walking around for a while. That soldier you have walking around there with this awareness in him is the final end production of the EVOLUTION OF A SOLDIER.

An essential part of this evolutionary process were intensive lessons in "the science of slaughter," which were set down in the diary of Sergeant Myles Babcock of the 37th U.S. Infantry Division. It included propaganda "combined with physical and mental hatred" that hardened soldiers and stripped away their inhibitions:

The psychological effect of lessons in hand-to-hand killing proved brutalizing. Lack of feminine companionship encouraged vulgarity, almost completely stilled courtesy. The individual civilians poured into the crucible of hate, brutality and organized murder undergo a subtle change. True they retain their identity and personality, but all bear the imprint of a common mold. The formula utilized in making a soldier is visualized to be an intangible called "discipline." No matter how forceful or unusual the personality, eventually it succumbs to habit, discipline, propaganda and mass psychosis. He becomes a soldier with salient characteristics and reactions. He embodies myriad vices, virtues and traits including profanity, vulgarity, chronic complaining, skepticism, irritability, brutality, respect for rights of colleagues, disrespect and envy of civilians, loneliness, hatred of monotony, a type of fatalism, despair, animalism, stamina, a Spartan reaction to pain and a burning hope that destiny dictates the return to the States.

European conscripts accepted this "crucible of hate" more readily than Americans, since war and military service had long been a part of the established British, French, German, Japanese, and Russian social order. In the United States it was significant that soldiers became tagged with the "Government Issue"— GI was an appropriate label for the expendable human elements in the mass-produced machine of twentieth-century warfare. They were distinguished only by the number on the dog tags that hung around their necks and military publications officially approved the title "GI Joe." Draftees were told to be "proud" of "the wonderful phrase that completely expresses the utter anonymity of the private soldier."

"Who in uniform would want it otherwise?" asked the *U.S. Infantry Journal* — and many agreed. As one wartime draftee explained: "The soldier liked being a GI. It was comforting to feel, in this radically different kind of life which so often involved fear and danger, that his own self was submerged in the anonymity of the mass. The role of GI made no undue demands on individual virtue or responsibility. Even if he continually bungled and became a 'sad sack' his fellows looked upon him with a kind of joking affection."

James Jones provided a graphic insight into the conditioning process that stripped away civilian privileges in order to make a man a GI:

Living in herds and schools like steers or fish, where men (suddenly missing deeply the wives or girlfriends they left so adventurously two weeks before) literally could not find the privacy to masturbate even in the latrines. Being laughed at, insulted, upbraided, held up to ridicule, and fed like pigs at a trough with absolutely no recourse or rights to uphold their treasured individuality before any parent, lover, teacher or tribune. Harassed to rise at five in the morning, harassed to be in bed at nine-thirty at night.

Many enlistees found especially embarrassing and painful the denial of privacy, especially for personal bodily functions:

Toilet taboos were suspended for the duration. Fifty of us shared one latrine and took turns at cleaning it, in a symphony of grunts and smells and flushing noises. There were no doors on the booths, nor privacy at the urinal. Answering nature's call meant subjecting yourself to loud and detailed criticism — perceptive and merciless descriptions of your sex organs, ranging from glowing admiration; brilliant critiques of your style of defecation, with learned footnotes on gas-passing. Expert discussions gave new meaning to your technique of urination — which hand, how many, or no hands at all — or how nonchalant you managed to look. We soon learned to flaunt our genitals and brag about our toilet mannerisms. Anyone who was modest about these was immediately and forever labelled a homosexual.

The military environment was oppressively masculine, emphasizing the break from the feminine and "civilizing" influences of civilian life. When it came down to the actual business of fighting, the conditioning needed to turn the World War II civilian into an aggressive soldier was a brutalizing process that often triggered the release of undercurrents of sexual aggression.

The precise relationship between sexuality and violence has been keenly debated since Freud's contention, in his 1915 essay "Reflections on War and Death," that resort to fighting "strips us of the later accretions of civilization, and lays bare the primal man in each of us." The frequency of war throughout human history indicates the power of the primitive psyche to reassert itself through the violence of armed conflict. The sex drive is the most intractable of human instincts. Normally repressed by religious taboos and social convention, it bursts these restraints when social life is disrupted by war and the demands of armed combat. Looking at it another way, the notion that a sexually aggressive man makes the best fighter has been universal throughout history and in all cultures, as a ranking U.S. navy medical officer observed in a 1941 review of the essential qualities to be instilled in a draftee:

The men in a successfully trained army or navy are stamped into a mold. Their barrack talk becomes typical, for soldiers are taught in a harsh and brutal school. They cannot, they must not, be mollycoddled, and this very education befits nature, induces sexual aggression, and makes them the stern, dynamic type we associate with men of the armed force. This sexual aggressiveness cannot be stifled. Recently, I read an article by a man who bewailed the effect army life would have on his son. Imagine, if you can, an army of impotent men. This very sexual drive is amplified because of fresh air, good food and exercise, and exaggerated by the salacious barracks talk. It cannot be sublimated by hard work or the soft whinings of Victorian minds. How important this libido was considered historically can be gathered from the words of Gian Maria, Duke of Milan, who after his defeat stated: "My men had ceased to speak of women, I knew I was beaten." The Mongol hordes, who conquered all Asia and most of Europe, recognized this fact too. "He who is not virile is not a soldier. He who lacks virility is timid, and what rabbit ever slew a wolf."

Soldiers in a world of ritualized masculinity subconsciously and consciously came to regard their weapons as extensions of their virility. They were encouraged in this view by instruction manuals such as that which informed the U.S. army infantrymen: "Your rifle, like your girl friend, has habits for which you must allow." Military discipline also produced, as a by-product of its emphasis on obedience and masculinity, profane language and rebelliousness in offduty pursuits. Hard drinking — a manifestation of virility — is a common feature of army life as soldiers outside the confines of their barracks escaped from boredom to exaggerate their self-assertion. Coarse language was adopted as a badge of masculine aggressiveness; barrackroom talk was — and is — punctuated with sexual expletives intended to convey male assertiveness and a general contempt for women.

Crude expressions for sexual and excretory acts were common parlance in barracks and bivouac, in language that scorned normal social restraints. "And, furthermore, by pronouncing those 'dirty words' which he never dared utter in the presence of 'Mom' or his old-maid schoolteachers, the GI symbolically throws off the shackles of the matriarchy in which he grew up," was the inference a sociologist drew from his wartime experience as an enlisted man:

The profane term that most clearly expresses this swaggering masculinity and revengeful, contemptuous (and defensive) attitude toward women is doubtless the most commonly used word (as noun, verb, adjective, adverb, and expletive) in the United States and British armies. In Anglo-Saxon popular culture, molded by Puritanism, this term suggests that the sexual act can only be "dirty" and animalistic; and, in keeping with a more nearly universal conception, it suggests that, whereas these qualities do not reflect ill on the male by virtue of his dominant and casual role, they ineradicably contaminate and degrade the human female.

The aggressiveness toward women that was enshrined in the military vernacular was evident in the bawdy verses of the chant to which the British Expeditionary Force marched to the French frontier in 1939:

> *I don't want a bayonet up my arse hole*
> *I don't want my bollocks shot away,*
> *I'd rather live in England,*
> *In merry, merry, England*
> *And fornicate my fucking life away.*

GI argot also developed a rich scatological and sexual slang. Conversation became "shooting the shit"; abuse of authority was "chicken shit"; bawling out was "ass-chewing"; and a downtrodden GI was "a sad sack of shit" — origin of the famous cartoon character "Sad Sack." The U.S. army's slang expression for a bungle was "situation normal all fucked up" or "Snafu." Many of these expressions were so universally used by the end of the war that they had been purged of their obscenity and passed into common parlance, such as Snafu's emendation to an acronym for "situation normal all *fouled* up!"

"Aside from the richness of the language, army conversation has a beautiful simplicity and directness. It is all on one solid, everlasting subject. . . . Women, Women, Women," wrote American author Irwin Shaw about his wartime experience as a soldier:

This makes it different from the talk about women and baseball. Occasionally a soldier will deviate a little and his control will leave him, like a pitcher tiring in the late innings, and he will talk about frivolous things like what he thinks ought to be done with Germany after the war. But very soon he will catch himself and start talking about the blonde girl he knew back at Purdue who measured thirty seven and three quarter inches around the chest, so help him God.

After a tour of Pacific bases, one senator, writing to reassure wives and sweethearts of the American serviceman's moral health, provided a somewhat different emphasis: "All GI talk revolves around two things — food and home. But their heads don't revolve, they're fixed, right above one spot in the world — the home and the girl they left there."

The reason that sex became the principal subject of conversation of troops everywhere was summed up by James Jones: "When the presence of death or extinction are always just around the corner or next cloud, the comfort of women takes on a great importance." This suggests one reason why women went to war by proxy as the pinups that were so ubiquitous that they gave a female face to World War II. The icons of female movie stars, along with the photos of wives and girlfriends, provided the individual serviceman some romantic escape from the horrors of combat. It was common practice for soldiers to vaunt the plainest sweetheart — or the most perfunctory sexual contact — and the most popular barrackroom ballads sang the praises of insatiable whores.

British troops in the Western Desert reworked the "Foggy, Foggy Dew" into a ribald ditty about a legendary Cairene Mata Hari who specialized in the seduction of high-ranking allied officers:

> They call me Venal Vera, I'm a lovely from Gezira,
> The Fuehrer pays me well for what I do.
> The order of the battle, I obtained from last night's rattle
> On the golf course with a Brigadier from GHQ.
> I often tarry on the back seat of a gharry,
> It's part of my profession as a spy,
> While his mind's on copulation I'm exacting information
> From a senior GSO from GSI.

The German Afrika Korps — and later the Allies who adopted her — embellished "Lili Marlene" with endless salacious verses. Another favorite of American GIs during Tunisian campaign celebrated the dubious attractions of the local whores:

> Dirty Girtie from Bizerte
> Had a mousetrap 'neath her skirtie
> Strapped it on her kneecap purty

Baited it with "Fleur de Flirte"
Made her boy friends most alerty
She was voted in Bizerte
"Miss Latrine" for nineteen thirty.

That there was a connection between the bold sexual talk and a deep-seated fear of death is suggested in the stanzas of the English soldier poet Jocelyn Brooke and a similar sentiment in a stanza from his Welsh comrade in arms Alun Lewis:

Browned-off with bints and boozing,
Sweating on news from home,
Bomb-happy and scared of losing,
This tent of flesh and bone . . .

And we talked of girls, and dropping bombs on Rome,
And thought of the quiet dead and the loud celebrities
Exhorting us to slaughter, and the herded refugees.

The procreative urge that was aroused by the ever-present fear of personal annihilation contributed to the aggressive masculinity of men in the armed forces. It was a powerful incentive toward promiscuity. Unlike civilian society, where merely dating a girl was socially acceptable proof of virility, men in military society were under constant pressure from their peers to demonstrate and brag about intimate details of their sexual conquests. The extended periods of separation from their womenfolk were felt most keenly by sailors who had traditionally boasted "a girl in every port." Their wartime behavior upheld that practice, as an enlistee in the navy confirmed:

I may say here that my memories of the sex life of the men I knew in the Navy, as I heard about it and observed it, fully supported the Kinsey report, especially in its emphasis on the different levels of education. The sexual life of these men was crude in the extreme, and when they had to be and could be, even most of the married men were freely promiscuous, but at the same time their loyalty to their wives and their best girls was deep, and I suspected that most of them were or would be good husbands and fathers — warmer, more unselfish, more playful, and more firm in their own rights and dignity, than their bosses in civilian life.

Soldiers, particularly those sent to overseas theaters of war, faced the same problems and sought the same solutions according to PFC Bill Mauldin, the cartoonist of the GI in World War II: "Drinking, like sex, is not a question of should or shouldn't in the army. It's here to stay and it seems to us here that the best way to handle it is to understand and recognize it, and to arrange things so those who have appetites can satisfy them with a minimum of trouble for everybody."

Some senior British and American generals had advocated establishing a system of military brothels similar to the French "*maisons tolerées*" that had provided women for their troops during World War I. The most powerful argument against this was that although the Axis powers had established military brothels, it was morally indefensible for the Allies to use women in this way. Sexual deprivation weighed most heavily on the American forces in the Pacific. U.S. army aircrews in 1942 actually wrote to General Marshall during the Guadalcanal campaign saying to win the long battle for the fetid island what they needed was not more bombs and bullets but women. Men of the 37th Army Division on Bougainville in the Solomons complained in 1943 that they had "seen only one white woman in nine months, and that is Lois, the nude on the chest of Private Albert Horton."

The chief of the U.S. army replied that while he "appreciated" the need, it was beyond the supply capability of the War Department. As John H. Burns described in his insightful account of GI life *The Gallery*, good military logistics clashed with Anglo-Saxon moral attitudes:

Sooner or later every man's thoughts start centering around his middle. The cold and scientific solution would have been to have brothels attached to all our armies overseas, as other nations of the world have always done. But the American people wouldn't have stood for that. I mean that American people back home — too many purity lobbies from old ladies who have nothing else to do but form pressure groups to guard other people's morals.

Individual commanders made unofficial efforts to provide brothel facilities for Allied troops, but the political penalties for doing so became apparent to the British government as soon as the British Expeditionary Force had been dispatched to France in 1939. Prime Minister Neville Chamberlain was soon being bombarded with protests from religious groups and organizations such as the Association for Moral Hygiene with demands for "action to protect the men of the Home and British Empire Forces by insisting that, in France and any other country where the system of licensed brothels still exists, these houses shall be immediately declared 'Out of Bounds.'"

The War Office advised that putting the *"maisons tolerées"* out of bounds "might reasonably be interpreted as an insult to the French authorities," whose licensed brothels helped prevent "the spread of VD in the present abnormal circumstances." A policy memorandum circulated to the Ministry of Health early in 1940 acknowledged: "Quite possibly the percentage of men with uncontrollable passions is small but the percentage of men who on very small temptation will do their best to obtain sexual satisfaction is not small, witness the patronage of licensed houses which are in bounds. . . . Presumably the houses are not advertised to the troops and to put them out of bounds because prophylactic precautions are taken in them seems to be no more justifiable than to put out of bound cantonment bazaars in India because of the chaklas (native whorehouses)."

The War Office confidentially accepted that what had failed in peacetime India was not going to keep British soldiers continent in wartime France: "moral inducements to chastity" or the "fear which every right-minded lad and man and every woman ought to entertain of the terrible consequences of impulsive sexual intercourse." Ministry of Health officials started contingency war-planning at the time of the 1938 Munich Crisis to expand venereal disease treatment centers. It was foreseen that the proliferation of RAF and army bases in rural areas would require a fleet of mobile VD units to make weekly inspection tours, but the Treasury refused to grant funds for staffing and equipping the proposed fleet of twenty motor vans.

On the outbreak of hostilities with Germany on 3 September 1939, a Ministry of Health circular alerted local health authorities: "It is well known that a state of war favours the spread of VD in the population." The repercussions of the "lack of self-control" and "excitement of war conditions" was by June 1940 causing alarm at "definite signs of the expected wartime increase" in VD rates, which was blamed on the Treasury's penny-pinching refusal to fund the VD vans. As a battle for Britain's health was waged in Whitehall committees that fateful summer, the RAF Spitfires and Hurricanes fought their famous battle for the supremacy of the skies over England. The Luftwaffe was beaten by mid-September, but it took another month before the Ministry of Health won its fleet of mobile VD units. A major factor in this victory was that the return of the defeated British Expeditionary Force from Dunkirk placed the burden of dealing with the consequences of wartime military promiscuity on the local health authorities.

Urgent meetings took place at Scotland Yard to discuss ways of controlling the sudden explosion of prostitution in London's West End. The police agreed to investigate whether, as vociferous moral campaigners believed, "big criminal interests" were behind the "new type of prostitute," dubbed "Piccadilly Warriors," roaming the blacked-out squares of central London. The increase in the numbers of prostitutes was blamed on what the National Vigilance Association termed "nasty young men" among the influx of foreign troops from France and Poland.

The number of women who plied the ancient trade in the streets of London and around the main army bases and in British ports in World War II rose in direct proportion to the number of men conscripted — an indication that a certain section of the female population was volunteering to meet the sexual demands of the armed forces. Any effort at controlling them was hampered in Britain because while a brothel — or "disorderly house" as it was quaintly defined by the law — was illegal, no action could be taken against street-walking prostitutes unless they actually accosted the man they were soliciting. Only then could they be charged and arrested for "obstruction" under an arcane bylaw. This encouraged the "amateur" whore and "good-time girl" to take to blacked-out streets. Venereal infections spread apace through the military and civilian populations. By mid-1941 the national incidence of VD had increased by 70 percent since the beginning of the war. In London and the seaports the rise was more dramatic, with Liverpool's health authorities reporting an alarming fourfold increase in syphilis cases, and the rate "still rising."

So many merchant seamen were reported infected in Britain's main ports that a sinister Nazi plot to aid the U-boats in the Battle of the Atlantic was suspected. "There is good reason to believe that in at least one neutral port, Lisbon, the enemy has a scheme for infecting British and Allied seamen through diseased prostitutes," reported a worried British Shipping Federation. Although no conclusive evidence was ever unearthed to show Hitler had enlisted the aid of the nefarious spirochete in Germany's bid to cut the Atlantic supply line, a special issue of prophylactic kits was rushed to Liverpool for distribution to the crews of cargo ships bound for neutral ports.

The arrival of the first American troops on British soil in the spring of 1942 sent venereal disease rates to almost epidemic proportions. But it was not until October of that year, after a series of parliamentary debates, that the Ministry of Health launched a radio and poster campaign to educate the public and to break down the traditional taboo on the public discussion of VD, and emergency powers for compulsory medical examinations of those infected were introduced.

The medical officers of the U.S. army were dismayed by the prevailing ignorance and lack of effective laws to combat venereal infection in Britain. Sex hygiene, as it was termed in America, had been a major part of the New Deal health education program since the mid-thirties, with annual "Social Hygiene Days" proclaimed by President Roosevelt. When sixty thousand of the first million American draftees were found to be venereally infected, public and congressional pressure mounted for a crackdown on the booming "red-light" districts that sprouted up alongside the expanding military training camps.

"Pay day for soldiers, sailors and marines are looked to with anticipation by practically everyone in the racket," stated a 1941 report by the American Social Hygiene Association, which was to play an instrumental part in the wartime "Blitz on the Brothels" in the United States. "On the last day of each month, and usually for two or three succeeding days, long lines of 'soldier boys' waited their turn to gain admittance. The operators, 'old timers' in the game, admitted one at a time only as many prospective customers as could be accommodated, and Military Police prevented those who were waiting from gate-crashing." Red-light district hotels advertised "rooms equipped with every human convenience," and bellboys and porters at legitimate hotels as well as taxi drivers were cut in on the racket. A national survey revealed that it was not just the commercialized vice rings but a burgeoning army of free-lance hookers who operated out of their own cars or taxis. The more enterprising girls had trailers, called "chippie wagons" by the GIs, which could be towed away from camps and city limits when police tried to crack down on prostitution. The magnitude of the problem confronting the U.S. military was outlined in the report of an experienced army doctor:

As to potentially infectious sexual contacts, soldiers may be divided into three categories: 15% of men will expose themselves repeatedly; for them disease prevention must be accomplished by prophylaxis. Another 15%, restrained by moral, aesthetic, or sanitary considerations, will not risk exposure at all; in them venereal disease control gives us no concern. The majority of 70% will expose themselves only under special circumstances, and usually not at all when more wholesome female companionship is available. For them a major element of disease control is the provision of such wholesome and normal feminine contact through organized recreational opportunity.

Precisely what substitute "recreational" opportunities could adequately compensate sex-hungry servicemen for these modern camp-followers was ignored by the supporters of Senator May's bill, passed in July 1941, that gave commanders of military bases the power to summon the FBI to close down local whorehouses. But many commanding officers preferred to "wink at prostitution" and ignore the official army policy directing a "vigorous repression" of prostitution. One camp colonel filed an official protest consisting of Kipling's pertinent observation that "Single men in barracks do not grow into plaster saints." But public moral outrage reached fever-pitch that July following publication of a book by the two ranking members of the U.S. Public Health Service, which charged that VD was the "No. 1 Saboteur of Our Defense." The *New York Times* reviewer found the sensational exposé "as fascinating as it is sinister." It charged that so-called panzer prostitutes, well-dressed women in smart automobiles, patrolled roads around army camps offering lifts to soldiers — to houses of ill repute. There were reports of "brothels on wheels" and a trailer camp, near Fort Knox, populated by elderly "parents" each with a surprisingly large family of dubious daughters available for hire by the hour.

Sackfuls of angry protest letters arrived at the White House and War Department demanding to know why the administration had not stepped up the battle against "the panzer prostitutes who nationwide are tainting our soldiers in increasing thousands." On the eve of the Pearl Harbor attack, U.S. army chief General George C. Marshall issued an official army directive on the need to repress prostitution. Commands were advised to invoke the provisions of the May Act, and enlistees were to be given sex hygiene brochures and shown anti-VD films regularly. "Unless extenuating circumstances exist, a high incidence of venereal disease in a command shall be regarded as indicating a lack of efficiency on the part of the commander concerned," the War Department circular warned.

"The guiding principle shall continue to be that continence and self-control not only develop character but are the only completely satisfactory methods of preventing venereal disease," directed War Department Circular No. 249. But the underlying hypocrisy of this directive — like all wartime attempts by the American and British to control military promiscuity — was that commands were instructed to continue establishing prophylactic stations and issuing free condoms "*when* the foregoing educational efforts have failed." This left the generals — more concerned with morale than morals — wide open to repeated charges from the morality campaigners and the Catholic Church that they were encouraging fornication by "making sin safe."

"Control" was interpreted as necessitating free contraceptives and establishing a defensive chain of prophylactic stations around naval and military bases. "Education" was hopefully to be achieved by posters, pamphlets, films, and regular lectures on the perils of prostitution and VD. The campaign was launched shortly after Pearl Harbor by former boxing champion Gene Tunney, then a naval commander, who urged American servicemen to pin what he called the "Bright Shield of Continence" on their uniforms and display "moral bravery when confronted by the rouged challenge" of "motorized brothels" and "diseased harlots." His homily, which was reprinted in *The Reader's Digest* and other popular magazines, cautioned:

Tally cards seized as evidence showed how much these prostitutes had earned in one day; three cards showed 49, 37 and 28 customers. . . . Can you imagine what happened to the 114 servicemen who visited them that day? . . . Can our sailors and soldiers, as champions of democracy, afford to indulge in sexual promiscuities scorned by most prize fighters? Dare they forget that in the First World War 7,000,000 days of service were lost to the U.S. Army as a result of venereal infections?

The appeal to continence was a failure; as Tunney's statement admitted: "Men don't get medals for practicing it." It was another failure in the long line of attempts made by generals and religious leaders to protect the health of their armies. Xenophon recorded that Greek warriors ignored warnings on "the issue of the flesh"; Julius Caesar had soldiers with symptoms of gonorrhea flogged; and Richard III had soldiers with the "pox" as it was known, hanged! It was the promiscuity of French soldiers campaigning under Louis XIII in Italy at the beginning of the sixteenth century that spread a sinister new venereal infection across Europe. Originally it was called *"Il morbo Gallico"* — the "French Evil." When it was discovered to be no respecter of nationality, it was renamed "syphilis" after the hapless Greek shepherd who was inflicted with a new plague for defying the god Apollo. The sinister scourge of syphilis has ever since been a consequence of wars. Although the long and painful "salvarsan" treatment had been introduced before World War I to offer a cure for the long-term effects of syphilis, it produced high casualty rates during the war and an extensive outbreak of congenital infection in infants following 1918.

As one GI put it, "A man is going to have sexual intercourse regardless of the price or danger to his health." Allied military commanders could therefore do little in World War II other than resort to the same lectures and disciplinary measures that involved reducing enlisted men in rank or forfeiting pay. The principal weapon in the armed forces was the regular exposure of servicemen to lectures and films. General Frank M. Richardson, one of the British army's senior wartime medical experts, vividly recalled his own first lecture just before World War II:

I rejected the advice of the experienced captain and waded into sex — masturbation, the lot; subjects then seldom voiced in public. I could feel the temperature falling to sub-Arctic, except above my collar where it was feverish. When I huskily announced that I was finished . . . into the dead silence burst the roar of a bull-voiced and popular subaltern, one year older than myself. "Well, doctor — you've certainly taken a load off my mind." The laughter raised the roof.

In the British army such lectures and "short-arm" inspections were yearly events in most regiments, but in the U.S. armed forces enlisted men were required to submit to the ritual of inspection and lecture every six months. Medical officers generally adopted the line "You absolutely must not; but if by chance you do," echoing the official attitude that took it for granted that soldiers would seek sexual relief regardless. "There was a colonel who scratched his pants crotch frantically as he warned us that we must never touch a woman," remembered one American enlisted man, "but that if we did, we should jump right out of bed and run to the nearest Pro Station. Then there were close-ups of male genitals undergoing an excruciatingly painful treatment. Have you ever seen genitals wince?"

The skills of Hollywood were mobilized by the U.S. army in 1942 to make a sex hygiene film that undoubtedly got across its message about the dangers of VD. "The day I got my wing and three stripes I was ushered into a cinema to see a horrifying film on V.D.," recalled an RAF flight sergeant. "God! There were people passing out right, left and centre." The problem with such shock tactics was that the film was considered too X-rated for teenage enlistees and the uncut version never received the widest circulation. The British army even primly restricted the censored version for fear of upsetting the sensibilities of its female projection staff.

Some chaplains devised a more up-to-date approach than the traditional homily of St. Paul's that "whatsoever a man soweth, that shall he reap." "Follow the red line to the shuttle train" was one original approach, which sought to compare the "moral red line for human conduct" to the directions in the New York subway. Other chaplains considered that the threat of hellfire for the "boasting sex-violators, your strutting libertine" was the most effective way of getting their message across. The British corps of chaplains, on the whole, avoided red-blooded language, appealing to the troops to respect "the perfect woman" and "loyalty to regiment."

The military chaplain's lot was not a particularly comfortable one. As a rabbi in the U.S. army confessed, "I have been asked if chaplains considered themselves as the guardians of men's morals. If we saw ourselves in that role, what an unhappy lot was ours. Advocating that the soldiers' language be laundered, that drunkenness be discouraged, that an army-operated brothel be abolished, was an invitation to unpopularity and transfer."

A sex survey conducted by the American army in the final year of the war revealed that only a tiny minority abstained from intercourse out of religious conviction. "Sure I am just as tempted as the next fellow, and just as human," explained one of the less than 1 percent of GIs who claimed to have remained continent in Italy in 1945, "but praying for strength to overcome temptation, I find it easy through Jesus." The overwhelming majority — more than 75 percent of American soldiers overseas — were restrained neither by prayer nor fear of disease. As a private observed of the failure of the British army to check the promiscuous behavior of soldiers, "We go in search of women. We know the risks. Doc said that we were sticking our pricks where he wouldn't put the heel of his dirty boot. Doc is worried. He says more soldiers fall from VD than from bullets. But as one old-timer said: 'Which would you rather have, laddie, a dose of VD or a packet of shrapnel up your arse?'"

Writer John Steinbeck, who observed U.S. servicemen at close quarters, criticized the hypocrisy of public opinion, which obliged the army to subscribe to the fiction that "five million perfectly normal, young energetic and concupiscent men and boys had for the period of the war effort put aside their habitual preoccupation, girls. The fact that they carried pictures of nude girls, called pin-ups, did not occur to anyone as a paradox. The convention was the law. When Army supply ordered millions of rubber contraceptive and disease-preventing items, it had to be explained that they were used to keep moisture out of machine gun barrels — and perhaps they did."

There was, however, little official recognition that wartime promiscuity was at least partially the product of the sexual aggressiveness induced by military conditioning. "In his image of himself" a sociologist, who served as a GI, noted "the soldier tends to feel a freedom from civilian society's taboos and controls."

★ [6] ★

Jagged Glass

Army life overseas wrecks these old emotional ties when it takes a man away from his wife or sweetheart, and leaves him with a set of memories.

— U.S. ARMY SEX SURVEY, 1945

The license to kill necessary in military service transgresses humanity's most sacred social taboo. It forces those at the "sharp end" of war to come to terms not only with ritualized murder but also the unconscious self's refusal to confront the possibility of extinction. Primitive societies had developed elaborate atonement rituals for the murders committed in warfare before their warriors were permitted to resume relationships with women. But, as Freud pointed out in "Reflections on War and Death," Western civilization, despite its frequent resort to war over the centuries, had abandoned such social remedies for releasing the extreme psychological tensions induced in fighting men.

Just how this pent-up guilt at the ferocity of modern warfare contributed to what was called "combat stress" was not to be fully appreciated until extensive World War II research revealed it to be one of the critical factors in cases of mental breakdown that were described as "battle fatigue." The startling discovery was then made that only one American soldier in six could be consistently relied on to open fire on the enemy — whatever the provocation.

"Fear of killing rather than fear of being killed, was the most common cause of battle fatigue in the individual, and the fear of failure ran a close second," was the conclusion of Brigadier General S. L. A. Marshall. *Men Against Fire* was based on the analysis of his interviews of combat veterans and the study of thousands of US army action reports:

The Army cannot unmake [Western man]. . . . It must reckon with the fact that he comes from a civilization in which aggression, connected with the taking of life, is prohibited and unacceptable. The teaching and ideals of that civilization are against killing, against taking advantage. The fear of aggression has been expressed to him so strongly and absorbed by him so deeply and pervadingly — practically with his mother's milk — that it is a part of the normal man's emotional make-up. This is his greatest handicap when he enters combat. It stays his trigger-finger though he is hardly conscious that it is a restraint in him.

"I remember myself potentially expendable according to the Rules of Land Warfare, trapped in a war which (I said) was none of my making," was how one GI rationalized this conflict about killing and being killed. Many soldiers steeled themselves emotionally before combat with thought of home and the wife or sweetheart in whose memory, or offspring, they would achieve some hope of immortality if their own flesh was shattered by high explosive. As one American soldier wrote, "I sometimes feel a little ashamed at the way I long to come back home."

" 'When I come back' is the soldier's solace — dreaming of home generally makes him a better soldier — home is where the heart is," wrote one GI. Another wrote that his vision of home was "fresh milk, strawberry shortcake, steaks, ice-cream, pie and, of paramount interest in lustful mind and sex starved imagination . . . women, women and women and more women and liquor."

Most soldiers were unwilling or unable to content themselves with thoughts of the women back home that they might not survive to embrace. "In the war a man gets lonely, a kind of loneliness which nothing can drive away except women — real ones and ones you can dream about waiting for you back home," a GI wrote to his father. "And it doesn't matter much if they aren't there when you come back. The important thing is to have this dream when you're lying in a dirty ditch with bullets whistling all about you."

That living with the prospect of death generated a high sex drive in the men who risked death on a daily basis was evident from the high VD rates suffered by Allied bomber crews. Unlike the infantryman who had few channels for sexual release at the battlefront, aircrews also found plenty of women around their bases.

Lieutenant Ted Binder, one of the 9,937 American airmen who perished in the great Allied bomber offensives over Germany, discovered when his turn came as mail censor just how promiscuous aircrews were. He was shocked at their boasts in letters to their pals of sexual adventures with English girls, while at the same time assuring their wives or sweethearts back in the States that they were their only love.

I have found fifty sets of letters of this nature: One is to the wife or steady girlfriend back home. English girls, Joe says, are a mighty poor substitute for females. But of course even if they were Hollywood glamour girls, he wouldn't be interested, 'cause he can't think of anything but his little Mabel back home. Letter No. 2 is to some girl Joe has met in England, who may or may not know of his previous connections, and who may herself have a husband in the Eighth Army. "Darling," says Joe, "I never knew what life was till I met you. I live for those hours we have together on my leaves. You're the luckiest thing that ever happened to me." And the third letter Joe put in the mail box that night is to his buddy working at Willow Run. "Pete," he says with enthusiasm, "you don't know what you're missing. These English broads really go crazy when they see a Yank. I've got a really nice little shack date lined up, and believe it or not, it's all free."

"You went to war for six hours," was the way one RAF bomb aimer explained it, "and you came back to clean sheets and when you did an operation you got ham and eggs. Nobody else did." Extra food was not the only compensation for Bomber Command's suffering the highest continuous attrition losses of all the Allied forces — its average wartime casualty rate of over 20 percent was exceeded only by the German U-boat crews. The high risks they ran on bombing missions acted as a subconscious aphrodisiac for aircrews. Many became adept at exploiting the relatively poor chance of survival, according to the tail-gunner of a Lancaster bomber:

While girls had a much stricter upbringing, they were sorely tempted when they knew what little chance their loved one had of returning unscathed. There was no doubt that wartime did make more opportunities, and caution was often not exercised under such stress. Equally, quite a lot of us chaps would play on girls' emotions by stressing the possibility of death, even though we as aircrew never believed it would be us who got the "chop."

The "chop" was something that all men in the armed force tried to put at the back of their mind, but could never completely ignore. Yet in the "reality of love and sex amid the conflagration," as one GI explained, it so often became "jagged glass," for a soldier seeking an outlet for sexual frustration intensified by combat:

The typical soldier gives himself up for dead before he ever sees combat. And then the combat experience itself merely reinforces this sense of doom. So every woman might be his last. This is a cliché, but a truthful and powerful one — particularly if you can imagine what it's like to make love while assuming that tomorrow you'll be dead. You are no more violent in bed than usual. In fact, you're not even necessarily more loving. But perhaps you clutch the girl's shoulders a little more firmly than you normally would.

The girl, meanwhile, even as she's dreaming of her real lover, knows what you're thinking. She herself is torn; while pretending you're someone else, she's simultaneously relating to the actual and awful fact that she's in bed with a man who knows he may die. So watch her face; she alternately opens and closes her eyes, sometimes in ecstasy, more often in a desperate attempt to grasp this essentially ungraspable situation. And she stares up at you with the slightest hint of guilt in her eyes, or is that knitted brow simply knowledge, flowing into her mind like you into her body, of what she herself must mean to you, a man whose name she'll not remember?

Just how traumatic this kind of sexual encounter could be was related by a GI who lost his virginity after a drunken spree with two French prostitutes:

After a while things began to go pretty blotty. Before I knew it, one of the girls got on my lap and was kissing me and whispering all sorts of things to me, and I all of a sudden I started to cry, tears rolling down my cheeks and she was trying to wipe them off, and it was so damned silly but I couldn't stop. I felt so sad and lonely. Then there was another girl trying to stop me from crying, and she was so sympathetic that she cried herself, and that made me even sadder. She gave me a glass of wine, and that was my end, because all of a sudden there was a blackout . . . and when I opened my eyes everything was dark. I looked around without seeing anything, and then I felt somebody's arm on me, and I groped in the dark and felt a girl lying next to me under the blanket. Well, that was a new experience and I got terribly excited. She must have wakened up because she pressed her body to mine, and it was so warm, and she kissed me, and before I knew it, it was all over. And when it was all over, I felt terribly ashamed and disgusted, and I was getting physically sick too, my stomach was turning and choking me, and I knew I had to get out.

A World War II combat infantryman confirmed that the "proximity of danger finds a man obsessed with a wild exhilaration, almost sensual. He feels impervious to missiles of a deadly nature, yet underneath this sense of power . . . gnawing like a rat in a sepulcher . . . is the knowledge that his fellows feel the same, yet some will die."

Procreation and death are after all the extreme parameters of human existence, and are brought into conjunction by war. Sex and violence shared an uncomfortable alliance in the minds of men in a battle. Hallucinations of an overtly sensual nature were not uncommon at the front. Author and ex-marine William Manchester recorded a vivid account in *Goodbye, Darkness* of a female apparition appearing before him at the height of fierce engagement with the Japanese which wiped out his comrades. His "Whore of Death" "rasped obscenities" and "hoisted her skirt to her hips and spread her legs," arousing in him "overwhelming" sexual cravings."

For the first and only time in my life I understood rape. I have never been more ready. Then from her sultry muttering, I learned her fee. I couldn't mount her here. She gestured toward the Japanese lines. I shrank back shaking my head and whispering "No, no I won't, no, no, NO." Just then a random shell rustled over and landed a few yards away. In the flash she disappeared. But my yearning for sexual release remained.

In Manchester's view a "close call with death is often followed by eroticism. It is characteristic of some creatures that they are often very productive before their death, and in some cases appear to die in a frenzy of reproductive activity."

In preparation for the advance into Germany in the spring of 1945, Supreme Headquarter Allied Expeditionary Force issued the directive "No social intercourse of any kind with Germans will take place." Allied military planners who persuaded General Eisenhower to adopt this strict nonfraternization policy had neglected to take into account the frustration of both their troops and German women. This became apparent after Cologne had fallen in mid-March when a disturbing report was received from an officer of SHAEF intelligence staff who had been amazed to hear the shouts of "Ve haf vaited fife years for you!" across shattered streets still littered with bodies of civilians killed during the fighting: "Girls put on their most seductive smiles . . . and the girls in the recently occupied territory don't seem to make any bones about the fact that the lack of young men in Germany left them in a rather receptive mood."

SHAEF tried to cool the ardor of this reception by issuing an edict that "such women can hardly be considered as the suitable mates for the defenders of democracy." "Women were told that it was right and patriotic to bear children for any soldier desiring the same," pointed out another report on the failure of the nonfraternization policy. "Many soldiers of the invading Armies found this situation very much to their liking and have done nothing to change it."

Heavy mandatory fines were also unsuccessful in curbing the American soldiers' appetite for liaisons with willing partners. Enlisted men defied the stiff financial penalties, claiming "65 bucks is dirt cheap, it was worth it!" Medical officers protested that such punitive measures only made it more difficult to check the spread of venereal infection, and officers who ignored the orders they were supposed to enforce did not provide a good example to their men. When the nonfraternization policy began to pose a real threat to good order and military discipline, confidential SHAEF memoranda reveal that Eisenhower's staff gave "very serious consideration that licensed houses should be provided under Army supervision," to be staffed by German prostitutes passed as morally and medically free of contagion.

Germany was particularly vulnerable to "moral chaos" because the war had not only reduced the cities and economy to ruins, but it had shattered the rigid dictates of the Nazi society. In a flourishing black market for the basic necessities of life, sex was a passport for survival for many German women.

"Two things our soldiers can't resist — kids and a glimpse of married family life," reported the *New York Herald-Tribune* from Cologne in a piece about the "$65 dollar question" — the fine stipulated for enlisted men convicted of intimate association with enemy civilians. "The biologic aspects of boy-meets-girl can be rigidly controlled. But the kids here look like the youngsters back home, and the old folks seem harmless and their houses are nice and clean and they appear to live about the same as we do."

The magnitude of the sexual problems confronting an Allied army of occupation had been foreshadowed in Italy and by the "liberation" of Paris and Brussels, which brought another leap in VD rates. On the other side of the world General Douglas MacArthur's army had driven the Japanese out of Manila in the spring of 1945 — only to lose the battle against venereal disease to an estimated eight-thousand-strong prostitute army of "native females wandering through military encampments and intimately associating with military personnel."

The introduction a year earlier of the "wonder drug" penicillin to treat venereal diseases had also removed another restraint on the sexual activities of Allied troops who set out to "liberate" Europe. Word of the availability of a "one-shot cure," instead of the long series of injections that had previously been the standard treatment — and painful punishment — for contracting gonorrhea or syphilis, had spread quickly among the invasion forces. The rapid upward leap in the VD charts kept by every regiment indicated that even the most cautious of soldiers were tempted to abandon "the bright shield of continence" now they knew that health and honor could be restored by the "magic bullets" of penicillin.

"When VE-Day finally arrived, the inevitable let-down took place and the rates for venereal disease soared," reported the U.S. army medical inspector. "Those of May were greater than April, and June saw the highest rate in the history of the theater, with every indication that the end was not yet in sight and that the army of occupation would have an experience with those communicable diseases greatly exceeding that of the period of wartime operations." The report blamed a lack of shipping space that delayed the arrival of seventy thousand VD posters and consignments of rubber contraceptives, and forced rationing to four per man per month — a rate that medical officers considered entirely inadequate!

The U.S. army had become so concerned by the early summer of 1945 about the tidal wave of promiscuity and the resultant casualties of VD that an extensive survey was launched to learn more about the typical soldier's sexual habits. Thousands of questionnaires were circulated and filled in by GIs with a promise of anonymity to encourage a frank response. The survey revealed that the level of promiscuity among the troops was far higher than officially admitted, and rates rose in direct proportion to the amount of time the men had spent overseas. More than eight out of ten soldiers who had been away from the United States for over two years admitted in the anonymous survey to having had regular sexual intercourse with the women they met "over there."

The extent and detail of the U.S. army survey left no doubt that after more than a year abroad, whether they were married or single, most American soldiers had thrown restraint to the winds. Fewer than a fraction of one percent of those polled claimed they had remained continent because "The Scriptures teach that it is sinful to have intercourse out of wedlock" — or as one shy GI confessed:

The reason I haven't as yet had intercourse is probably that I never bothered about it in civilian life when school took up most of my time. I think about it a lot over here and wonder if I'm not being too prudish about it. I'd like the first time to be "nice." Usually I lose my nerves when I feel in the mood for slobbing it. Don't shy away from it as a subject of conversation, but think I'll let it go now that I might return to the U.S. soon. Boy! am I glad you don't ask for names.

"Sex patterns of males are established relatively early in life a the matter of being in the army had little influence upon the dividual's willingness to expose himself to VD," the report nounced. Three out of four men were having intercourse w Italian women, on average once or twice a month. Of these, percent paid for their favors in cash, 27 percent paid nothing gave gifts of rationed food, and less than 1 percent said they pa with cigarettes or clothing.

Nearly a third of all enlisted men who filled in the anonymous report forms admitted to having wives back in the States, while almost half the respondents indicated they intended marrying their girlfriend in the United States. That over three-quarters of all men with such stated attachments did not consider the "girls they left behind" a bar to sexual adventure overseas was a measure of the war's dramatic impact on the average soldier's morality. Typical of the responses was one from a soldier who had been married for six years who confessed:

Until 9 months ago when I came overseas I had never had intercourse with any woman other than my wife since I married her. When an older married man is in the same tent with a bunch of unmarried boys that are out most of the time, it puts him in a bad frame of mind.

Still more significant was the discovery that fewer than half the men who anticipated returning to marry the girl they had left behind had any conviction that she had "stayed loyal" to him. One respondent insightfully noted, "The army gives us plenty of beautiful posters and interesting movies on sex and how to avoid diseases and why we should not indulge in sexual intercourse — NOW — How about producing some really good shorts on the same stuff to show our wives and sweethearts back in the United States?"

"There is a new set of accepted rights and wrongs in this overseas situation," concluded a senior U.S. army officer in his review of the sex survey from the Mediterranean theater, "it is right to have intercourse with any available women, it is not wrong to get VD unless one fails to go on sick call, it is wrong to punish a man for VD — even for repeated offenses."

This is the apparent situation with regard to sexual intercourse among those overseas men. The normal (in the case of civilian) disapproval of intercourse is missing except as one is reminded by memories or by letter. It has been shown for instance, that having a *loyal* sweetheart somewhere else is *not* a powerful deterrent for all the men overseas, although it is for a minority. Under normal conditions this is one of the most powerful sanctions, leading to abstinence with other women.

The survey concluded that there was "no evidence that frequent VD talks or movies cut down the exposure of men to VD over-

seas." Not only did the troops repeatedly ignore advice by chaplains and medical officers to "keep it in your pants" but fewer
than half the respondents used sheaths or prophylactics because,
as one soldier put it, "Most GI rubbers are so damn thick you
can't enjoy yourself"; and another explained, "GI condoms are
no good. Half of them bust anyway. Try one sometime."

Why are officers allowed to keep their service records clear when they
contract VD by having their medical record marked with everything from
a bloody nose to a strain. They know that rank is no barrier to disease.

One factor that persuaded many enlisted men to ignore the
repeated lectures on continence and prophylaxis was that the officers who gave it failed to practice what they preached. The
widespread habit of officers who persuaded WACs and native girls
to share the privileges of rank by "shacking up" was bitterly resented:

What's sauce for the goose is sauce for the gander. We should not be
handicapped *because of rank* in our search for clean women or in our
ability to entertain them. And this means using government vehicles too.

As for the officers having all the WACs, I believe there is an Army
regulation out which states that an officer is not to associate with an
enlisted WAC. Why isn't this adhered to? Give the enlisted men a chance
to be with and talk to a few American WACs and also have a dance
with them.

It therefore came as no surprise to the officers who analyzed
the questionnaires to find that one out of five respondents also
favored "GI whorehouses." They wanted the U.S. army to do "as
most other armies do, put up government sanctioned and inspected houses" to reduce the dangers of disease and to "keep
their price down." Another soldier suggested that "five to a company" would be adequate — "Of course this would have to be kept
from the press."

The U.S. army survey of 1945 that provided such a frank and
detailed record insight into the sexual life of American troops was
to be kept a classified secret for nearly forty years because it reflected badly on the public image of the GI as a clean-living cru-
sader for democracy. While no such detailed research into military sexual habits appears to have been conducted by British

forces, their very similar VD statistical trends suggest that soldiers in both armies shared the same sexual habits.

The most revealing aspect of the U.S. army sex survey was that it exploded once and for all the traditional belief that "a man who *knows* a girl is waiting for him somewhere will be true to her; he will not seek outlets with other women."

A soldier would have been a "peculiar man" if he refrained from having intercourse. "When 3 out of 4 soldiers engaged *in any* given activity which the Army would like to control, the problem is numerically staggering," noted the report. "When it is an activity which is approved of by the group as a whole, not only by a man for himself but the for the other fellow too, this powerful social sanction makes the activity almost uncontrollable." The American survey concluded with an observation that was appropriate to the sexual lives of all soldiers in all the armies who fought in World War II:

However, the man in this study is *not* having an unusual amount of intercourse at all for men of their average age (26 years). Any man of age 26, and certainly any married man in the theater (32%) can rightfully feel that he is being cheated sexually by this overseas situation which is not of his making. The steady rise in the frequency of intercourse with time overseas gives credence to this notion of being cheated of the sex life which society taught him was his as soon as he becomes a man. Furthermore, only 10% of all those men are having intercourse at least once a week, which is certainly not an indication of anything like abnormal sexual activity. The average frequency of once to twice a month is certainly not high, if we hazard guesses as to the probable frequency of intercourse for this group if they were in normal civilian life . . . the Army would make a mistake in either charging these men with sexual abnormality or threatening them as such.

⋆ ⟦ 7 ⟧ ⋆

Comrades in Arms

Sodomy is specifically denounced as an offense under the provisions of the 93rd article of war. Administrative discharge in lieu of trial in cases of this character is not only contrary to the War Department policy, but to the express intention of Congress.

— U.S. ARMY POLICY CIRCULAR, 1941

Sex was not really an issue on the *Dido*. There was much the same atmosphere as at a fairly easy going public school.

— SEAMAN GEORGE MELLY, ROYAL NAVY

"What ain't we got? We ain't got dames!" In real life on a "No women atoll" like Eniewetok, GIs had chanted less elegant choruses that advocated the so-called Pacific Prescription:

> *Masturbation is the fashion*
> *For your unrequited passion*
> *If the girls can do it, why can't we?*
> *But out here in the Pacific,*
> *Purely as a soporific,*
> *Nothing equals simple self abuse!*

What U.S. navy white-hats referred to as "the sordid imitation" was so widespread among servicemen that one British army doctor "had no hesitation" in advising the men in his unit that masturbation "was perhaps the easiest and the safest way of obtaining relief, there being no reason why they should not embellish this experience with some fantasy of their loved ones at home."

But Victorian taboos died hard, even in the army. Another officer in the medical corps, however, admitted he was "shocked to learn how openly, even boastfully, masturbation was performed in some barrackrooms."

"Formerly my wife was my right hand," a World War I soldier had quipped; "in the army my right hand became my wife." In World War II many servicemen resorted to the same substitute to satisfy their sex hunger, although "masturbation guilt" was still considered a medical disorder in the psychiatric textbooks of the period. But as long as men in the armed forces kept their hands to themselves, no military regulations were broken. If their comrades, however, provided the stimulation, servicemen risked a court-martial, imprisonment — and in the case of German SS officers after 1942, the firing squad. Yet the military, because it segregated millions of young men at the height of their potency into a life devoid of female companionship, exposed many men to what was called "emergency" or "deprivation" homosexuality.

Unlike the ancient Greek armies, which had not only tolerated but exploited the amorous bond that developed between comrades in arms, modern military organizations had long proscribed homosexual activity. Not only did it offend basic Christian sexual taboos, homosexuality was perceived as a threat to the essential aggressive "manliness" of soldiers. But above all, homosexual relationships were "prejudicial to good conduct and discipline" by breaking down the divisions between military ranks. Deprivation homosexuality had long been recognized as a problem by navies. Historically it had been dealt with either by toleration and a complex hierarchical code, as in the galleons of the Spanish Armada where there was a complex pecking order for sex code, or by making it a capital offense, as in the Royal Navy when as late as Nelson's time officers had been hung from the yardarm for the offense of sodomy. "Ashore its wine, women and song, aboard its rum, bum and concertina" ran the nineteenth-century sea shanty that doubtless prompted Winston Churchill's aside during World War II: "Don't talk to me about naval tradition. It's nothing but rum, sodomy and the lash."

In World War I it had been a constant concern for military leaders that the lack of feminine company in the trenches of the Western Front would lead to an epidemic of homosexual behavior. The German Army High Command, which had been touched by prewar scandal, was especially sensitive to the issue and had launched periodic witch-hunts in regiments where excessive numbers of requests for frontline duty suggested that homosexual partners might be attempting to emulate Spartan military tradition by fighting alongside their lovers. The war also offered many confirmed homosexuals — or urnings, as they were then called — not only the opportunity for male cameraderie but the chance to prove their masculinity and defy social stigma.

In World War II the scant military data that has been made available suggest that homosexuality in the armed forces was as widespread as in society as a whole. According to Professor Kinsey's wartime surveys, one in ten American males between the ages of sixteen and fifty-five was more or less exclusively homosexual, three out of ten admitted to some adult sexual experience with other men, and one in five was bisexual. He therefore concluded that "nearly 40% of all males in town could be arrested at some time in their lives for similar activity, and that 20 to 30% of unmarried males could have been arrested for homosexual activity that had taken place that same year." The official records, however, reveal that the American Selective Service boards had rejected only 1 percent of draftees as homosexuals unfit for military service, and that less than .5 percent of the men in the military were subsequently discharged for homosexuality.

"History paints in lurid pictures abnormal sexual practices which become associated with men at sea," Captain Joel T. Boone of the U.S. navy medical service proclaimed in 1941. "We have no place in the service for the homosexualist, the panderer or the pederast. He is — as soon as discovered — and this happens with amazing speed, taken to one of the naval psychiatric institutions for treatment." Yet for all the "amazing" efficiency of the navy's ability to purge itself of homosexuals, the 1941 records of new admissions to the two main naval prisons at Portsmouth, New Hampshire, and Mare Island, San Francisco, disclose that over a quarter of them were there as a result of homosexual charges. That only thirteen navy and seven marines were committed that year was indicative that either the prevalence of homosexuals in the navy was far below that of the population, or that shipmates and commanding officers were turning a Nelsonian blindeye to the old "naval tradition."

This appears to be confirmed by the degree to which homo-

sexual activity was tolerated aboard Royal Navy warships provided relationships did not cross the disciplinary divide between
lower and upper decks. In his memoir appropriately titled *Rum,
Bum and Concertina,* author and jazz singer George Melly describes the relatively relaxed attitudes he found as a seaman just
after the war aboard one of His Majesty's cruisers:

Sex on the *Dido* was comparatively low key, but uncensorious. There
were a few obvious homosexuals, the doe-eyed writer for one, many total heterosexuals and a fair number of those who would, on a casual
basis, relieve sexual pressure with their own sex. It was accepted, for
instance, on my mess deck, that on our Saturday "make 7 mends" (half-
days off) anyone who fancied some mutual masturbation would crush
down in the coat locker, a structure of closely-meshed wire like a medium sized cage. As an open part time invert, I was often solicited on
these occasions and usually accepted. Sometimes my masculine role both
surprised and disappointed those who had misread my predilections.
Mostly, however, it was no problem and there was as relaxed and tolerant an atmosphere as any I've ever encountered. I had a sometime
affair with a corporal of the marines who shared my watch on the quar-
terdeck, but this was only in the middee watch and, mostly, from his
point of view, to allay boredom.

Ashore and afloat the undeclared policy in naval establishments on both sides of the Atlantic appears to have been to crack
down on cases of homosexuality only if they posed a real threat
to discipline. Attempts by some commanding officers to institute
purges of homosexuals led to witch-hunts and blackmail that
proved even more destructive of good order and morale. Although stern penalties were laid down by navy regulations, cap-
tains dealt with homosexual cases aboard their vessels with a
latitude that derived from their sole authority. The more liberal-
minded dealt with offenders in a manner that caused the least
disturbance to the functioning of their ship as an efficient fighting unit.

Army commanders, however, had neither the same degree of
control nor the same problems with sexual offenses, since troops
were not usually denied contact with women for such long spells.
Nonetheless, wartime medical studies appear to confirm that the
percentage of homosexually inclined servicemen in the armies of
World War II was also greater than in the population as a whole.

"Many conscious homosexuals have found their way into the army, and of these only a certain number have come to psychiatrist, either at their own request or because their odd behavior has brought attention to them," reported a British army psychiatrist in a study of "conscious and unconscious homosexual responses to warfare." His conclusion was that 4 percent of all military psychiatric cases admitted for "war neuroses" were "conscious inverts." "Sexual inversion does not necessarily imply a corollary of military uselessness," the study pointed out, citing both the "acceptable homosexual warrior of warfare in classical times" and that many of the men under examination had been mentioned in dispatches. Nor were offenders unpopular with the other men, and he gave the example of guardsman who worked out his masochistic homosexual fantasies polishing boots. This particular trooper's commanding officer made "urgent representations" for the soldier's speedy return to his battalion.

One postwar psychologist suggested that military society attracted homosexuals because its comradeship and discipline were founded on "sublimated homosexuality." An American sociologist, while observing that "homosexuality is repellant and was unconsciously repressed in army life," said that as a GI there had been "continual joking about homosexual practices." He noted that "there was an apparent total lack of awareness of homosexual attitudes and inclinations. . . . This contrast between blindness to the reality and concern with the idea doubtless implies strong tendencies and equally strong repressions."

"There is frequently a homosexual bond between the leaders and the led," noted British military historian Brigadier Shelford Bidwell: "This may be entirely free from actual homosexual relations (although these do occur, for quite different reasons, in most young, virile, all-male societies) but there is a natural tendency for leaders to collect a subgroup of able and brave young men around them to act as their champions, aides, favorites and even jesters, who are permitted to take liberties that even the leader's senior lieutenants would not dare take."

Homosexual charisma undoubtedly contributed to the success of such famous military leaders as Alexander the Great, Richard Coeur de Lion, Prince Eugene of Savoy, Charles XII of Sweden, Frederick the Great, General George Gordon, and Lawrence of Arabia. The popular conception of homosexuals as weak and effeminate men does not square with the courage and manliness demanded of such commanders on the battlefield. But their valor has never been in question, nor has history questioned the bravery of the three-hundred-strong Sacred Band of Thebes, "every man the sworn lover of another," who died to a man at the Battle of Chaeronea in 338 B.C. Indeed, the very success of the classic Greek phalanx depended on the front-rank and rear-rank men who called each other "comrades in arms." As one British general observed, "Being what they were, they were probably found in one another's arms more often than would accord with modern ideas of military discipline."

The percentage of World War II servicemen who ended up in each other's arms — either by inclination, or out of "deprivation homosexuality" — is a matter for speculation. "For several obvious reasons there is very little authoritative or accurate information concerning the true extent of sexual disorder in the services, and the relevant published literature is sparse" was the opinion of wartime army psychiatrist Colonel Harry Pozner:

Those military personnel suffering from sexual disorder and voluntarily reporting on this account to their service doctors are comparatively few, and in general only seek advice from some ulterior motive or when threatened by disciplinary action for indiscreet sexual behavior. That they represent only a small section of sexual deviates in the services is confirmed by police reports, sociological surveys and semi-documentary modern novels indicating the active participation of service men of all ranks and social status in the homosexual underground of every large port and city.

The experience of prisoners of war and concentration camp inmates confirms that "deprivation homosexuality" was not an uncommon practice among men of otherwise heterosexual inclination. A married Belgian officer, for example, wrote about his awareness of homosexual feelings watching a blonde stripper after three years in a German Stalag:

This innocuous display occasioned palpable discomfort among the audience, and the actors were much less enthusiastically applauded than the members of our P.O.W. troupe, who usually collect generous plaudits. I myself was as shocked as a fifteen-year-old. Our compulsory chastity must have turned us into Puritans. My first response was actually: "God how ugly the female body is! Most of the boys I see in the showers are more pleasant to look at." I was disturbed at discovering this tendency "à la Gide."

The same phenomenon was noted by a British prisoner in Malaya: "I had always considered myself the normal male and it was with a sense of shock that, during the latter months of Pudu and our stay at Changi, I found in myself certain homosexual tendencies." In the Japanese camps the poor food and heavy work diminished the libido of the fifty thousand young men and the POWS became "so debilitated that sex, in deed and in thought, failed to exist."

"Deprivation homosexuality" was also to become endemic in the Nazi concentration camps, and not only among those men convicted under Article 175 of the German penal code, who were forced to wear identifying pink triangle arm patches. Hoess, the commandant of Auschwitz, records in his autobiography how at Sachsenhausen an attempt was made to reduce homosexuality by dispersing the pink triangles throughout all the huts instead of confining them together in one section. This only increased homosexual activity, and the decision was taken to establish brothels in the camp to check it.

A 1945 study by the U.S. army confirms that most homosexuals did indeed manage to adapt to the military environment. "Many of those who were caught were normal heterosexuals who were accused of homosexual behavior on a single occasion, usually while under the influence of alcohol," observed Lieutenant Colonel Lewis H. Loeser. His study concluded that there had been "gross inequalities" because the "true homosexual who admitted to repeated acts of sodomy was brought to trial infrequently, while the infrequent or first time offender was usually court martialed." The colonel pointed out that the equivalent in civil life was "habitual criminals and repeat offenders are permitted to go free while single first offenders are punished."

The situation was remarkably similar for the British forces. According to one army doctor's assessment, "the frequency of men *known* to be suffering from any form of sexual disorder was less than one in a thousand." The inference was that the reported cases represented only a very small percentage of the military homosexual community. This was given credence by the assertion in a British army medical journal that the "impression was also gained that there was more sexual disability amongst officers and less amongst other ranks than would seem at first evident from the available official data."

King's Regulations clearly stated that "confirmed homosexuals whose rehabilitation is unlikely should be removed from the Army by the most expeditious and appropriate means." The discrepancy between actual cases and the statistical estimate of the homosexual population was evidently a question of semantics, subterfuge, and tolerance by some commanding officers. A British army study of sexual offenders concluded that homosexuals "achieved gratification from those of their comrades who turned towards them as substitutes for women, but this fulfillment was so tempered by fear of detection and punishment that the inverts came to avoid even those who sought them out — usually while drunk."

An example of the lengths that some British soldiers went to in concealing their tendencies was that of a forty-two-year-old sergeant. He was a highly regarded soldier who had repressed his homosexuality to the point of mental instability and left letters from a fictitious son lying about the barracks. Fear that he would be exposed had finally resulted in a suicide attempt and, while hospitalized, he demanded to be castrated or imprisoned. The same study also revealed that the active military homosexual often exerted excessive authority "to dominate the male group, obtain love, respect, and acknowledgement of his prowess. He must lead, cannot be led and finds it intolerable to be in a passive position of obeying." Over a third of the cases examined "had Fascist leanings and were facile exponents of power politics."

The British report concluded that homosexuals "form a foreign body in the social macrocosm" and vindicated the wartime policy that offenders were best dealt with by being "quietly invalided out of the service, with appropriate advice about medical treatment, unless they had to be brought up before courts martial." Formal charges were usually instituted in the British armed forces only for those sexual transgressors who had committed a flagrant breach of discipline, especially between officers and other ranks, or civilians.

One such case was that of the writer G. F. Green, who had confided to his wartime diary that he had "chosen a way of life deliberately not the way preferred." As wartime army lieutenant in Ceylon, he had insisted on pursuing his chosen way and flaunted his homosexuality to the fury of the Mess. He pursued his amorous attachment for native youths despite warnings. He was court-martialed, cashiered, and sentenced to two years in a grueling military detention center. According to a brother officer, his colonel had no choice but to let the case be tried by a military court because Green was "found on his bed, all lights on, in the wrong place, at the wrong time, with someone whose company, in the circumstances, could only be regarded as conduct unbecoming, to say the least."

Some duration-only officers with little or no service experience treated every sexual offender strictly by the book. The professional officer corps, many of whom had seen service in India where homosexual activity, particularly among the Sikh regiments, was not uncommon, were prepared to be more lenient. One British major recalled how, just before the Battle of El Alamein, a potentially embarrassing court-martial was hushed up:

A sergeant in our brigade was discovered masturbating with a private in a tent and they were both put on a charge by the sergeant major. Our colonel, who was himself a homosexual, was absent, and so the case went right up to the brigade headquarters. The brigadier, who had been a boy soldier promoted through the ranks and to whom nothing in army life was a surprise, dismissed both men with a reprimand. He was absolutely furious that it had got as far as it did. "The battalion's been out here for two years, these two youngsters had never had home leave," he stormed afterwards in the mess. "Out in India when I was in the ranks, reveille brought every man tumbling out of everyone else's bunks. What the hell does Brigadier G. want his men to do for sexual relief, go down to the brothels in the bazaar, chase Arab women and catch syphilis?"

In wartime such tolerance was practiced wherever possible because the potential loss of one soldier in ten would have left British frontline regiments badly under strength. "When the conservation of manpower was an essential priority," admitted one army psychiatrist, "it was often considered practical and realistic to post known homosexuals of good intelligence and proved ability to large towns, where their private indulgences were less likely to be inimical to the best interests of the service." In practice this

unofficial policy often resulted in the transfer of sexual offenders to the Pay Corps, where they could still make a useful
contribution to the army.

The 93rd Article of War laid down that "soldiers ascertained
to be sodomists" were subject to "dishonorable discharge, forfei-
ture of all pay and allowances, and confinement at hard labor in
a Federal penitentiary for five years." Nonetheless, unofficial policy
in the U.S. army was also to avoid courts-martial proceedings by
resorting to "administrative discharge." Fearing that draft dodg-
ers might feign homosexuality to get "administrative discharges,"
the War Department in the fall of 1941 issued a directive that
"administrative discharge will not be used for summarily ridding
the service of undesirable soldiers, who by their misconduct, have
rendered themselves liable to trial by court martial." Six months
later, however, when the United States was at war and facing
a severe military manpower crisis, the adjutant general's office
relaxed its previously inflexible policy on administrative discharges.

A spate of embarrassing courts-martial in the months after Pearl
Harbor, in particular an investigation into allegations of widespread homosexuality at Moffet Field, California, resulted in a
new policy directive that was set out in a report from the adjutant general's office titled a "Study of Sodomy Cases." Concerned to avoid the "wholesale discharge of soldiers," the judge
advocate general of the U.S. army established the criterion that
the "primary consideration should be the interest of the service
of men possessing a salvage value." It designated three classes of
sexual offense. The "true sodomists" were to be court-martialed.
Homosexual offenders in "extenuating circumstances" or where
there was insufficient evidence for a conviction, were to be given
an administrative discharge. The final category was "men who
through either alcoholic overindulgence or curiosity, will submit
to unnatural relations"; they were to be "studied carefully by a
qualified psychiatrist and if not found to be moral perverts will
be returned to duty after appropriate disciplinary action."

Draft boards were supposed to screen out sexual inverts, and
examiners at induction centers were advised to be on the lookout
for "effeminacy in dress or manner." In practice it was not difficult for homosexuals to slip through the screening process —
often with the sympathetic assistance of members of the board.

"I walked into this office and here was a man who was a scream-
ing belle," recalled one homosexual New York draftee. "He was
a queen if ever I saw one and he asked me the standard questions, ending up with, 'Did you ever have any homosexual experiences?' Well I looked him right in the eye and I said, 'No!'
And he looked right back and said, 'That's good!' — both of us
lying through our teeth."

Identifying homosexuals proved difficult, even for trained
psychiatrists. One ranking medical officer in the U.S. army found
that less than half of the homosexual cases he had studied were
effeminate. Because it was the "intent of the War Department that
homosexuals be discharged from the service, or in the case of officers be permitted to resign if they are not deemed reclaimable,"
he provided an aid to "diagnosis." Army doctors were urged to
make themselves familiar with "the extensive homosexual vocabulary" and note how "homosexuals tend to group together and
it is interesting to observe the speed and certainty with which they
are able to recognize one another."

Administrative discharge became the preferred method of
dealing with those homosexual offenders deemed "nonreclaim-
able" because it avoided time-consuming courts-martial. It was
intended as neither an honorable nor dishonorable discharge,
merely listing the section of U.S. army regulations for which the
individual was "not eligible for re-enlistment." But because the
blue discharge form soon came to indicate to civilian employers
that the bearer was a homosexual, the ex-servicemen who received them took to calling themselves "Blue Angels."

Like the army, the U.S. navy was obliged by January 1943 to
amend its strict prewar policy of court-martialing all sexual offenders "as a result of a probable large wartime influx of homosexuals." Prior to the secretary of the navy's confidential letter to
commanding officers, navy regulations had required that all homosexual offenders be charged under Article 22. Officers found
guilty of "scandalous conduct tending to the destruction of good
morals" could be punished with dismissal and a maximum of
twelve months' hard labor, while enlisted men faced a dishonorable discharge and ten years' imprisonment.

Naval prison records, however, reveal that the actual maximum penalty handed out for sodomy conviction in 1941 was only
half the potential maximum, and the small number convicted in

a year that the navy was rapidly expanding suggests that most homosexual cases were dealt with as psychiatric cases. By 1944, administrative discharges were approved for self-confessed homosexuals or in cases where there was no proof of offenses committed in uniform. But there was apparently so much inconsistency that the following year the Navy Department issued a directive requiring commanding officers to submit all administrative discharge cases to the Bureau of Personnel for review.

One sailor who escaped a general court-martial under the revised wartime policy was Roy, a seaman second class at the Jacksonville Naval Air Station. He was arrested and charged with "willfully, knowingly, indecently and lewdly" permitting an act of oral sodomy with a civilian. Under questioning he admitted to a variety of "homosexual acts with soldiers, sailors, and civilians" in hotels, parks and restrooms." Naval investigators also obtained a confession from one of his partners that Roy was "very gay." A naval yeoman at the naval air station testified to "association with members of this gay circle." The psychiatrist's diagnosis was "homosexual" and that the seaman was "unsuitable for retention in the naval service." The accused's naval career came to an end when he signed "an undesirable discharge for the good of the service and to escape trial by General Court Martial."

There were many inconsistencies in the application of the revised policy toward homosexuals in the navy. Evidence of two zealous Miami police officers resulted in the discharge of a navy lieutenant for "scandalous conduct" after they had arrested him for "kissing and fondling the buttocks" of a sailor. Jim, a seaman first class, was arrested in 1944 for desertion and then compounded his crime by seducing the three inmates of the brig at the U.S. naval base in Texas. Jim confessed that he had engaged in repeated homosexual acts throughout his service career. He admitted that "on average I have been performing the acts on men every other night." But this seaman's request to be allowed to plead guilty only to the desertion charge was denied, and a full court-martial convicted him of "scandalous conduct" in addition to desertion.

In the case of Bob, a seaman second class in the U.S. coast guard from Virginia, he was held to have provided all the evidence needed for a general court-martial for "scandalous conduct" in an explicit letter to an army lieutenant which contained a graphic description of the sexual exploits they anticipated the following weekend and concluded "all soldiers very understanding" — an opinion proved wrong by the one who censored mail at Fort Bragg, North Carolina, and who promptly filed a report. When confronted with what the Office of the Inspector General of the War Department described as a "very obscene" letter, both the lieutenant and the coast guard sailor "resigned for the good of the service."

There was strong opposition to the introduction of a more flexible U.S. navy wartime policy toward homosexuals, particularly the review of those already serving sentences for "scandalous conduct." In 1944 a strong protest was made to the Navy Department from the Eighth Naval District where an investigation of a "homosexual ring" had resulted in the arrest of seven officers and twenty-three sailors, as well as ten officers and seven enlisted army men.

"It is not believed that the present hush hush manner of handling homosexuality and perversion is effective," complained the memorandum from the commandant and admiral commanding the Eighth Naval District. They argued that the administrative discharge policy was "in error" because it granted homosexuals "complete liberty to pursue their practices at will." They charged that "the practice is widespread throughout the naval service"; and it was a "criminological rather than a medical problem"; and that all homosexuals should be court-martialed and confined to "an institution for the insane, to remain there for an indefinite period." In extreme language, the alarmist district medical officers reported a threat to the navy and nation from the "dry rot" of "homosexualists" bent on "racial suicide."

The Navy Department in Washington, significantly, adopted a less alarmist view of the New Orleans affair. If those charged with "scandalous conduct" had been convicted, the homosexual population of the naval prisons would have been doubled! "Homosexuality is a problem which extends beyond the narrow confines of naval jurisdiction," advised the chief of naval personnel in his August 4 memorandum, which concluded:

The Bureau does not believe that incarceration would appreciably reduce homosexuality in the Navy. . . . Whatever the defects of the present policy, it has provided for a period of eighteen months a policy easily applicable, resulting in the speedy elimination and equal treatment of officers and enlisted men."

Only a very small fraction of the homosexual population of the U.S. armed forces were eliminated from the service, and the majority certainly served their countries no less bravely and efficiently than their heterosexual comrades. According to the only available official study of homosexual soldiers in the U.S. army during World War II, their performance "ratings average considerably higher than in the Army as a whole and would indicate that the group is superior in ability and technical skill to the average." Yet the report's author — a psychiatrist who was a lieutenant colonel in the Medical Corps — concluded nonetheless that "the group is lacking in temperament and skills necessary to the combat soldier."

Individual cases that have emerged since the war do not support the contention that homosexuals who served in the military lacked the "temperament and skills" to distinguish themselves in action. One of the foremost American carrier task force commanders of the Pacific war was avowedly homosexual. When his predilections brought investigators from naval intelligence to question him, he unceremoniously ordered them off his ship. His "scandalous conduct" was brought to the attention of the chief of naval operations in Washington. But Admiral Ernest J. King, although a staunch disciplinarian, was himself a womanizer. He ordered investigations to be dropped in order that this particular officer's service continue to play a vital role in defeating Japan.

The concern about such cases does not appear to have stemmed from doubts about the bravery of homosexual officers, nor from fear of public scandal. Rather it stems from a fear that a senior officer's homosexual entanglements might distort his military judgment. In at least one case, a shipboard romance in the Royal Navy would appear to have cost Britain a capital ship and the lives of many men. A. L. Rowse's *Homosexuals in History* contains the intriguing reference:

Some of us know of such episodes as that in the Second World War, when the captain of a battleship lost one of his planes at sea and had the great ship put about to search, to be torpedoed by a submarine: the commander was in love with the young flight lieutenant who had not returned.

Such a catastrophe, if it did occur as described, has to be measured against the military advantage which accrued to the Allied cause as a result of the determination of most homosexuals in the armed forces to prove that they were as courageous as their heterosexual comrades. Testimony to their bravery was given by an officer in a frontline infantry regiment:

During the last war I met "queers" in all ranks from private to general. One of the bravest was a Battle of Britain fighter pilot who won his DFC and Bar shooting down German 'planes over England. Twice be bailed out of blazing Spitfires. Once his parachute landed him in a greenhouse. Twice the King congratulated him. Eventually he became a group-captain, although he had started his Royal Air Force career as an air-craftman. He was a highly emotional man, but he willed himself to do everything his companions did. He shot down more enemy planes than most of them, was a likable and highly efficient fellow, and he really loved the RAF. So his companions accepted him readily and regarded him with affection. He commanded a squadron of Polish fighters, among the best and most reckless of airmen. Most of the leading pilots who met him suspected or knew that he was homosexual, but no one minded.

This former British infantry captain discovered to his relief that no one at British Middle East GHQ in Cairo appeared unduly concerned that the famous Shepheard's Hotel was the rendez-vous for a wide circle of the homosexual military elite. At the beginning of 1943 he was a regular at the bar, which he noted was the favorite gathering place for the officers of Colonel Stirling's Long Range Desert Group. One evening a decorated Battle of Britain ace made a pass at him. The man was then the group captain in command of an RAF base in Egypt, and the two struck up an intimate friendship, socializing with other homosexual officers in parties held at the flat of one of the senior secretaries at the American embassy.

Shepheards Hotel and its discreet coterie of Allied military and diplomatic officers was largely immune from the periodic efforts made by British military police to crack down on the wartime homosexual network in Cairo. Like Algiers, Naples, and later Paris, Cairo and the port of Alexandria were meccas of sexual adventure for servicemen of all proclivities. In back streets Arab boys lurked who were willing to provide sexual satisfaction for many a serviceman whose inhibitions about homosexuality were less than his fear of venereal disease. These brief encounters did not turn the average soldier into a confirmed homosexual — any more than did sharing a blanket for warmth in a slit trench at the front.

During the final tense hour of the earthshaking bombardment before the second battle of El Alamein on 24 October 1942, a major recalled how a young married lieutenant crawled over: "In a few minutes this boy was groping me and we were kissing passionately. It was a powerful emotional climax for both of us, although I knew that he was married and not a homosexual at all."

In *Goodbye, Darkness,* William Manchester describes how a Japanese barrage unhinged his veteran sergeant, who was "macho in ways which, we thought, were the exact opposite of homosexual." None of his company had apparently taken seriously the heavily muscled six-feet-two sergeant's drunken boast that he intended to write a book he proposed calling "Famous Cocks I Have Sucked." That was until the sergeant's image crumbled during a bombardment during the bloody battle for Okinawa in April 1945, when Manchester had to relieve his "mewling" superior and escort him out of the firing line. Later, while lying wounded in hospital, he learned that the sadistic sergeant major was a self-confessed homosexual who had been court-martialed for "scandalous conduct."

"There was so much excitement (and apocrypha) about heterosexuality," Manchester wrote of his wartime sexual experience, "that we seldom gave it [homosexuality] a second thought." But the recollections of another Pacific veteran suggest that in the Pacific theater homosexual activity was far from uncommon. Many of the GIs, he claimed, took advantage of a variety of homosexual substitutes for the "dames" they sorely lacked:

In the Philippines, a section from one motor pool used to requisition a jeep for "midnight reconnoitering," stopping at MP guardposts in isolated positions. When the MP leaned down to confirm directions to the area requested, you kissed him full on the mouth. The driver then stepped on the gas, leaving an amazed, sometimes annoyed military policeman in the dust thrown up by spinning tires. Once when I was in the "action seat" I gave the MP on solitary duty a big wet smack and waited for the driver to roar off into the darkness. This time the motor failed! To my surprise, the MP put an arm around my neck and kissed me back. My traveling companions were startled, and then jealous when the guard undid his trousers and I complied readily.

The other nighttime outlet was on an army transport truck shuttle to the Seabees, down the stretch from Naha, to see a film. If you wanted to get blown you tried to sit on the side benches of the canvas-covered truck. Depending on how horny you were and how badly you wanted to see Betty Grable, you could ride the trucks until you were satisfied. Daytime sexual relief could be obtained at a spot on the seashore marked by three reddish rocks soaring up like phallic symbols at the beach where many units went bare-ass bathing.

Perhaps because of official realization that there were fewer available women in the Pacific, the prevalence of such extensive male-to-male erotic activity indicates at least that American military authorities adopted a somewhat more tolerant attitude to homosexual behavior than in Europe or the United States.

The U.S. Marine Corps preferred a speedy discharge for officers who committed sexual offenses at the front. But enlisted men were not always so fortunate. The U.S. army attempted to preempt such problems by offering Pacific GIs who admitted "homosexual tendencies" a passage home and discharge without loss of benefits. "We were treated as insane people," recalled one soldier who felt he was cheated after nearly two years of service in the Pacific when he reported his "tendencies" to his medical officer. Half of those who came forward were sent to hospital psychiatric wards and the other half incarcerated behind barbed wire in a "queer stockade." When they arrived back in the United States, this contingent of homosexuals from the Sixth Army were stripped of their campaign medals and given "Blue Angel" administrative discharges.

The regular attempts that were made throughout the war to purge the armed forces of their homosexual element were motivated by wartime studies that indicated that so-called sexual inverts were less resistant to the stresses of combat than heterosexual troops. A British report cited the example of a sergeant, "an active homosexual who had been an excellent fighting soldier," who had to be invalided out of the army as a psychotic when his long-standing passive partner broke up their relationship to get married. Other such cases included soldiers who had concealed their sexual nature with wartime marriages. One suffered a mental breakdown when his wife was unfaithful, and another was hospitalized when the birth of his child was taken as "signal proof of his partner's femininity."

Military psychiatrists also identified homosexuals as being especially vulnerable to breakdown when their male lover was killed in action. "Prolonged mourning tendencies are found in those to whom the loss of a comrade means the loss of a homosexual love-object, and the grief is all the more profound in that its occasion is neither apprehended nor formulated," advised a British army doctor. Invariably the surviving partner complained, "The bullet should have got me, not him." In one case the survivor had discovered his friend with the top of his skull blown away — and within a few hours developed a hysterical sense of numbness and constriction. Another witnessed the sudden amputation of a comrade's legs and became a hysterical paraplegic when he heard of his lover's death. Not all the patients studied were conscious homosexuals, as in the case of a twenty-five-year-old private who had suffered for two years from intense headaches, battle-dreams, and weeping. He was reluctant to recognize the sexual nature of his attachment to his dead comrade until, as his case notes reveal, he was hypnotized by the doctor treating him:

Under light hypnosis he expressed a rather odd relationship with his dead comrade. "He held my hand when I was frightened and gave me confidence. He is the best pal I ever had. We were like a loving couple, like husband and wife. I saw him shot and his neck was covered with blood. I tried to bring him back to life with water but he died while I was holding him up." In most of the nightmares that beset him, his friend would come back to life together with his bloody injury, and on a few occasions there were emissions during these episodes. Occasionally he dreamed he was dressed in ATS uniform walking arm in arm with his chum, along the streets of his home town. The meaning of these simple wish-fulfillment dreams was very obvious and puzzled no one save the patient. He was in fact an evident and glaring example of the usually more subtle homosexual mourning reactions.

The "mourning reaction" of homosexuals in the military was often made all the more intense because the surviving lover was forced to hide the real reason for his grief for fear of exposure. One GI whose long-standing homosexual buddy died in the battle for Manila recalled:

I went into a three-day period of hysterics. I was treated with such kindness by the guys I worked with, who were all totally unaware why

I was hysterical. It wasn't at all because we were being bombed; it was because my "boyfriend" had been killed.

"No one asked me if I was gay when they called out 'Medic!' and you went out under fire and did what you were expected and trained to do," observed a homosexual medical corpsman who had enlisted at the age of eighteen. "Buddies from medical training days were dying like flies and it became lonely. I was wounded at Cherbourg during the Normandy invasion and during the Battle of the Bulge. There were so many gays in the medics and so many of them gave their lives."

Yet despite such unfairness and the fear of discovery and persecution, the military experience of homosexuality in World War II chipped away some of the old taboos. Servicemen living in close proximity to one another were made aware that men who chose a sexual relationship with other men were not suffering from a deadly disease or were not cowards or effeminate. Many thousands of homosexuals discovered a new consciousness of their collective identity in the subculture of bars and camaraderie that expanded to meet the wartime demand. An indication that public attitudes to the taboo of homosexuality were also shifting came with the appearance of homoerotic advertisements in American magazines, which began featuring male "pinup" such as those for Musingwear underwear and Cannon bath towels.

In the postwar reaction against the liberal morality of wartime, there was an inevitable homophobic campaign. But World War II, by the very act of bringing so many homosexuals together, helped sow the seeds of a collective consciousness that was to contribute to the evolution of the so-called Gay Liberation movement in the United States twenty years after the war had ended.

★ [8] ★

Sentimental Bullets

I was reminding the boys what they were really fighting for,
the precious personal things rather than ideologies and theories.

—VERA LYNN, "THE FORCES' SWEETHEART"

There'll be love and laughter
and peace ever after,
Tomorrow, when the world is free.

—"THE WHITE CLIFFS OF DOVER"

"We want to give Hitler a more audible razzing than we've
been doing," announced the chairman of the United
States Office of War Information's Music Committee in October
1942. The sentimental bullets being turned out by American
songsmiths lacked the verve of World War I hits like "Over
There." He complained that Tin Pan Alley was letting down the
war effort with "just love songs with a once-over-lightly war
background — 'boy meets girl' stuff." The "Arsenal of Democracy" needed more aggressive songs like "Dev Fuehrer's Face"
featuring a rude chorus of Bronx cheers that were considered so
vulgar that radio stations refused to give it air time. This was the
sort of number that rallied the offensive spirit, according to the
OWI spokesman, who told *Variety* that they wanted more "freedom songs" like "Praise the Lord and Pass the Ammunition."

Popular composer Frank Loesser, who had written America's
first wartime hit, claimed that there was no incentive to repeat its
success because the advertising sponsors of radio shows believed
that housewives were put off by music that sounded overtly martial.

You stay in the middle sort of. You give her hope without facts; glory without blood. You give her a legend with the rough edges neatly trimmed. . . . If you want to sell a housewife Jell-O you don't tell her: "Madam, it is highly probable that your son is coming home a basket case, or at least totally blind, but cheer up, tonight choose one of the six delicious flavors and be happy with America's finest dessert."

Radio undoubtedly played a role in denying "Tin Pan Alley Patriots" the chance to repeat their foot-stamping successes of World War I, most of which were written for marching or dancing to. In World War II, swing was all the rage in the wartime dancehalls, and sentimental love ballads dominated the radio. The short-lived success of the flag-wavers such as "This Is Worth Fighting For" or "Let's Put a New Glory in Old Glory" soon gave way to a revival of prewar songs with strong nostalgic themes, like "You'd Be So Nice To Come Home To" and "You Made Me Love You," that reminded servicemen and their sweethearts of each other.

Patriotism had given way to sentiment two years earlier in Britain. "We're Going to Hang Out Our Washing on the Siegfried Line" epitomized the brash optimism of 1939. But as the British Expeditionary Force retreated to Dunkirk, a polka — "Roll out the barrel, we'll have a barrel of fun" — expressed the collective "we're all in it together" mood as the nation braced itself for the military storm that was about to hurl itself across the Channel. Throughout the critical summer of the Battle of Britain, the BBC musical broadcasts provided a reassuring diet of nostaliga and saccharine sentiment as a counterpoint to the ringing Churchillian rhetoric promising "blood, sweat, toil and tears." During what the prime minister called the nation's "finest hour," references to the "thumbs-up" optimism of young RAF fighter pilots "braving the angry skies" endowed "The White Cliffs of Dover" with a painful topicality. It was of little significance that bluebirds were not native to Dover, nor anywhere else in the British Isles, but they symbolized romantic togetherness in an England safe from enemy bombs when "Jimmy will go to sleep in his own little room again."

That this most unashamedly sentimental and patriotic of all the British wartime songs went on to become a favorite in the United States was in no small measure due to Vera Lynn. This plumber's

daughter from London suburb of East Ham had no special sex
appeal, but her evocative vocal style endowed nostalgically romantic wartime songs with a personal sincerity that only Bing
Crosby could match. "Radio's Sweet Singer of Sweet Songs," as
one wartime billing described her, attributed her popularity to
her "bath voice, when I'm pretending to be in opera," in which
she delivered "songs that spoke for very ordinary people." An
echo of her childhood cockney pitched her songs precisely on the
fine line between sentimentality and mawkishness. It endowed
their often trite lyrics with an inspiring sincerity and made her
voice an unforgettable part of World War II.

"The words of her songs may have been so much twaddle,"
wrote a radio listener after hearing one of her troop concerts.
"But she treated them with as much tenderness as if they were
precious old folk songs, as though they meant something, something she believed in and assumed her audience did too."

Vera Lynn, who had sung with the Ambrose Band that had
been the toast of prewar London's fashionable Embassy Club, had
by 1940 become the nation's most popular vocalist. Her records
were being played by the BBC more often than those of America's top singers of sentimental ballads, Bing Crosby and Deanna
Durbin. "Yours," "Faithful For Ever," "Somewhere in France with
You" and "There's a Boy Coming Home on Leave" were aimed
at the lovers who were parted by war, making her the favorite
singer of the British Expeditionary Force. When the *Daily Express*
of 17 April 1940 announced "British Girl Wins BEF Radio Vote"
in a poll conducted by the BBC Forces Network, Vera Lynn acquired her enduring title of "The Forces' Sweetheart."

"We'll Meet Again," which had done more than any of her songs
to make Vera Lynn so popular with the service audience, had been
first recorded in the autumn of 1939. She attributed its immediate success to the fact that it was a "greeting-card song" which
expressed sentiments that ordinary people, parted by war, needed
to say to each other, but did not find it easy to express. It was
perhaps *the* World War II song, which better than any other typified the desperate optimism felt by separated couples who were
enjoined to "keep smiling through" until "sunny days" returned
and "the blue skies drive the dark clouds far away."

Vera Lynn was the first to admit that there was a measure of truth in the flippant observation made by one postwar critic that "during the war years, Vera Lynn had history working for her as an agent." In Britain, as in the United States, the popular demand was not for patriotic marching songs but for romantic sentiments as a morale booster on the home front as much as behind the battle lines. Vera Lynn had a "genuine respect for simple, sentimental lyrics, which I could sing as if I believed in them because I *did* believe in them." It was this instinctive judgment that, as she describes in her memoir *Vocal Refrain,* made her a better judge of the national wartime mood than the army chiefs and parliamentarians who felt, like the U.S. Office of War Information, that too much sentiment made for poor fighting morale:

Certain belligerent MPs and high military officers — none of whom was actually doing any of the fighting — jumped to the conclusion that a sentimental song produced sentimental soldiers, who would become homesick and desert at the first catch of a crooner's voice. What the boys were supposed to need was more martial stuff, a view that completely overlooked the experience of a previous world war, which, as it got grimmer, produced steadily more wistful songs. As I saw it, I was reminding the boys of what they were *really* fighting for, the precious personal things, rather than ideologies and theories.

That romantic sentiment was an antidote for wartime cares was confirmed by the semiofficial "Mass Observation" surveys which, in 1940, reported that "plain love songs" were proving by far and away the most popular item in the national menu of wartime entertainment. Many of the early hits like "Yours" gave expression to "faithful isolation" with its pledge of constancy "till the stars loose their glory" for couples separated by the military call-up. But devotion "to the end of life's story," after two years of war, had to come to terms with the snatched love affairs that by then had become the staple reality of wartime romance. Anne Shelton, a blond vocalist with Ted Heath's band, scored her greatest success with "That Lovely Weekend." Its haunting melody underscored gently suggestive lyrics that told of the romantic, but all-too-fleeting intimacies of "Those two days in heaven you helped me to spend."

For many British girls, the wartime craze for dancing provided the opportunity for making new boyfriends. Like the cinemas, theaters, and most other forms of entertainment — except the radio — the nation's dance halls had been shut down by government decree on the outbreak of war because of exaggerated fears of enemy bombing raids. But by early 1940 many places of public entertainment were permitted to reopen. People flocked to them as never before. The attitude of those in search of companionship and fun was that "if Hitler was going to drop a bomb on you, he might as well catch you enjoying yourself as huddled under the stairs."

London's Hammersmith Palais — later to become a favorite with GIs — and the Paramount in Tottenham Court Road staged jitterbug marathons and swing contests. Their significance was not lost on one newspaper, which noted that "this noisy exhibition of abandoned convulsions was all in keeping with a mad world in which madmen are conflicting to dominate the continent." To satisfy the wartime demand for dance bands rather than grand opera, the management of Covent Garden installed a dance floor over the stalls of the historic theater in Drury Lane. Dancing was the most popular social antidote to anxiety and loneliness, and the desire for close bodily contact soon made swing and jitterbugging less popular than chain-dances like the "Lambeth Walk" and "Hokey-Cokey," which gave the wartime dance halls a party spirit — and soldiers the excuse to hold any pretty girl on the floor. Foxtrots and slow waltzing enjoyed a wartime revival accompanied by the classic romantic love songs such as Cole Porter's "You'd Be So Nice To Come Home To," or the lilting melodies of "Let There Be Love," "You Made Me Care," and "You'll Never Know" (just how much I miss you).

A short-lived "Lambeth Walk" variant called "The Blackout Stroll" urged couples to take advantage of the darkened streets. Such frivolous sentiments, however, could not survive the ordeal of the Blitz. But the scantily clad chorus girls at London's Windmill Theater did manage to keep on dancing through the air raids to inspire other theater managers to launch a morale offensive against Hitler with lines of high-stepping chorines. The Coliseum reopened early in 1941 with the revue *Strike Up the Music*, and the even more exotic vaudeville *Nineteen Naughty One* played at the Prince of Wales Theater.

Sexual titillation became an established feature of London's wartime entertainment. Although the almost-but-not-quite nude

Windmill Girl had to remain statically posed by decree of the Lord Chamberlain, there was more than enough female flesh exposed to arouse the passions of the uniformed men in the audience. The moralists protested at this public display of depravity, but the Windmill Girls were a regular feature of magazines like *Picture Post, Reveille, Blighty,* and *Tid-Bits* that were popular with the troops.

While sex became a more overt ingredient in wartime entertainment on stage, radio remained remarkably chaste and programs such as Vera Lynn's "Sincerely Yours" broadcast servicemen's requests for songs that were laced with nostalgia and romantic sentiment. The average GI or British soldier might not have been aware of what an important role these songs played in sustaining morale, but they often were the sentimental bullets that provided musical talismans and fortified the spirits of the men fighting their way across the world's deserts, and jungles. It was romantic yearning for the girls left behind that provided the inspiration for the songwriters who kept the ammunition lockers of Allied morale replenished with sentimental ballads like "Always in My Heart," "A Little on the Lonely Side," "I'll Walk Alone" (because to tell you the truth I'm lonely), "Rose Ann of Charing Cross," "A Boy in Khaki, A Girl in Lace," "Silver Wings in the Moonlight," "I'll Keep the Love Lights Burning," "My Devotion" (is endless and deep as the ocean), "Paper Doll," and "When the Lights Go on Again All over the World."

American lyricists churned out ballads such as "Rosie the Riveter," which celebrated the women in the factories who were "making history working for victory." But these songs never featured in the forces radio request programs, because the men fighting overseas wanted reassurance that their girls were waiting for them and not abandoning cozy homes to rivet bombers and weld Liberty ships. It was not a wife laboring at a lathe, but the comforting image of her back home, that accounted for the immediate success of Irving Berlin's "White Christmas." Soon after it was featured in the 1942 film *Holiday Inn,* it had become one of the most widely sung, hummed, and whistled tunes of World War II. Crooner Bing Crosby, whose talent for delivering every song as though it was the greatest number in the world, endowed "White Christmas" with an appeal that long outlasted the war and made it one of the most popular hits ever written. But its evocation of family, fireside, and home ensured that it reached the top of the wartime Hit Parade no fewer than nine times. "It came out at a time we were at war and it became a peace song, nothing I ever intended," Berlin was later to confess.

"White Christmas" may have been the most popular ballad with servicemen and their loved ones back home, but it was a German marching song that was destined to become the undisputed favorite of soliders in every army by the end of World War II. "Lili Marlene" was a haunting song about a German soldier's girl that crossed the front line in North Africa in 1942 to be adopted by the Allied troops. Her popularity surpassed World War I's "Mademoiselle from Armentières," and the lyrics telling of a girl waiting in the lamplight before the barracks gate were to be bawdified by military versifiers — and bowdlerized by the civilian songsmiths of half-a-dozen nations. The Italians added a verse that began "Give me a rose, and press it to my heart." The French gave it an explicit sexuality with the line "And in the shadows our bodies entwine." British troops of General Montgomery's Eighth Army, who had first picked up the song from Afrika Korps radio request broadcasts and soldiers captured from Rommel's desert army, added sexually explicit stanzas and their own refrain: "We're off to bomb Benghazi, we're off to bomb BG."

The United States Office of War Information at first tried to have it banned from American radios — on grounds that it was enemy propaganda that would harm GI morale. British WAAFs were ordered not to whistle or sing it within earshot of German prisoners of war because it might lead to fraternization. The BBC, concerned about the salacious unofficial translations as much as by the infectious popularity of a German song, commissioned "official" English words. Their evocative romance and its simple marching melody made it inevitable that recordings by Vera Lynn and Bing Crosby and later Marlene Dietrich became big hits:

> *Underneath the lantern*
> *By the barrack gate*
> *Darling, I remember*
> *The way you used to wait:*
> *'Twas there that you whispered tenderly,*
> *That you loved me,*

You'd always be
My Lilli of the lamplight
My own Lilli Marlene.

The secret of "Lilli Marlene's" phenomenal success was the universality of its sentimental theme: a soldier's parting with his sweetheart. Her remarkable international career began, according to Lilli's creator, World War I soldier/poet Hans Leip as a "private little love song" about the two girls he became involved with on an officers' course in Berlin in 1917. Lilli — real name Betty — was a greengrocer's daugher at his billet. Marleen was a part-time nurse and doctor's daughter whom he encountered in an art gallery. Dreaming of Lilli while on guard duty one rainy evening as the lamplight flickered in the puddles, he saw Marleen pass by waving her feather boa. It was while lying on the guardroom's iron cot that Fuselier Leip composed his sentimental poem. "Their names could no longer be coupled together with an 'and.' They melted into one, not too shapely, as a single pleasure and pain."

The poem expressed the sadness of a soldier's last farewell, with its final stanza anticipating his death in action and his ghost returning to meet his girl again under the lamplight in front of the barrack gate. Norbert Schultze, a struggling composer in Berlin, set the words to a wistful march he had written. The song was first recorded by a Swedish cabaret artist, Lale Andersen, after it had proved popular on her Radio Cologne broadcasts in the year that war broke out. But its downbeat theme was not considered inspiring enough to celebrate Germany's victorious conquest of Western Europe — and Lale Andersen's records were dispatched to the basement storerooms of the Reich radio networks in 1940.

A year later an army corporal, dispatched to Vienna in 1941 to collect a consignment of records to be played in Belgrade Radio's nightly broadcasts to German troops in North Africa, included it in his selection. An officer, hearing its bugle-call introduction, decided that it would make ideal signing-off music — and that was how "Lilli Marlene" received its first reairing on 18 August 1941. Within a week the station was flooded with thousands of requests, and it was thenceforth played every night at 9:55 P.M.

for three years on the Belgrade station — the only day it was not heard was when Hitler banned all entertainment the day after the fall of Stalingrad.

"Lilli Marlene's" popularity quickly spread to home audiences and although Dr Goebbels was initially afraid that it might depress rather than boost morale, German stations were soon spinning the record up to thirty times a day. Lale Andersen became one of the most requested singers for troop broadcasts — in the course of the war she received over a million fan letters from German soldiers. What she was to call "my fateful song" saved her from the Gestapo after she failed to make good her attempt to join her long-standing Jewish boyfriend in Zurich while on a 1942 concert tour of German army camps in Italy. The security police who arrested Andersen told her that it was the end of her career. "But a BBC broadcast saved me," she was to write. "The BBC put out a report that I'd been taken to a concentration camp and died. Goebbels saw it as a golden opportunity to prove that the English radio told lies. He needed me alive."

British troops who fought in the Western Desert never forgot the important psychological contribution that the symbolic "capture" of their opponent's marching song made to their victory in the battle of El Alamein. "Look here, this is our song! This is the song we hear on our radios in the tanks in the North African desert," an Eighth Army officer claimed shortly after El Alamein. "Mouth organs strike up 'Lilli' at night. We sing it in day charges against the Germans. 'Lilli Marlene' gets us right in our guts. 'Lilli Marlene' is the theme of the Desert War and get that straight!"

Lilli marched with the British Army to Italy, where she also became a favorite with the soldiers of the American Fifth Army who added new verses that were derived from the more sentimental Italian version:

> When we are marching in the mud and cold,
> And when my pack seems more than I can hold,
> My love for you renews my might,
> I'm warm again, my pack is light.
> It's you, Lilli Marlene, it's you Lilli Marlene.

GI's "fell victim" to the "captured" German ballad because, as the celebrated cartoonist with the Fifth Army Bill Mauldin explained, "Our musical geniuses back home never did get round to a good, honest, acceptable war song, and so they forced us to share 'Lilli Marlene' with the enemy. Even if we did get it from the krauts it's a beautiful song, and the only redeeming thing is the rumor kicking around that 'Lilli' is an ancient French song, stolen by the Germans. It may not be true, but we like to believe it."

General Eisenhower did not subscribe to this commonly held belief among Allied soldiers. In 1945 he credited Schultze with being "the only German who has given pleasure to the world during the war." A reporter for the army newspaper *Stars and Stripes* succinctly summed up that it had done "something that all Tin Pan Alley has failed to do" by giving the GIs a song that was "good for marching, cafe singing and humming to oneself on lonely outposts."

It was not for the want of effort that British and American songwriters failed to deliver the song that matched the universal appeal that "Lilli Marlene" had for all servicemen. The initial war years produced the songs of yearning for absent sweethearts like "Always in My Heart," "I'll Wait For You (Always)," "I'm in Love with the Girl I Left Behind Me," and "I'm Thinking Tonight of My Blue Eyes" (and wonder whether she's thinking of me?). These all reflected the perennial concern of soldiers over the constancy of their girls back home. "Stick to Your Knittin', Kitten" and "Be Brave, My Beloved" became the U.S. armed forces' favorites as the war dragged and men overseas began to doubt whether the little lady really was waiting for her Johnny to come marching home. "Somebody Else Is Taking My Place," was too direct an expression of this fear to compete with the enormous success of the Andrews Sisters' vibrant revival of the World War I song "Don't Sit Under the Apple Tree" (with anyone else but me!).

Whatever comfort was afforded the overseas GI in 1943 by "They're Either Too Young or Too Old" and "What's Good Is in the Army" was undone by "You Can't Say No to a Soldier" and Sophie Tucker's gently wicked "The Bigger the Army and Navy" (the better the loving will be). It was not so much that the GIs worried that new stateside recruits might seduce their girls, but "draftdodgers" and those young men who enjoyed the benefit of a reserved occupation to stay out of uniform.

In 1944 when thirty thousand bobby-soxers rioted in New York's Times Square before a Frank Sinatra concert, the wiry young man with the quaff and 4-F classification that kept him out of uniform increased the resentment many servicemen felt about the sex appeal of the young crooner with the intense blue eyes and mellow bedtime voice. Although Sinatra was already married and had a child, a Columbia University psychologist surmised that "this little fella represents some kind of an idealized hero, much like the story of Prince Charming" to explain the new phenomenon of "mass hysteria" among his teenage female fans. When Frank Sinatra finally made his much-publicized and often-delayed overseas concert tour for the USO in 1945, he was greeted at first with derisory yells until he melted the GIs' hostility with his talents as a balladeer.

In the final year of World War II the hit songs anticipated the need to heal the wounds of separation with the passions of homecoming reunions. "It's Been a Long, Long Time" was followed by Perry Como's overtly suggestive rendition of "I'm Going to Love That Gal" (like she's never been loved before). And in Britain, "I'm Gonna Get Lit Up" (when the lights go up in London) looked forward to a national binge on "the day we finally exterminate the Huns," when the singer promised "we'll all be drunk for months and months." The biggest hit of all the homecoming songs was "I'll Be Seeing You" (in all the old familiar places). Its lyrics were given a more explicit sexual reinterpretation than its composers intended by British and American servicemen. "We'll Meet Again" also offered limitless possibilities for barrack-room songwriters by changing "meet" to "mate."

If the popular songs were the sentimental bullets in the morale war, the dance bands were its heavy artillery. They sustained a romantic musical barrage throughout World War II, which an RAF serviceman evocatively recalled:

In a smoke-hazed aeroplane hanger "somewhere in England," the floor crowded to capacity with uniformed boys and girls swaying gently or "jiving" wildly according to the dictates of that essential commodity, the dance band, the vocalist, his (or her) face almost obscured by an enormous microphone, singing of love not war. . . . The dance was on and all we were conscious of was the music (and what music it was) the exhilarating rhythm and of course, the girl in our arms. She may have been a little WAAF cook, or an ATS orderly, but as the orchestra wove its spell, she was Alice Faye, Betty Grable, Rita Hayworth or whoever our "pin-up" of that particular week may have been.

No bandleader excelled Glenn Miller for capturing the wartime mood in a sensual brassy appeal that could shift effortlessly from the upbeat tempo of "American Patrol" to the dreamy sentiment of his orchestra's "Moonlight Serenade" theme. The tragic disappearance of Colonel Miller on a 1944 concert tour added a heroic dimension to the mystique of the band's music: Glenn Miller was *the* sound of World War II for many people. There were of course plenty of other popular bands, including those of clarinetist Benny Goodman — "The King of Swing" — Tommy Dorsey, and Harry James in the United States. In Britain the BBC made millions familiar with the piano tesssitura of Victor Sylvester and the Geraldo Orchestra's lush strings. In the dance hall many preferred the brasher tones of the Joe Loss Orchestra's silver trumpets or the sweeping syncopations of the RAF musicians who played the popular "Squadronaires."

The wartime tours of military camps by famous bands were just a part of what, by the end of the war, had become a massive logistical campaign that sent popular singers and entertainers to the most distant battle theaters to raise the morale of troops thousands of miles from home. The American USO (United Services Organization) and Britain's ENSA sponsored and organized regiments of singers, dancers, comedians, and musicians who volunteered to undertake these grueling overseas tours that played on improvised open-air stages, in bombed-out theaters, or from the backs of army trucks. Allied entertainers endured dust storms, tropical downpours, the mud of the European front — and in some cases the distant rumble of frontline guns — to ensure that the show went on.

Vera Lynn donned an ATS uniform in March 1944 to make an arduous four-month trip to entertain the troops battling the Japanese in the jungles of Burma. The men of the so-called Forgotten Army never forgot the resourcefulness of Britain's most popular wartime singer when she toured the Far East Front. It also proved an unforgettable mission for her. Braving humidity, baggage mishaps, endless truck breakdowns, lost pianos, and rough beds, "The Forces' Sweetheart" never failed to bring the men the songs that reminded them of their faraway homes. Often this meant standing before the makeshift microphone in a borrowed pair of army pants while tropical beetles, attracted to the spotlights, swarmed around her hair. In another jungle performance, as she recorded in her memoir, "my pale pink dress grew steadily darker as I sweated, until it was hanging on me limp and sodden." She sang to thousands at base camps in India and to small groups in the Arakan behind the front line. Her "smallest audience ever" consisted of two men in a hospital tent: "They were both terribly wounded and they asked me to sing 'We'll Meet Again.' I could see what they were thinking. In the end only one of them got home."

"Munitions and movies are just about equally vital to American fighting men," proclaimed Paramount's leading sex symbol Paulette Goddard after her thirty-eight-thousand-mile tour of the China-Burma-India theater in 1944. Hollywood vied with Broadway in these USO show tours that made the more limited British ENSA concert party seem like amateur theatricals. *Four Jills in Jeep* was a film compiled from sequences shot during a five-month USO tour of North Africa, Italy, and England, by Carole Landis, Martha Raye, Alice Faye, and Mitzi Mayfair as they gave up to five GI shows a day.

The leading light behind the mobilization of American show-business talent overseas was comedian Bob Hope. After a dozen overseas tours accompanied by a bevy of stars and entertainers that took him to every major theater to play before an estimated seven million troops, he was named the United States number one "soldier in greasepaint." His machine-gun delivery of gags that were a good deal more risqué than he dared use on his radio show never failed to appeal to soldiers. But the loudest roars of approval in these makeshift troop shows were always reserved for the goddesses of the silver screen who braved the weather and the wolf-whistles no matter what time of day to bring glamour to what they called the "foxhole circuit."

"Carole Landis and the girls dressed to the hilt in evening gowns, although the rain came down in sheets almost constantly," recalled Jack Benny admiringly after a tour of the Pacific. "They never covered themselves with coats — after all, the boys wanted reminders of the girls back home." Female stars knew better than anyone what the men really wanted. "Miss Legs," as she was affectionately called by GIs, always made good on her reputation by wearing her famous sequined sheath dress on concert tours and during her many hospital visits. "I may have seemed slightly incongruous walking into hospital wards in long slim gowns," Dietrich was to recall, "but the look in the men's eyes when they saw me made up for the inconvenience of trying to pretend I was just strolling onto a Hollywood movie set."

The GIs wolf-whistled their delight, but prudish churchmen in America roared with anger that Marlene Dietrich's act constituted "indecent and sexually exciting entertainment" after the legendary gams that had been bared before a thousand American soldiers had appeared in a *Life* photo-spread. "Miss Dietrich's legs, as you know, have been publicized for many years," replied the executive vice-president of USO Camp Shows Inc.:

This leads me to the conclusion that if Miss Dietrich makes a personal appearance she will be asked to show her legs, and the question arises then as to: 1. Whether or not her granting this request is indecent and 2. If it is not, whether her manner of exposing her leg to the knee is indecent.

The final decision on this vital issue was left to the senior chaplain of the European Theater of Operation. Whether he was a fan of Miss Dietrich is not recorded in the official correspondence, but the legendary Marlene continued to show a leg for victory!

In similar vein another chaplain filed a formal protest at "the most vile, obscene thing I have ever heard" after listening to a female USO entertainer's performance:

In seductive language she, in her song, is describing why she wants to get married. At the close the mistress of ceremonies yells through the mike, "Men, you could all get twenty years for what you are thinking!" — and then lets out a vulgar laugh. If what I hear as I sit here trying to write this letter is a fair example of modern cinema, society is truly in a pitiable state.

The USO directorate clearly had to tread a very delicate line in balancing the sensibilities of the military chaplaincy with Hollywood's enthusiasm for satisfying the GI sense of humor. "We had two roosters that got caught in the rain; one made a run for the barn, and the other made a duck under the porch," and "Jack and Jill went up the hill, and each one dollar and a quarter; Jill came down with two dollars and fifty cents. You can't tell me she went for water!" were so mildly blue that they could not have brought the faintest blush to the cheeks of any soldier accustomed to the racy talk of the barracks. But after one USO show they sent a chaplain rushing for his typewriter to protest to Washington.

Even Jack Benny and Carole Landis came in for criticism over their suggestive jokes during their 1944 Pacific tour. Miss Landis was censured by one chaplain because "of the large number of men she promiscuously kissed." He was not included, which was perhaps why he felt so bitterly that she had failed in her duty to remind the men of "the finer qualities of their own women folk back home." Two comedians were discharged from their USO contract for "indecent language," but sexual titillation and saucy humor remained an indispensable part of the "foxhole circuit" entertainers' kit bag — although the increasing number of protests from field chaplains forced the theatrical officers of the USO to approve the contents of every script.

The demand for shows was so great that even the USO, which tapped the combined resources of Hollywood and Broadway, could not satisfy them by 1945 when the curtain was going up on a performance somewhere in the world round the clock. The Special Services Division of the army therefore arranged for distribution of "do-it-yourself-manuals" for soldiers to put on their own shows. *Hi Yank!* was based on the famous GI cartoon strip "Sad Sack" — the "army's unluckiest guy." With music by Broadway songwriter Frank Loesser, it was billed as a "lusty fast moving show" by the *New York Times*. It came with complete instructions for crepe-paper skirts for the all-male chorus and for outfitting Carmen Miranda look-alikes and choreography sketches for the all-male chorus line. Its supposedly "actor proof, audience proof script" included a sexually suggestive chorus, calculated to bring hoots of delight from the GI audience, in which Sack laments:

I had so much romance in me I thought I would burst;
I hurried off to see my gal, my line was all rehearsed;
I rang the bell — she said, "So sorry, the Marines have landed first!"
With full equipment — !

Even without entertainment manuals, music, and crepe-paper costumes, some frontline units contrived to put on variety shows. In Bayreuth, which was captured in the final weeks of the war by Patton's troops, the "4th Armored Follies" took over Wagner's hallowed Festspielhaus for a revue billed as "All the pretty ladies in the world." Hitler's favorite composer "definitely turned in his grave" according to a member of the audience:

Actually there were far too few females. Instead, we were treated to half the noncoms in the 4th Armored (myself definitely excluded) in drag, kicking up hairy legs and intoning "See What the Boys in the Backroom Will Have" and lecherous verses to "Lilli Marlene."

Such soldier-show pastiches were cheerfully vulgar slurs on the cultural ammunition in the enemy locker, but throughout the war both Axis and Allied sides had hurled a more sinister form of sexually loaded entertainment at each other across the airwaves. Sentiment and the romantic hit parade were essential ingredients in the daily Radio Tokyo broadcasts in English. Beginning in the early summer of 1942, they had featured female announcers who interspersed recordings of popular dance bands and light classical music with exaggerated threats of the numbers of GIs about to die in forthcoming operations and frequent reports of the infidelities of their wives and sweethearts back home.

In a theater where long spells of boredom between bouts of fierce fighting went unrelieved by little entertainment and less sex, the female voice of Japan's sirens of the airwaves and the sweet music that was intended to make them homesick, actually made one particular announcer who was dubbed "Tokyo Rose" into a popular "radio pinup." Although there were about a dozen female announcers, "Tokyo Rose" became the legend and the name was applied by GIs to "at least two lilting feminine voices. One of these belonged to Iva Toguri d'Aquino, a Los Angeles–born nisei girl in her mid-twenties who joined Radio Tokyo as a typist after the outbreak of war barred her passage home, and who was persuaded to assist the team preparing the "Zero Hour," the nightly propaganda broadcasts aimed at undermining the morale of American troops.

Far from undermining the morale of GIs, "Tokyo Rose" became a boost to their spirits. "If a radio popularity poll could be taken out here among American fighting forces," the *New York Times* reported in March 1944, "a surprisingly large number of votes would go to Tokyo Rose and other of the programs beamed from the land of the Rising Sun." For American troops garrisoned in lonely bases in Alaska, it was "Madame Tojo" who brought them the same nightly fare of popular music and ineffective invective. And although much was later to be made of the vicious and sinister propaganda intended to make the GIs homesick, "Your favorite enemy, Annie" as the seductive female announcer liked to introduce herself was awarded a spoof US navy citation in August 1945:

Tokyo Rose, ever solicitous of their morale, has persistently entertained them during these long nights in fox-holes and on board ship, by bringing them excellent state-side music, laughter, and news about home. These broadcasts have reminded all our men of the things they are fighting for.

Yet despite such testimony to the contribution she made to American morale, the unfortunate Iva Toguri d'Aquino, whose U.S. citizenship made her a convenient scapegoat, was tried in 1945 and convicted as traitor. She was sentenced to ten years in prison and a $10,000 find for the entertainment she had provided to millions of GIs. The same fate was also meted out to another siren of the enemy airwaves, whom the GIs called affectionately "Axis Sally." Mildred E. Gillars, an American woman, became the German equivalent of "Tokyo Rose" in propaganda broadcasts that were beamed to American troops fighting in Europe during the final year of the war.

If the Axis efforts at using seductive female broadcasters to undermine the morale of Allied servicemen backfired completely, postwar evidence was to show that the intensive British and American efforts to turn sexually loaded propaganda against the enemy met with no greater success.

Britain's "black propaganda" was sponsored by the government's Political Warfare Executive, which had been set up to counter Dr. Goebbels's skillfully directed radio offenses. Stations were set up which purported to be broadcasting secretly from inside the Reich, run by various anti-Hitler groups. The German authorities with their sophisticated direction-finders quickly identified them as an enemy propaganda operation and announced severe penalties for anyone caught listening to these unauthorized broadcasts. To attract an audience, British stations often included salacious or pornographic material — a favorite theme was to broadcast the intimate details of the sexual eccentricities of Nazi officials or Hitler Youth Leaders.

The mastermind behind Britain's black sexual propaganda was Sefton Delmer, an Austrian expatriate, who invented and played with great relish a tough Prussian character known as "Der Chef." Night after night he took to the airwaves to condemn the depravity and corruption of the Nazis. His scripts' potent brew of patriotism and pornography apparently attracted quite a following in Germany. Station GS-1, which was the identifying call-sign for "Gustav Seigfried Eins," was condemned by the German High Command for its "quite unusually wicked hate propaganda."

Nor were the Germans the only ones to complain about the diet of sex and sadism with which "Der Chef" was spicing up his reports of the Reich's administrative corruption and military bungling. After a broadcast by GS-1 in the summer of 1942, which graphically related the supposed sexual acrobatics of a Kriegsmarine admiral, a strong Foreign Office protest was made after the transmission had been picked up in Moscow. Sir Stafford Cripps, the austere British ambassador to Russia, raised a bureaucratic storm about the propriety of such broadcasts. Delmer's chief submitted a retort that drew an interesting parallel about the way that the undercover war was being fought:

If the Secret Service were to be too squeamish, the Secret Service could not operate. We all know that women are used by them for purposes which we would not like our women to be used, but we say nothing. Has any protest ever been made? This is a war with the gloves off, and when I was asked to deal with black propaganda I did not try to restrain my people more than M [the head of the Secret Service] would restrain his, because if you are told to fight you just fight all out. I am not conscious that it has depraved me. I dislike the baser sides of human life as much as Sir Stafford Cripps does, but in this case moral indignation does not seem to be called for.

Delmer, who was described by his director as "a rare artist," was instructed to tone down the pornographic element of "Der Chef's" scripts, but was otherwise encouraged to continue his contribution to the black propaganda radio war with his gloves off. His artful exploitation of sexual themes was to find its way into the broadcasts made by the other "secret" British wartime radio stations such as the "Atlantiksender" station that beamed its transmissions to U-boat crews and the various "Soldatensenders" which broadcast news and music to German troops in Europe. Actual news was peppered with items that reported the scandalous sexual behavior of Nazi party bosses with the wives of absent Wehrmacht troops; that Wassermann tests had revealed that a large quantity of blood in German army field hospitals was contaminated with syphilis; and announcements of the birth of children to the wives of U-boat men who had not been on home leave for a year.

These stations offered, like "Tokyo Rose," plenty of music and a clever concoction of personal information and names of actual people gleaned from captured German sailors, soldiers, and airmen that was intended to upset the morale of the men at the front. They were reinforced by thousands of leaflets like those dropped over the French U-boat bases in 1943. These emphasized the high casualty rates in a captioned picture strip that made great stress of the awful suffering caused to seamen's widows and families in the fatherland.

Yet for all Delmer's acknowledged genius at inventing credible sexually loaded propaganda, postwar evidence suggests that such broadcasts had little negative impact on Germany. As a leading member of Britain's wartime Political Warfare Executive put it: "I am very dubious whether black propaganda, despite its brilliance in radio work, had any marked effect on the course of the war. It had to be so entertaining that it probably maintained morale!"

The wartime broadcasts and sexually explicit leaflets may, by their very entertaining nature, have initiated changes in Western society's definition of pornography. By exploiting sex as a legitimate content for propaganda, both the Allied and Axis powers may have unwittingly helped initiate the shift in public attitude that permitted the explicit treatment of sex in postwar novels as well as the reinterpretation of the magazine publishing laws that made popular what came to be known as the "Playboy Philosophy."

★ [9] ★

Ammunition for the Heart

We're all in this fight together. Women as well as men sharing our responsibilities. I want to be part of you — the part that goes with you into the battlefield.

— THIS IS THE ARMY, 1943

In trench or camp or ship,
Here's wishing you Good Luck from Jane —
And she hopes you like her strip!

— "JANE" CARTOON, *Daily Mirror*

After German troops overran Europe in the summer of 1940 and Churchill defied Hitler to invade Britain, a military draft in the United States was making Americans apprehensive that they might soon be dragged into the fight. Films like the previous year's blockbuster *Gone With the Wind*, with Clark Gable at romantic loggerheads with Vivien Leigh, had set a trend and struck a powerful chord of contemporary concern among millions of men and women who were worried about how their lives and loves might be affected by a war.

Leigh, Britain's leading star, was back on the screen again in 1941, playing another romantic heroine battling the tides of war in *Lady Hamilton*. Producer Alexander Korda described the movie as "propaganda with a very thick coating of sugar." But the sugar-coating on the passionate love-affair of Britain's famous naval hero Lord Nelson, played by Laurence Olivier, was not thick enough to stop American isolationist protests that the movie was yet another effort by Hollywood's anti-Nazi Jewish community to undermine United States' neutrality.

Prime Minister Winston Churchill, who had cabled production

instruction to Korda, pronounced *That Hamilton Woman,* as it was known in Britain, his favorite wartime film. He had every reason to be delighted at the way in which Hollywood was turning public sympathy against Germany while boosting British morale with Charlie Chaplin's caricature of Hitler in *The Great Dictator,* while movies like *Four Sons, The Mortal Storm,* and *Escape* alerted audiences to Nazi brutality against women and exposed the concentration camps.

Despite the isolationist outcry, American filmgoers' attention continued to be directed to Britain's struggle, with Vivien Leigh's 1941 remake of *Waterloo Bridge* about a melodramatic love affair in the Blitz. Mickey Rooney and Judy Garland in the teenage musical *Babes in Arms* sang "Chin up, Cheerio, Carry On," which promised to "turn the Blitz on Fritz!" Meanwhile, Hollywood was doing its bit for United States mobilization. *Sergeant York* retold the saga of the all-American World War I hero, and in *I Wanted Wings* Veronica Lake and Ray Milland managed to combine romance with a recruiting campaign for the army air force. Dorothy Lamour made army life bearable for Bob Hope in *Caught in the Draft.* In *Navy Blues* Ann Sheridan broke into passionate song to convince her sailor boyfriend why it would be unpatriotic of him to go back to his Iowa farm, and Jimmy Durante and Phil Silvers in *You're in the Army Now* gave a musical endorsement of Selective Service: "The draft has begun / I'm number two-eighty-one / I'm glad my number was called." But it was romance against the backdrop of the war in England that proved to be the biggest draw of the year. Tyrone Power, in *A Yank in the RAF,* helped save English soldiers stranded on Dunkirk beaches and found time to marry his dancer sweetheart. This was made possible after the British government had intervened to have the screenplay rewritten so that Betty Grable did not die, as originally intended, in an air raid on the eve of her marriage.

The formula was perfected in the 1942 Academy Award–winning movie *Mrs. Miniver* which successfully brought to the screen the drama of war's impact on the lives and loves of a "typical" British family. Its distortion of middle-class archetypes promoted one English critic to disown "a world which seems to consist of giggling housemaids with their bucolic young men; doddering servile station masters; glee singers in their feather boas; duchesses and their granddaughters, blackmailing comic grocers and

truculent ever-leaving cooks." But for all its glossy sentimentality, *Mrs. Miniver* presented an evocative cinematographic tribute
to the quiet courage of women in World War II. Greer Garson
was the epitome of genteel feminine resolve which triumphed over
enemy bombs. The emotional demands placed on married women
in wartime were characterized by the manner in which Mrs. Miniver, both as mother and mother-in-law, stoically confronts the
prospect of widowhood: "If I must lose him, there'll be time
enough for tears, there'll be a lifetime for tears," announces her
daughter-in-law on the eve of her wedding.

In a powerfully emotional finale, Mr. and Mrs. Miniver con-
sole each other at the funeral service for their daughter-in-law,
killed by a strafing German fighter while their son lives on to fight
in the RAF. As Spitfires roar the bombed-out church, the rector
defiantly proclaims Hollywood's inspired epitaph on World War
II:

This is not only the war of soldiers in uniform, it is a war of the people — of all people — and it must be fought not only on the battlefield,
but in the . . . heart of every man, woman and child who loves freedom. **This is the people's war.**

The climactic panegyric of *Mrs. Miniver* became a rallying call
for the democracies in their fight against totalitarianism as the
film's 1942 release coincided with the United States' entry into
the war. Romantic films were no longer purely entertainment, but
ammunition for the heart and inspiration for the fighting spirit
of men in battle as well as the women who labored in war production on the home front. In *Mrs. Miniver* Hollywood had made
good on the promise made in 1941 by the deputy director of war
information that "the screen can be used to give the people a clear,
continuous, and total pattern of total war."

Romance, nonetheless, remained the staple ingredient in wartime film production. As the flyer for a B-movie called *China Girl*
succinctly put it, "An American will fight for only three things —
for a woman, for himself and for a better world." The studios
found it more difficult to sustain the love interest during the first
year of the war when most of the top-flight male stars, including
Clark Gable, Tyrone Power, William Holden, Alan Ladd, James
Stewart, and Robert Montgomery, patriotically joined the armed
forces. But neither the shortage of glamorous male leads nor of

steel hairpins and film stock, stopped the romantic glamour factory. In the absence of the top male box-office stars, Hollywood promoted women into the major movie attractions. This gender switch in the film industry's promotion satisfied both the serviceman's demand for sexy symbols and the ego of a largely female wartime home audience. It also proved a box-office bonanza.

World War II brought Hollywood its second golden age as moviegoing became the main form of wartime entertainment. Hollywood stars became national heroines. They raised millions of dollars in War Bond drives and toured the home and overseas fronts entertaining servicemen. January 1942 brought Hollywood the first war casualty when Carole Lombard was killed in a plane crash on a bond promotion tour. Dorothy Lamour stepped forward to complete the tour. She became known as the "Treasury's Sweetheart" when the cash poured into the federal coffers after her trip around the shipyards and defense plants.

Booming wartime box-office receipts encouraged the American studios to marshal their huge resources toward turning out an average of four hundred new motion pictures a year. Hollywood's war output included propaganda documentaries and patriotic tributes to the American fighting man. Films like *Wake Island, Bataan, Five Graves to Cairo, Thirty Seconds Over Tokyo,* and *Guadalcanal Diary* satisfied the demand of the wives and sweethearts for films about the way the war was being fought while spurring on the efforts of the war production workers. Keeping the wartime audiences laughing on both sides of the Atlantic were Bob Hope and Bing Crosby who took *The Road to Morocco* with Dorothy Lamour, whose clinging sarong made her a favorite of the GIs. *Swing Shift Maisie* sent the irrepressible blonde Ann Sothern into a war plant while *Buck Privates* put Abbott and Costello into uniform. In 1942 Humphrey Bogart's enigmatic affair with Ingrid Bergman in *Casablanca* elevated the anti-German espionage film into a romantic art form. The same year Judy Garland, George Murphy, and Gene Kelly in *For Me and My Gal* started a wartime craze for musicals featuring men and women in uniform.

"Motion pictures are as necessary to the men as rations," insisted an American general. *Time* magazine was to publish a 1944 poll that indicated : "GIs like musical comedies best, comedies next best, then adventure films and melodramas." When General Eisenhower was planning D-Day, he demanded, "Let's have more movies" — and the troops cheered. "Without movies we'd go nuts," wrote a GI from the Pacific. Soldiers' favorite movies were those that were light on patriotism and heavy on sentiment, like Rita Hayworth's *My Gal Sal* and Judy Garland's *Meet Me in St. Louis* — or cartoons such as Donald Duck's hilarious effort's to battle Hitler in "Der Fuehrer's Face" and help the war drive with "Get in the Scrap."

Films were uniquely suited to boosting the morale of the armed forces, they were prepackaged sentimental bundles of home which could be easily shipped behind the front lines. They were sent where no live concert party dared to go and cans of film and projectors reached jungle camps, desert bases and Nissen huts in arctic tundra. Testimony to the unique contribution that wartime Hollywood made to boosting allied morale came in a 1943 letter from a marine private who had seen six months' action in the Pacific:

I know what it is to be cut off from everything . . . to sit on my bunk with my head in my hands . . . to walk a post in some lonely nowhere . . . to wait and wait for God only knows what. Those hours can stretch into centuries — and would, if it weren't for a movie now and then. Movies that stop us from thinking of ourselves and our surroundings. Movies that remind us that there are such things as pretty girls, gay music, and a civilization worth living for . . .

Of all Hollywood's outpouring of wartime entertainment, it was the musicals that provided the biggest boost to the wartime morale of servicemen and civilians alike. The movies whose flimsy boy-meets-girl plots were disguised in a lavish package of sexy glamour and cheerful songs offered the tonic of a few hours' respite from the grim realities of war. The musical, which had buoyed American spirits through the Depression, had become a faded box-office attraction until its popularity was revived by the wartime demand for escapist entertainment. No greater contrast to the war could have been concocted than these frothy visual sundaes whipped up around nubile female chorus lines and topped off with the glittering stars such as Betty Grable, Ginger Rogers, Ann Sheridan, Judy Garland, Rita Hayworth, Marlene

Dietrich, Dorothy Lamour, Barbara Stanwyck, Alice Faye, and Carmen Miranda.

The wartime Hollywood musical which made their female stars into national cheerleaders at the same time promoted them as sex symbols in "pinups."

The bands and chorus lines at Warner Brothers studios were in full patriotic blast for *Yankee Doodle Dandy*. The enormously popular movie was a timely salute to the flag-waving music of composer George M. Cohan. It won an Oscar for James Cagney in the rags-to-riches title role and revived the World War I hits "Over There" "Give My Regards to Broadway," and "You're a Grand Old Flag" just in time to rally American spirits after Allied fortunes hit rock bottom as the flood tide of Japan's military conquest rolled over the Philippines, Malaya, and Burma.

Two years later the same studios produced Irving Berlin's no less red-white-and-blue soldier-boy love story *This Is the Army* which set the pattern for a spate of parade musicals. This patriotic salute and tribute to the GI with its rousing title song also made a hit of the wistful "I Left My Heart at the Stage Door Canteen." More convincingly than most of the parade musicals, it managed to tie the knot between patriotism and love with Ronald Reagan as the draftee soldier who is reluctant to wed his sweetheart before he goes off to war. In a symbolic wartime reversal of the traditional roles, it is Joan Leslie who finally persuades *him* to marry her with lines that doubtless put the seal on many real life wartime romances:

We're all in this fight together. Women as well as men sharing our responsibilities. I want to be part of you — the part that goes with you on the battlefield. This is a free United States. If we want to get married — let's get married.

The success of *This Is the Army* prompted the other Hollywood studios to adopt the same formula in which romantic plots were less important than the number of stars and dance routines that could be mustered onto the screen. *Stage Door Canteen* from United Artists was set in one of the wartime service clubs staffed by show-business personalities. Not to be outdone, Warner Brothers retaliated with *Hollywood Canteen*, a musical pegged on the improbable story of a sailor in from the Pacific who finds himself the millionth serviceman to enter the famous Los Angeles club founded by Bette Davis. For his prize he chooses as his weekend escort the "as American as apple pie" Joan Leslie. The Andrews Sisters performed the film's calloused title song, which celebrated the Hollywood Canteen where "GI Joes can forget their woes and boogie with any movie star." America's most popular wartime female trio then went on to complain in close harmony of the pain they endured from "patriotic corns" from jitterbugging with too many GIs.

Thank Your Lucky Stars was Columbia Pictures' entry in the "musical parade." it was notable for Bette Davis singing up at a huge Victory poster of U.S. soldiers, sailors, and marines, and lamenting the men who were left were "either too young or too old" and "there is no secret lover, the draft board didn't discover." Star-Spangled Rhythm was Paramount Pictures' contribution. It featured an irrepressible Bob Hope introducing Paulette Goddard, Dorothy Lamour, and Veronica Lake in a slyly sexy ditty: "A Sweater, a Sarong and a Peek-A-Boo Bang." The big chorus routine "On the Swing Shift" was a musical salute to the girls in the home front factories in which Betty Hutton saucily sang "I'm Doing It for Defense."

These wartime musicals not only made female talent their main feature, but they also contributed to the wartime blurring of the sex roles by casting men in women's roles for comic situations. This Is the Army and Hi Yank featured dance routines for soldiers dressed up in female costumes. In other wartime comedy films, Danny Kaye had to don a WAC's skirt to date his officer girlfriend, and Red Skeleton dressed as a ballet dancer to pursue Esther Williams into a posh Eastern girl's academy.

The ultimate symbol of wartime gender confusion was the aggressive sexuality of Carmen Miranda. The "Brazilian Bombshell," as she became known after the 1940 release of Down Argentine Way, became famous as a Latin American "femme fatale" whose Mickey Mouse mouth, clattering maracas, and exotic headpieces made her an outrageous parody of a woman out to get a man. Her most stunning screen appearance was in the 1944 musical The Gang's All Here when she sashayed through a tropical fruit salad chorus routine concocted in glorious Technicolor by Busby Berkley to sing "The Lady in the Tutti-Frutti Hat" in her unique "south-of-the-border" style. Carmen Miranda, as one critic noted, "projected about as much sex-appeal as a Christmas tree in July," but she sent up the traditional notion of female allure with rolling eyes, ruby lips, and a suggestive turn of phrase that delighted audiences. By the end of the war she had become the most travestied star, and no improvised vaudeville all-male army show was without a hilarious impersonation of the Lady in the Tutti-Frutti Hat.

If Carmen Miranda represented the kind of nonthreatening sexual confusion that servicemen could laugh at, GIs found less to joke about in those movies that presented women taking over the customary male role. The 1943 film *Broadway Parade* was intended as Hollywood's musical tribute to the female war workers and it opened with a masterpiece of choreographic cinematography in which a high-kicking chorus line dissolved into a marching battalion of female welders while a soldier sang:

Once they had so many dates life became a bore,
Now they're in defense work making bombers by the score.
They gave up fancy clothes and are happy in navy blue,
They are wearing cotton hose and are happy in khaki too!

There was not much sex appeal or glamour for the service audience in such movies, as Paramount found when it had welded together *Rosie the Riveter*. The tortuous plot of this 1944 musical strained even Hollywood's power of romantic invention as it told the "inspiring" tale of a pretty girl who delays her marriage so that she can take a job in an aircraft factory because "winning the war is more important." Although it played to packed audiences of female war workers who shared the heroine's belief that they "typify Miss America today," its interest for GIs was on a par with the large notice over the factory set: "IF YOUR SWEATER IS TOO LONG, LOOK OUT FOR MACHINES — IF YOUR SWEATER IS TOO SMALL, LOOK OUT FOR MEN!

Rosie the Riveter was not a hit with the American male audience, nor were the other wartime "women's pictures" in which Hollywood catered to its large female wartime audience with films that depicted women coping with the war by fulfilling traditional male roles. The novel situations of women in wartime offered Hollywood producers scope for new dramatic plots and situation comedy opportunities. *Swing Shift Maisie* was about Ann Sothern's trials as an aircraft worker, *Government Girl* featured Olivia de Havilland as a Washington bureaucrat, and Lucille Ball played a film star turned defense worker in *Meet the People. Keep Your Powder Dry* featured Lana Turner as a pert heiress who joined the WACs only to burst into tears when she was commissioned, and Betty Hutton frolicked in uniform through *Here Come the Waves* playing twin sisters.

In Britain, where the cinema industry could not compete with Hollywood in glamour or output, the so-called women's films were so "American" that their psychological impact was muted. Although German bombs demolished one in ten cinemas, attendances trebled through the Blitz as the total weekly attendance grew to over thirty million. Twice-weekly changes of program ensured that there were always queues waiting in the blackout at the local cinema. The principal fare was more likely to be popcorn romances or musicals rather than home-produced Gainsborough comedies such as *It's That Man Again—ITMA.*

Plagued by shortages and the Blitz, the British film industry struggled to produce documentary salutes to the "people's war" like *London Can Take It* and *One of Our Aircraft Is Missing.* There were a spate of patriotic features made about spies and fifth columnists such as *Night Train to Munich* and *Gestapo.* But it was not the story of a Polish flyer escaping to join the RAF and his love affair with a British girl that made *Dangerous Moonlight* popular, but Richard Addinsell's Rachmaninoff-like score with its so-called "Warsaw Concerto." Three years later it was his "Cornish Rhapsody" theme that saved *Love Story* from the sentimental oblivion to which it was destined by its plot about a concert pianist's romantic obsession with a blinded RAF pilot. The wartime British film industry paid patriotic homage to national heroines. *They Flew Alone* told the story of aviatrix Amy Johnson and *Nurse Edith Cavell* was an anti-German tribute to the World War I heroine for whom "Patriotism was not enough." Alexander Korda returned to England in 1943 to direct a documentary on the RAF, *"The Lion Had Wings,* and made *The Perfect Stranger* with Robert Donat and Deborah Kerr playing a husband and wife struggling to rebuild their marriage after three years of wartime separation.

Noël Coward and David Lean nonetheless succeeded in producing the most memorable British war film. *In Which We Serve* won an Academy Award in 1943 and was praised by *Newsweek* magazine as "The finest film to come out of the war." It celebrated the courage of the men on a Royal Navy destroyer and their families, with Coward playing the captain of HMS *Torrin,* a role modeled on Lord Louis Moutbatten. Coward's 1944 production, a sentimental celebration of a working-class family in two wars which was based on his play *This Happy Breed,* was a wild success when it was released at home, but it generated less enthusiasm in the United States.

The "pinups" of World War II originated in the French *cartes postale suggestive,* which appropriately described the artful semi-nude girls in frilly negligees that had made Paris famous for its "naughty postcards" with the Allied troops in World War I. The "cheesecake" tradition of a teasingly exposed female was supposedly socalled after a New York newspaper editor had approvingly exclaimed in 1915 that such pictures were "better than cheesecake!" By the 1930s the Hollywood glamour cameramen had streamlined the pinup. The World War II model had been liberated from her frilly hourglass corset in favor of shapely legs in seamed stockings and a slim figure defined by a skintight bathing costume that emphasized a full bosom. Only her teasing "come-on" smile remained unchanged.

Such was the display put on by Betty Grable, the undisputed leader of the wartime pinup parade. She best exemplified the sex appeal of the all-American girl-next-door. Women liked her too, which suggests that Grable's real appeal was less erotic than as a wholesome symbol of American womanhood. Her reign as queen of the pinups owed less to her unsensual, plumpish figure or her much-photographed "Million Dollar Legs" than to a carefully groomed exploitation of her good-natured hominess by 20th Century–Fox.

The year after the enormously popular *A Yank in the RAF* had taken Elizabeth Ruth Grable to number eight in the box-office ratings, she made a trio of movies — *The Dolly Sisters, Sweet Rosie O'Grady* and *Coney Island.* These were sentimental roles that enhanced her image of naïveté and girlish exuberance. In the 1943 musical *Song of the Islands* she romanced Victor Mature, establishing a special brand of wholesome eroticism that made her Hollywood's biggest wartime star and the highest paid actress in the United States. Her studio lost no opportunity to exploit her image as the American serviceman's favorite. In *Guadalcanal Diary* William Bendix, as the rugged marine hero, shaved in front of her famous bathing suit pose, suitably pinned to a palm trunk.

Darryl Zanuck, the astute boss of 20th Century–Fox, backed up his hunch about the special "apple pie" sex appeal that the pert blonde would have for servicemen with glamourous big-budget Technicolor films that highlighted what he termed her "pastel charms." His fears that Grable's "Number One Pinup" status might be harmed by her 1943 marriage to bandleader Harry James proved groundless. It only increased her appeal for many soldiers — and their wives. "We ought to be mad at you for marrying the sweetheart of our camp, but it couldn't happen to a nicer guy" was typical of the letters her husband received from GIs who wrote asking for her wedding photo. The birth of her child the same year only enhanced her popularity. The combination of glamour girl and mother undoubtedly gave a tremendous boost to the receipts of her 1944 film *Pin-Up Girl,* which was less than critically acclaimed by the *New York Times* as a "spiritless blob of a musical."

What *Pin-Up Girl* lacked in plot, it more than made up in its lavish staging and star turns. Military and civilian audiences flocked to see a befeathered Grable playing a chorus girl against a cloud of black tulle. There were twenty thousand requests a week for her famous bathing suit photograph, making her by far and away the most popular pinup with the American forces in World War II.

If Grable's enormous wartime success owed more to her image as the girl every GI dreamed of coming home to, there was an array of Hollywood stars whose appeal was more erotic than wholesome. Rita Hayworth was the runner-up to Betty Grable in the wartime pinup stakes, a position secured after she sang and danced with Gene Kelly in the 1944 musical *Cover Girl.* Hayworth, a brunette who had originally been stereotyped a "Latin firebrand," was an undeniable beauty who exuded the sultry sex appeal of a mature woman. Hayworth leaped into the wartime pinup stakes in 1941 after *Life* magazine published a classic photograph of the star on a bed of satin sheets, captioned, not without justification: "The Goddess of Love of The Twentieth Century."

The prize for the sexiest pinup photographs of the war, however, went to Jane Russell, a relative unknown, whose thirty-eight-inch chest was shamelessly exploited by Howard Hughes to publicize his RKO production *The Outlaw,* an otherwise unmemorable remake of the legend of Billy the Kid. Grable's famous back-to-the-camera stance was innocent cheekiness compared to Russell's passionate sprawl on the hay. Photographer Leslie Hurrel was hired to get what Hughes called "production out of Jane's breasts." The publicity stills provoked a furious public discussion when Hughes advertised the forthcoming film in 1942 with the slogan: "What are the two great reasons for Jane Russell's rise to stardom?" This began a four-year struggle with the Motion Picture Association to get approval for public release of the *The Outlaw.* Hughes spent $1.5 million, most of it on promoting the sensational physique of its star. Russell's flamboyant sex appeal made her pinups wildly popular with GIs overseas, and her fans relished reports of the scandal that her full figure was stirring up back home. "How would you like to tussle with Russell?" made her so celebrated that when a skywriter outlined two cirles over San Francisco, everyone knew what was being advertised.

While female "cheesecake" became a wartime staple for most men in the armed forces of World War II — even the Wehrmacht's magazines included glamour shots of popular German actresses and singers — the military authorities in women's auxiliaries took exception to male "pinups." The female libido was apparently not aroused by the exposure of male muscle according to Hollywood, so most of the publicity photographs showed its leading men clothed. Even so, in many ATS barracks in Britain pictures of famous male stars like Tyrone Power, Errol Flynn, and Clark Gable were banned from the women's lockers by many female commanding officers who considered them unhealthy and bad for military discipline.

Men in uniform were more fortunate. While some officers had at first adopted a prudish attitude to pinning up "pinups" in barrackroom lockers, by the end of the war these pictures had become a universal accoutrement of the Allied armies. They were featured in magazines like *Life* and *Look* as well as encouraging a wartime boom in the publishing of so-called girlie magazines featuring "pinup parades" such as *Tid-Bits of Beauty* and *Glamorous Models* in the United States and *Tid-Bits, Blighty* and *Reveille* in Britain. Other publications carried more blatantly erotic presentations, keeping the mail censors busy on both sides of the Atlantic because the law banned from the mails what was later to be termed "soft pornography."

Esquire magazine, like the American and British *Men Only,* had catered to a middle-class male audience since before the war with the exclusive artistic eroticism of the artists George Petty and Albertos Vargas. The Petty or Vargas Girl was a fantasy, whose airbrushed skin beneath a wispy negligee suggested the color and texture of a ripe apricot. These luscious full-color spreads were much sought after by servicemen, a market that *Esquire* was quick to cultivate by adding the Stars and Stripes, or a medal, to the Vargas or Pretty Girl's minimal costumes.

Such blatant commercialization of sex directed at GIs grated on the stern Catholic morality of the U.S. Postmaster General Frank C. Walker. In 1944 he finally canceled the magazine's mail privileges because of obscenity. *Esquire* commenced a lengthy legal battle and hearings took place on Capitol Hill with clergymen, academics, and representatives of women's organizations lining up to testify. But until the magazine was acquitted of publishing "lewd and lascivious" pictures, the American serviceman overseas was deprived of his favorite color pinups. Angry protests flooded the editorial offices and Capitol Hill. One letter from an army private minced no words about their outrage:

You won't find one barracks overseas that hasn't got an *Esquire* Pin-Up Girl. I, for one, have close to fifteen of them, and none of them seems to demoralize me in the least. Those pictures are very much on the clean and healthy side and it gives us a good idea of what we're fighting for. What will these ignorant specimens think up next?

"Such pictures are objectionable to all persons of refinement and good taste" was the official view of the U.S. army chaplain general. Others supported the postmaster general's view condemning all pinups: "Their suggestiveness does not add to moral practices nor to the production of virtuous thoughts." That at least one GI agreed was evident from a letter received by a Catholic priest from a soldier who condemned the army magazine *Yank* for pinups and cartoons "that should make any decent man blush with embarrassment. . . . Why does the Army always try to play up upon a man's sensual appetite? . . . I was lonely many, many times. I needed a morale booster; however, these sensual appeals tended to lower my spirits, rather than boost them."

The War Departmnet found itself with a fine bureaucratic conundrum, since the most popular feature of the semiofficial service publications *Yank* and *Stars and Stripes* were their full-spread pinup parades. The same was true for the officially approved British service magazine *Reveille,* which had carried pictures of girls in bathing suits since the beginning of the war. "Bathing suit 'art' " and "pictures of the comparatively undraped female form" presented a moral dilemma to the chaplaincy. It was eventually addressed by the acting chief of U.S. army chaplains in a 1945 memorandum which concluded:

It is not one of the primary functions of Army information channels to provide beauty for the adornment of dugout walls. . . . However, one cannot refrain from quoting from a lengthy editorial salute by an Army newspaper at an isolated post in Alaksa to a New York strip tease artist who has posed for special pictures for their small publication. "You are the bear grease in our lupin-root cakes. You are the seal blubber in our bowl of salmon berries" is a touching acknowledgment of the fact that the life of this isolated garrison, the likeness of the obliging young woman was more warming to the quonset hut than any mere coal fire!

Confirmation, if any was needed, that pinups did indeed warm the cockles of many a soldiers heart came in the flood of mail that arrived at *Yank* magazine after they printed a Sergeant O'Hara's complaint about a pinup of starlet Irene Manning: "I would much rather wake up in the morning and see a picture of a P-51 or 39 hanging above my bed or the picture of my wife."

"Don't slam our pin-ups. If I had a wife I would make sure her picture was up, but Irene Manning will do until that big day," was how one sailor defended the military value of pinups. "Maybe if some of those 'panty-waists' had to be stuck some place where there are no white women and few native women for a year and a half, as we were, they would appreciate even a picture of our gals back home" was the retort from GIs in Alaska. "We nasty old Engineers still appreciate *Yank* **with** its pin-ups." Another letter demanded an apology to Miss Manning: "I have her picture over my locker and I like it very much. I suggest Sgt. O'Hara go out and learn the facts of life from someone who has been around. . . . Keep the pictures coming. We like them."

It was one of the sexual ironies of World War II that service-men transferred the most popular female icons to their ma-chines of war. By 1945 there was hardly a tank or a plane in the U.S. military that was not adorned with its own painted icon of feminity as a good-luck talisman that also showed the enemy what is was that red-blooded Americans "were fighting for."

In one U.S. army bomber squadron based in England the cus-tom grew of pasting the latest Vargas Girl and pinup clipped from *Esquire* and *Men Only* onto the center section of their Flying For-tresses:

One navigator had most of the film stars, including Gypsy Rose Lee, accompanying him on day trips to Berlin, and in his enthusiasm, had pasted pin-ups on both the inside and outside of the Fortress. On each flight down the "Kraut Run," the navigator's skipper swore that their particular plane was singled out for special attention by the German fighter pilots who "wondered what all the queer pictures were about."

In the Pacific theater at least, the pinup may actually have played a direct role in the United States' victory over the Japanese. The Pacific Fleet intelligence officer included sexy pinup sketches in some of the intelligence summaries sent out to the ships, calcu-lating that this would ensure that proper attention was paid to his reports! Unfortunately the practice had to be halted after a prudish kill-joy officer sent a message of complaint to CINPAC headquarters. But no one protested that Captain Dyer, one of the navy's leading codebreakers at Pearl Harbor, housed under his glass-top desk one of the finest pinup collections in the fleet. What became known as "Dyer's Desk" was one of the main at-tractions of the subterranean chamber where its occupant con-tributed to the decryption of Japanese messages which led to the American victory at the Battle of Midway. Whether the sight of so many pretty females under the piles of intercepts assisted Dyer in his vital wartime codebreaking is a matter about which even he was reluctant to speculate!

There can, however, be no denying the tremendous success achieved by the British cartoon heroine "Jane," whose adven-tures were also to be chronicled in *Stars and Stripes* as "that girl who picks 'em up and lays 'em down, puts 'em on and takes 'em off!" Jane and her pet dachshund, called Fritz, who became the

"You're in the army now, Miss Jones." (left) A British ATS driver receives training. (bottom) WAACS parade in Miami, 1942.

Commander of a U.S. Army tank crew on the testing range at Aberdeen, Virginia.

Marine recruiting poster

ATS recruiting poster

British Civil Defense worker during the Blitz

British ATS recruits service a Churchill tank.

"What did you do in the war, Mommy?" Women welders and shipyard workers were the muscle behind the 200 percent increase in American shipbuilding.

Welders come off shift after working on submarine hulls at an East Coast shipyard.

ABOVE AND RIGHT: *Young welders at an East Coast yard*

Checking "1000 pounder" bombs at Firestone Rubber's Oklahoma plant

At work on the locomotive of the B&O Railroad

A "lumber jill"

Blast furnace flue cleaners at U.S. Steel, Gary, Indiana

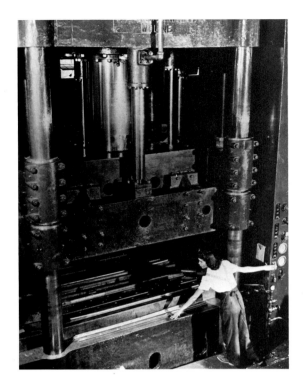

A press operator at San Diego's
Consolidated Aircraft plant.

An engineer at General Electric's
flight test center

RIGHT AND BELOW: *"Rosie the Riveters"* at work on aircraft

Women workers were urged by advertisers to keep the ''femininity quotient'' high in the factories. ''She does a man's work in the ground crew, but she hasn't lost any of her glamour, sweetness and charm'' ran a McCall's headline.

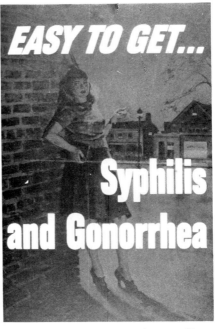

Images of women in poster campaigns: (top left) the patriotic contributor to the war effort on the home front; (top right) the tough-minded independent wage-earner; (bottom left) the seductress; (bottom right) the prostitute

The World War II pin-ups: (top) Ann Miller and Jeanne Crain in the pages of Yank *Magazine; (bottom) Rita Hayworth and Ann Sheridan.*

"This picture issued primarily for use in publications by and for servicemen." (top left)
Athlete of the Year; (top right) Jane Wyman; (bottom left) Jane Kean; (bottom right)
Betty Grable

The legendary Marlene Dietrich on tour

Entertaining the troops

The "friendly invasion": U.S. GIs on their way to Britain

*Irish wives of U.S. Navy personnel stationed in Northern Ireland arrive in New York.
Originally captioned: "They have left their old homes to find new ones in the U.S. . . .
This is the first mass shipment of war brides from the European Theater."*

LEFT AND BELOW: *Loneliness and companionship during wartime*

army's girlfriend, the mascot of the Royal Navy, and the pet of the RAF, had begun her modest career in a 1932 comic strip about a feckless "Bright Young Thing." When war came, it seemed quite natural that she should begin to do her part to boost national morale in the dark days of the Blitz. Jane became a special favorite in submarines on long patrols. They carried a special newsheet which reprinted her cartoon strips, and a new installment was passed around to eager hands each day. Only once was this strict rule broken, during a depth-charge attack that had sent one of His Majesty's submarines to the bottom with damaged engines. To relieve the tension, a crewman asked "What's Jane doing tomorrow?" The coxwain peeled off three weeks' worth of issues to men who did not expect to live that long. When the engines were restarted, the crew naturally attributed their lucky break to Jane.

It was popularly believed that the morale and effectiveness of RAF bomber crews on their night raids over Germany depended on how much clothing Jane had left off in the *Daily Mirror* that morning. "I remember at the Admirality during the war no admiral ever settled down to his day's work until he had looked to see whether the young lady's clothes were on or off," recalled one member of Churchill's coalition government. "During periods of bad news, the editor always kept up morale by keeping her clothes off."

The legend quickly grew up that Jane always disrobed for victory. It was said that the first armored vehicle ashore on D-Day carried a large representation of naked Jane. True to form, when she finally lost the last vestiges of her modesty during the Normandy campaign, the word was passed round the front that "JANE GIVES HER ALL" — and the Allied breakthrough followed a few days later!

★ ⟦ 10 ⟧ ★

A Woman's Work
Was Never Done

Earlier I buttered bread for him, now I paint grenades and think this is for him.

— GERMAN WOMAN MUNITIONS WORKER

It's no longer a question of what is the most comfortable arrangement for each family. We are fighting for our lives — for our freedom and our future. We are *all* in it together, and what is already being done by other women, you can do!

— BBC BROADCAST, MAY 1941

The burden of total war falls upon the women of the country with ruthless impact.

— BRITISH OFFICIAL HISTORY

"The British girl who has taken her place in the War Machine," wrote a wartime journalist, "has little in her life now except work and sleep." This was the lot of the female work force, which was to increase by a dramatic 40 percent to bring an additional two million pairs of hands in the United Kingdom and nine million in America to help turn the wheels of the Allied war effort. After the British government had taken the unprecedented step of beginning a compulsory female mobilization in 1942, the Ministry of Labour estimated that over 80 percent of all single women between fourteen and fifty-nine, 41 percent of wives and widows, and 13 percent of mothers with children under fourteen were at work or in uniform of the auxiliary forces. Even without conscription of women in the United States, that same marked wartime increase in the employment of wives and mothers was also to be reflected in the numbers of married women at work. Making up almost a quarter of the total labor force, married women outnumbered single women in the workplace for the first time.

The involvement of such a large percentage of wives and mothers in the the World War II production battle was to accelerate the erosion of the sexual division of labor and the traditional reluctance of mothers to join the industrial work force. It was the redistribution of the jobs they successfully undertook, as much as by the overall increase in the numbers of employed, that sowed the seeds of a far-reaching change in attitudes to what constituted "woman's work." Custom had combined with the high unemployment to ensure that more than a third of British women at work during the 1930s were in domestic service. The textile industry, historically the largest employer of female labor, was contracting, but jobs had increased in the service and distributive trades and the tobacco industry — and especially in the expanding electrical and vehicle assembly factories. The accelerating technical revolution of the so-called new industries increased the opportunity for repetitive, unskilled light-industrial work, which was considered by male-dominated craft unions and employers as particularly appropriate for female hands to perform.

Yet the majority of working women who entered the pre–World War II work force were, in keeping with tradition, unmarried, under thirty-five, and paid at less than half the male rate. Notwithstanding the 1919 Sex Disqualification Removal Act, which in theory had opened up all the professions except the top grades of the civil service, women remained concentrated in the lowest grades and most poorly paid sectors of teaching and civil service. In industry, although mining and working in the lead-paint industry were the only jobs specifically excluded from women by law, in practice they were denied entry into much of heavy factory work by parliamentary legislation, which prohibited the employment of women on night shifts, Sunday work, or laboring for more than the statutory maximum forty-eight-hour week. Many feminists suspected that such regulations, ostensibly passed to protect the female labor force from an unhealthy and unsuitable working environment, were a subtle means of depressing the average female industrial wage by excluding women out of high-paying "men's work" in the steel, engineering, and shipbuilding industries.

The opening year of the war did not bring any major shift in the traditional sexual distribution of Britain's industrial labor force. Although manpower mobilization began in earnest on 3 September 1939, with all males between the ages of eighteen and forty-one eligible for call-up for military service, no attempts were made to redistribute the female work force until Churchill became prime minister in May 1940. Less than a third of a million additional women were recruited, and few opportunities were opened up to them except when the call-up began to remove men from the retail, food, and distributive trades and the transport industry.

In the vanguard of what would later become a major wartime female invasion of the workplace were the conductresses who, by the spring of 1940, had become a familiar part of the British travel scene. "To be a good bus conductress, you had to be a dab at figures, juggling and back-chat," reported one journalist after a week as a "clippie" plying across Birmingham in a red double-decker bus. Her first journey "was a riot" on an early run picking up factory workers coming off night shift with loud demands to be introduced to the new girl friend. The "top deck passengers got going with a cheerful, if insinuating song." Her advice to other women considering becoming a wartime "clippie" was:

Whether you'll like a conductress's life (in preference, say, to munitions work, nursing or the services) depends on your temperament. This is no job for the cool, aloof or misanthropic character. It's essentially a jolly job. A human, sociable job, involving perhaps six or seven hundred separate human contacts a day. The life is varied and independent, and you get plenty of breaks and fresh air. Against this you must set the fact that the hours are long; that you are always on your feet; that passengers can be exasperating and rush hours exhausting.

So many girls were recruited into the transport industry to take over jobs previously done by men that by April 1940 British women won a significant, if limited, objective on the long road to equal status when the Industrial Court ruled that women over twenty-one were to be paid the male rate after six months on the job. It was an advance toward equal rights that was not reflected in the manufacturing and engineering industries vital to the war effort, where powerful craft unions vigorously resisted what they saw as attempts by employers under government pressure to dilute the skilled and semiskilled male work force.

Even in the state-run munitions factories during the first year of the war there was neither equal pay nor much employment offered to the daughters of the women who had packed shells with cordite powder in World War I. Not until the national emergency became acute after Hitler's divisions had overrun Europe and the threat of an invasion loomed did the engineering industry, which had one of the lowest proportions of female workers, agree to allow the training of women in some of its skilled trades such as fitting and welding — but they would be permitted to work alongside men only as what were termed "dilutees" and for the duration only.

After May 1940 there was major shift in government policy. The "Durkirk Spirit" and the ringing rhetoric of Winston Churchill rallied the nation for the fight and — it was hoped — would open war-plant gates to a flood of female war workers. The new prime minister made an integral part of his "blood, toil, tears and sweat" policy the concentration of labor and production on the war effort by closing "inessential" industries for the duration. Many of those factories that ceased to operate or were turned over to war production were the textile, clothing, hosiery, shoe, paper, and pottery works that employed high proportions of women.

Many women did take the opportunity to join the rapidly expanding production lines turning out the fighter planes for the RAF and the tanks and guns to rearm the British army, which had abandoned almost all its weapons on the beaches of Dunkirk. Ten-, eleven-, and even twelve-hour shifts were not uncommon. While young able-bodied men were called up and those overage for military service drilled with pitchforks and improvised antitank bombs, the women of Britain turned their hands to unfamiliar and unfeminine work with lathes, heavy presses, and drills.

The national peril that confronted all British people in 1940 was immediate enough to forge an emergency alliance in the workplace that was far more extensive than during World War I, when women had been brought into aircraft factories only to apply their traditional skills sewing fabric and applying dope to wings and fuselage. In every aspect of weapons production, women played a part in World War II — from machining and assembling engines to riveting, wiring, and testing complete aircraft systems. Like the burgeoning wartime electronics industry, the aircraft production lines offered plenty of opportunity for the lighter industrial work for which the female hand and eye was considered well suited.

"At first you think you'll never do it," a former Blackpool grocery store assistant told a fresh female trainee in the machine shop of a Ministry of Aircraft Production plant that built fighter aircraft. "You drop your tools and everything. But the men are very good. They teach you. To anybody with common sense, it's quite simple. And when you can do it — well, it's a real man's job."

Early in 1941 the government training centers were opened for the first time to females who sought skilled training in the engineering trades — and within two years, four out of ten workers in the British aircraft industry were women, who were performing half of all the production tasks needed for building fighters and bombers. But considerable hostility met the steadily increasing invasion of the traditional male workplace by women. "In they came, brunettes and blondes and gingers, quiet women and cheeky ones," recorded a shop steward at a railway engineering factory in 1941. "The men watched them with curious eyes, wondering whose jobs they were going to take."

An opinion survey of steel workers revealed that while most agreed emphatically "It's not women's work here," their real concern was not that the environment was unsuitable for women but that their jobs be protected against what they considered an invasion by a rival labor force. In some plants the men would tamper with the lathes during the night shift to cause problem for the day shift of women. "They don't like you to be working on this machine," one male worker confided. "Here's one woman doing it — they'll be getting other women in and then we'll be out of jobs and sent into the army."

Such deep-rooted male hostility came as a shock to women like Rosemary Moonen, who left a hairdressing salon to learn to weld, solder, drill, and rivet at one of these centers. Her semi-skilled fitters certificate "seemed such a waste of effort" when she encountered the resistance of the male factory workers:

I was sent with a group of die-hards to report to a certain foreman. He surveyed us all grimly, gave each one a job to do, with the exception of yours truly. No doubt I looked nervous and scared. He ignored me, and as he turned to walk away, I said, "What shall I do?" He turned toward me, sneered, "Oh, yes! We've forgotten sunshine here! What shall *you* do? — Here! Take this!", indicating a broom, "and sod around!" — With that he threw the broom at me and walked off. I was stung to humiliation before the rest of the girls. . . . As time went on I found my niche. As they discovered I could work a certain machine and get good results, I was transferred to another department. The girls by now accepted me and I was no longer treated with suspicion. Many of the men with whom I worked tried to "date" me, but as most of them were married, their wives and children evacuated, I declined all invitations. Even the foul language began to flow over my head, and the coarse jokes which prevail in factory life, I ignored.

Honor Balfor, perhaps because she was a well-known writer and broadcaster, was more fortunate when she did her spell as a forty-three-shillings-a-week war worker turning out fighter planes. She found the main vexation was the boredom of repetitive work:

On the final assembly line, there is interest and variety. The work is light, but you must be agile enough to nip up and down ladders, or haul yourself into unfinished cockpits, over half-made wings or through an incomplete fuselage. Light is good and the place is airy. On some jobs, you may smoke. On all of them there is a chance to pass a word to your workmates, or rest if you feel tired. At 10:30 A.M. the tea trolley comes round — tea 1d a cup, piece of cake 1d — and at mid-day you knock off for dinner. Some bring their own food; they can get hot drinks in the canteen. For the rest, there is a variety of snacks or a full-course meal. Food is plentiful, freshly cooked and quite cheap — soup 3d, meat (more on one plate than I've seen for months!), potatoes and two veg. 9d, jam tart 3d, coffee 2d. Back on the job at 1 o'clock. Tea-trolley at 2:30 P.M. Knock-off at 5:30 P.M. unless you are working overtime.

Food was an important attraction at a time when strict rationing was forcing a national belt-tightening, but the principal incentive for most women to leave their homes was the chance to earn relatively good pay. Even so, by the end of 1940 it was clearly not enough. Veteran civil servant Sir William Beveridge, who had masterminded the mobilization of the labor force in World War I and headed the Manpower Requirements Committee in 1940, estimated that the country was less than halfway to the target of bringing two million additional women into the war industries. Accordingly, the minister of labor and national service told the House of Commons that "we shall have to call into service many women who in normal circumstances would not take employment."

Apprehensive about the public reaction to a general call-up of the female population, the government decided that this mobilization would have to be achieved without direct compulsion by inviting women to register at employment centers under the wartime regulations which actually gave the minister of labor the power "to direct any person in the United Kingdom to perform such services" as ministry might require. The Women's Consultative Committee was set up in March 1941 and consisted of the two leading women parliamentarians — Dr. Edith Summerskill representing the Labour Party and Irene Ward the Conservatives — together with representatives of national women's organizations and the unions, under the chairmanship of the minister of labor's parliamentary secretary, who promised Ernest Bevin that "by presiding over the ladies on your behalf I think I could resist their charms."

It met to advise on wartime recruiting "from the woman's point of view" and although only consultative, the WCC took the lead in addressing such issues as "Should we pay any special regard to the marital status of women? Should a young married woman without any family responsibilities be treated differently from a single woman?" It was also instrumental in shaping the "voluntary" policy that required all single women aged twenty or twenty-one without household responsibilities and full-time employment to register at government employment exchanges as "mobile" labor. They could then be directed to filling vacancies in "essential" war factories.

The voluntary scheme for directing the so-called mobile women was not to prove the success that the Women's Consultative Committee had hoped. A principal cause for the failure of enough single women to volunteer for jobs in the war factories was that not all of them had ended up in the more "glamorous" war work such as riveting Spitfire cockpits and driving buses or cranes. A special survey commissioned from Mass Observation discovered that most of the jobs available to women were routine, undemanding, and distinctly unglamorous, as a typical interviewee explained:

My machine is a drilling one, and I am given a heap of small brass plates to drill holes in. . . . It is quite dark when we come out — which strikes one with a curious shock of surprise. For one feels not so much tired, rather as if one has missed the whole day.

The boredom of repetitive factory work was one reason why the war plants failed to attract half the female work force laid off by the closures of "inessential" factories in the first twelve months of Churchill's national coalition government. Ernest Bevin, the socialist minister of labor, was also extremely reluctant to introduce compulsion into the mobilization of the female labor force. "The release of a specified number of women did not add the same number to munitions manufacture," according to a report made by an observer for the U.S. Department of Labor: "Some workers thrown out of employment were lost sight of altogether, some remained jobless or drifted into occupations other than munitions, and many eventually filtered back into their original employment." By the autumn of 1941 Lord Beaverbrook, whose Ministry of Supply was struggling to keep the armed services equipped, protested in an October memorandum to the Cabinet that it was necessary to "recall these women for work in the war factories." Because only half those released had taken jobs in munitions, he called for a drastic change in labor policy:

There should be more expedition and ruthlessness in combing out women from non-essential occupations. Too many are still allowed to stay in kiosks and the distributive trades generally which still absorb over one million women.

The stringent rationing in force hardly made this "bogey-woman" a credible image, and the minister of labor, with a trade-unionist's instinctive aversion to government direction of workers, continued to argue for voluntary measures — even though the first step toward female mobilization had already been taken in March 1941 with an "invitation" to all women, paid and unpaid, to register their occupations with the local employment exchanges. Two million had dutifully registered by August, but of the half million of those who had been interviewed, only eighty-seven thousand had been recruited into the Women's Auxiliary Services or the government munitions factories.

This meager increase was in spite of a massive Ministry of Labor advertising campaign launched in 1941 to persuade British women to leave the clean comfort of their homes for the production battle. Brightly colored posters stressed the heroic nature of factory work with proclamations such as "WOMEN OF BRITAIN COME INTO THE FACTORIES." The same theme was reinforced in broadcast appeals by the BBC:

Today we are calling all women. Every woman in the country is needed to pull her weight to the utmost — to consider where her services would help most and then let nothing stand in the way of rendering such services. Like her, many women have made their sacrifices already and are doing their utmost to help win this war. But to these thousands who have not yet come forward I would say that here and now *every one of us* are needed.

Slogans were hammered home from hoardings, pamphlets, and newspaper advertisements that urged the women of Britain to take up the challenge of war work in a variety of jobs that had been the exclusive prewar preserves of men:

Did you know that over 10,000 women are doing men's work on one British railway alone, acting as platelayers, and permanent way labourers, helping with maintenance work, clerks, ticket collectors, porters etc?
GO TO IT!
Want a job to stick to? Then try billposting!
BRAVO THE WOMEN FLIGHT MECHANICS!
Ever thought of yourself as an electrician?
BE A WELDER!
COME INTO THE FACTORIES!

A series of "War Work Week" parades staged in November 1941 brought a temporary carnival-like atmosphere to bombed cities such as Coventry, with women dressed in overalls and gowns adorned with V-signs riding on tanks followed by truckloads of girls busily demonstrating filing, riveting and drilling airplane components. Yet while the banners enjoined "DON'T QUEUE

LIKE SHIRKERS, JOIN THE WOMEN WORKER," those to whom the slogans were addressed were reluctant to take full-time work. "We would get war in our homes if we took it," one potential recruit told the officer who interviewed her at the employment exchange. Surveys soon revealed that for most married women, their primary duty was to husband and home. One woman who gave up her war work explained:

My husband's on night shifts and I used to get home about six — it wasn't time to cook him his dinner and he was losing sleep doing it himself. Then they wanted us to stay and do overtime till 6:30 or more — I couldn't do that.

Another housewife had considered volunteering, but rejected the idea:

I feel very guilty sometimes, but there's my husband to think of. I know our homes are not supposed to count any more now, and it's only my husband and myself, but you have to do *something* in a house, or you'd get overrun by rats and mice.

Many women evidently felt their contribution to the war effort was at home. So did many of their menfolk. As an air raid warden put it:

If married women are called up home life will vanish, and it will be very hard to revive it after the war. Coming home on leave will find that they can only see their wives for an hour or two a day. Men in reserved occupations will come back to cold, untidy houses with no meal ready. Friction in the home will be greatly increased, and with children evacuated there will be nothing to hold it together.

It was not surprising, therefore, to find that employment exchanges reported by the end of 1941 that women were growing increasingly choosy about leaving their homes to take full-time war jobs that were not compensated for by the glamour, high pay, and excitement they had been led to expect by the posters and broadcasts. It was becoming apparent that, in addition to the animosity of the unions in heavy industry to a dilution of jobs and wages by female labor, and the lack of glamour in most factory work, the government campaign had overlooked the realities of homekeeping.

Long hours on a factory shift left women little opportunity for shopping and still less time for the chores necessary to looking after a family. The plight of one woman war worker was typified by a house that was a "complete mess" as reported by one survey taker who arrived to interview her as she was struggling to catch up with a pile of dishes at the sink, a bundle of washed but un-ironed clothes, and a table covered with crumbs and dirty crockery. The woman distractedly explained that it was impossible for her to take care of her housework before rushing back to the factory:

It's no good, I can't keep up with it. I thought I'd like to do a bit and bring in some money, but I can't keep up with it. If I could just have a couple of days to get straight, then it would be all right, you could keep it under, but I just can't manage like this.

Nearly two years of contributing to the war effort had boosted the female membership roster of British trade unions by a million and a half, but women shop stewards were all too often ignored when they complained that their special problems were being neglected by the male leadership who negotiated working conditions with the employers and the government:

We have no objection to working in the factories but we do object to the conditions we have to work under. Women in industry are called upon to bear burdens that are beyond imagination. Many are soldiers' wives who are obliged to go to work to keep their homes together as their allowances are so inadequate. . . . Our hours are ordinarily an eight-and-a-half-hour day, but with overtime this is brought up to ten hours. In the morning we feel fresh and do a good amount of work but the ventilation is so bad that by the afternoon we are weary. Then down goes the output.

Those married women who did go into the factories soon found that they were, in effect, doing a double job. The burden that war work and housework put on the shoulders of Britain's women was felt especially by young mothers like twenty-three-year-old Mary who was discharged from an ATS battery because she "got herself in the family way."

As soon as my son was a year old I found someone to look after him so that I could do my bit for the war effort again. I became a riveter, using a hydraulic gun to seal the rivets holding the metal skin to the frame of the bomb doors. These were made in sections and joined together when they were put in the planes. There were about ten of us girls and we made the doors for a couple of planes each day. We worked from 7:30 in the morning to 5 in the afternoon, with only a half hour off for lunch. I was up every day at 6 to get the tram to take my baby boy, half asleep, to his daytime mother. I was too busy and tired to miss my husband much.

The old adage that "a woman's work is never done" was never truer than in wartime when women were expected to work the fifty-seven- to sixty-hour week reported by the Factory Inspectorate's survey of 5,493 war plants. Such long shift hours made the mundane problems of housekeeping almost insurmountable as the *New Statesman* reported in December 1941:

In an industrial centre such as Birmingham a number of shops close at five o'clock or even earlier, which makes it impossible for those employed on a normal working day to do any shopping. In a London area it was found that over half the women shopped Friday nights, and two thirds of them on Saturday afternoons. Half the women had difficulty in obtaining their meat supplies, whilst it was practically impossible for them to get cooked meats or any of the non-rationed foods because they could not go to the shops in the mornings. The great majority of the women questioned had to do their own shopping, and normally had to queue. As a solution to the shopping problem it is suggested that the shops remain open until late on certain evenings of the week and remain open during the lunch hour. Some firms give weekly morning leave of up to three hours, or a shopping break before the lunch hour, but such schemes inevitably reduce production. And even greater difficulty than the shopping problem arises if the women have any children. Creches and nursery schools are seldom available, and meals are not obtainable at a considerable proportion of the schools.

Absenteeism was to become a chronic wartime problem for those factories employing large numbers of married women, many of whom could attend to essential household duties like shopping only by taking time off. A 1942 Ministry of Labor study was sympathetic to their plight:

A married woman with a house, a husband and children, already has a full-time job which is difficult to carry out these days. Yet thousands of them are working long hours in factories. They are trying to do two full-time jobs. If they can carry on with a mere half-day per week off the ordinary factory hours they are achieving something marvelous.

"While winning the war is the only big consideration," warned a 1942 Mass Observation report on women at work, "if the bonds of family and continuity are weakened beyond a certain point, the morale unity and work effort of the country is weakened." Yet the provision of adequate time off for shopping, or day-care facilities for the children of married workers had not even rated a mention in the 1941 ministry circular. It was left to a journalist to point out that "a whole family of five to eight people is looked after entirely by one woman, and if she is sent into full-time work, her jobs have to be taken on by no fewer than six different groups of workers, i.e. for day nursery, shopping, washing, meals for school children, evening meal for husband, care of children after school."

The minister of labor himself admitted he was not "anxious to increase the employment of women with young children if it were possible to obtain the labour otherwise" — but by the end of 1941 Bevin was obliged to concede that the voracious manpower requirements of total war would oblige the government to tap every available resource, including the contribution to be made by young mothers with preschool-age children.

The provision of nursery facilities for a quarter of a million children did not become a government priority until the labor crisis became acute at the end of 1941, forcing the government to encourage even mothers of children under fourteen into the factories. It was only then that the issue of the provision of school meals and nursery education had to be addressed on a national level. A bureaucratic dispute then ensued between the Ministry of Health's local officials, who irrationally campaigned against expanding factory-run nurseries because of exaggerated fears of epidemics of infantile disease. The mothers themselves were not squeamish, and the Ministry of Labor argued that the provision of adequate creches was essential to expanding the female work force. The minister of labor became the target of a public attack that he was not making good on his promise that "Every woman will have work who wants to." They took to the streets and staged what the press dubbed "Baby Riots" — traffic-stopping demonstrations of women wheeling strollers daubed with protests such as "WE WANT WAR WORK — WE WANT NURSERIES."

While Britain's wartime government, probably out of fear of the political repercussions of tampering too far with the traditional role of married women in the home, never made adequate provision for a national child-care system to serve the needs of working mothers, it did, however, attempt to improve their working conditions in the factories. Managers were sent a circular offering suggestions on how firms might clean up their shop floors and toilet facilities so as to make industrial work more attractive to women. Employers were advised to give "reasonable leave of absence" to wives when their husbands got leave from the services and to create a "sympathetic attitude" in the factories by improving canteens and "cloakroom arrangements." Management was warned that despite the disruption this might cause, "the paramount consideration is to make it as easy as possible for women to enter the factories and, to that end, there is no alternative but to adapt factory practice to the present situation."

Blacked-out windows increased the gloom and noise level of the older factories. In steel and heavy-engineering plants, the din and grime of this alien environment made them veritable "caves of Vulcan" where women were often deafened by the din and depressed by the dirt.

Working in factories is not fun. To be shut in for hours on end without even a window to see daylight was grim. The noise was terrific and at night when you shut your eyes to sleep all the noise would start again in your head. Night shifts were the worst. . . . The work was very often monotonous. I think boredom was the worst enemy.

To lighten the monotony and long hours of wartime labor, the BBC had in 1940 introduced the twice-daily program "Music While You Work" of lively popular tunes that proved so popular that it endured as a national broadcasting fixture for a quarter of a century. When they were not singing along to the music blaring out over loudspeakers, women crowding the long workbenches or hunched over drilling machines struck up their homespun patriotic war songs; one that achieved wide popularity in the Midlands aircraft factories ran:

> *I'm only a wartime working girl.*
> *The machine shop makes me deaf,*
> *I have no prospects after the war*
> *And my young man is in the RAF*
> *K is for Kitty calling P for Prue*
> *Bomb Doors Open.*
> *Over to you!*

"Music While You Work" and government "War Work Weeks" proved insufficient incentives to attract enough women into the factories. After the minister of labor had reported to the war cabinet in November 1941 that the number of women recruited into war production was a third lower than planned, Churchill's cabinet reluctantly decided in December 1941 to introduce a compulsory female mobilization. The National Service Act No. 2, which was passed by Parliament just ten days after the Japanese attacks of December 7 had brought the United States into the war, made Britain the first nation in history to formally conscript women. But the government, still sensitive to possible public hostility, was careful to announce it as a measure of "direction" rather than compulsion, which gave women the choice between going into the auxiliary services, civil defense, farm labor, and the munitions factories.

Churchill and the chiefs of the armed forces had argued that there was a national sentiment "against *any* compulsion of women" and the cabinet eventually compromised on the call-up of all single women aged twenty or twenty-one to begin in January 1942 — although married women were specifically exempted, "they should be allowed to volunteer." The mobilization was extended in February 1942 with the Employment of Women (Control of Engagement) Order, which directed that women between the ages of twenty and thirty could be hired only through employment exchanges. This was extended at the beginning of 1943 to women up to forty when it was announced that the Ministry of Labor had the power to direct them into part-time as well as full-time work. In deference to service opinion, both single and married women with responsibilities for running a home could apply for exemption as "Household R(eserve)" status. So from January 1942, the British government effectively instituted a limited but nationwide female mobilization order that affected childless widows as well as single women in the respective age groups, who were by law required to make themselves available for service in "vital war work" or as auxiliaries to make up the recruiting shortfalls that had been as great as thirty thousand behind the monthly targets. The list of occupations defined as "vital war work" included jobs in munitions factories, civil defense, nursing, the Women's Land Army, aircraft manufacture, the NAAFI (Navy Army and Air Force Institute — a civilian outfit that provided catering and recreation facilities to the armed forces), Royal Observer Corps, radio industry, tank manufacture, and the transport industry.

Women who refused to register and take government-approved employment, or who left vital war work, found that "direction" and compulsion amounted to one and the same thing. They could be fined up to five pounds a day and even imprisoned. Jehovah's Witnesses objected to being assigned nursing work, but the first of several hundred female pacifists to be brought before the courts under Section 5a of the Defence of the Realm Regulations was Constance Bolan, a former housemaid who was sentenced to a month's imprisonment in January 1942 for declining hospital work, which she held would indirectly assist the war effort. While in jail she insisted on hewing to her strict pacifist principle by refusing to knit socks for the army.

The vast majority of British women wanted no truck with pacifism and many rallied to the call from prominent parliamentary activist, Dr. Edith Summerskill, who formed the Women's Home Defence. Angry that women were denied the chance to join the Home Guard militia, this voluntary organization "gathered size and speed like a snowball." Its newly formed units met once a week to learn how to fire rifles, throw hand grenades, and deal with German parachutists. The government encouraged this patriotic display of female militancy and approved regular army officers, and the Home Guard provided instructors.

Yet so severe did the labor crisis in Britain's factories become by mid-1943 that the government suspended recruiting for the women's forces for twelve months. The factories rather than the ack-ack batteries were where womanpower was directed as the battle for production reached its peak. The only alternative to factory work for those women that were called up was to take a job on a farm.

The Women's Land Army had a marching song "Back to the land, we must all lend a hand,/To the farms and the fields we must go." Few of the eighty thousand who eventually joined up "to do their bit with a hoe" regarded it as a soft option. "The recruiting officer of the Women's Land Army won't quarrel with me if I say quite plainly that it's no rest cure," wrote Jane Morgan, who was one of those who donned the bottle-green sweater and khaki dungarees which the government supplied. A forty-eight-hour week brought them just thirty-two shillings in pay. Like most city women, Jane found that wartime work away from the grime and din of the factory healthy, but no country picnic:

My first job was to help pulling the beetroot. That looked easy. Our gang started on a large field which had been marked out into sections. Row by row, the tractor drove down and lifted the beetroot ready for us to pull out, clean our hands, twist off the tops and throw tidily into the line of boxes alongside; row by row we kept pace with the tractor. After two hours I loathed that tractor and its unfailing, inhuman progress up and down the field. The other land girls were sympathetic enough to call out inquiries about what they knew would be my breaking back. It was consoling to be told that they all went through it, and that the third day would be the worst. It was. After that the muscles began to do the work intended for them.

"If you think you are going to make ornamental garden gates you can think again," an employment official informed one young woman who wanted to take her call-up in "Rural Industry" after her Polish boyfriend was killed in the RAF. She found herself "pitchforked" into the Land Army but eventually came to enjoy the work and the nickname of "Buttercup" which the farmworkers gave her:

The life was quite strange at first. Each time I cleaned out the pigs, I brought up my breakfast! But I soon got over that. I made up my mind right from the start that I was going to "make a go" of this Land Army business, for who was I to grouse? I was lucky to be alive, not too far from home and with kindly country people. That boy just killed had been through hell to get here and he had always been cheerful and never groused. I was not going to let him down. I could take it — and take it I did.

During my service in the WLA I changed jobs several times between milking and general farm work on small and large farms. Then I worked with a gang of four girls going round Wiltshire farms with a steam engine and threshing tackle. It was hard and dirty work. In the spring and summer we did field work, hoeing and "singling" root crops and spud picking. We were not always treated with respect by farmers, but we learned how to put up with that and how to throw back the appropriate remarks along with the piles of dung we had to spread over the land.

I worked with all kinds of folks, countrymen and women. Some of the womenfolk thought of the WLA as "tarts" after their farmer husbands, but they got used to us in the end. I worked with gypsies and prisoners of war as well as quite a few younger women who had got out of Hitler's Europe. One cannot forget any of these men and women. But for me it started with that young Polish man who taught me how to stand on my own two feet. Unfortunately he never knew it, but I have never forgotten him.

The Land Girls, although most enjoyed better food and conditions than their sisters in the factories, like most World War II conscripts resented their long hours and the hard work, their discontent often surfacing in songs of humorous protest like their version of the famous soldiers' complaint from World War I.

> *When this silly war is over*
> *Oh how happy I shall be*
> *When I get my civvy clothes on*
> *No more Land Army for me*
> *No more digging up potatoes*
> *No more threshing out the corn*
> *We will make that bossy foreman*
> *Regret the day that he was born.*

The government, to its surprise, found that extending the National Service Act to women proved neither as unpopular nor as unworkable as Bevin had feared. So registration and "direction" were extended in August 1942 to women up to age forty-five, and fire-watching duty was made compulsory unless they were employed for a minimum of fifty-five hours a week. Only women with children under the age of fourteen were exempted — whether married or not.

"Nothing that a woman can do, or can learn to do, should be allowed to absorb a man of military age," proclaimed Labor Minister Bevin after a 1943 report recommended the extension of the female labor force in the shipyards and heavy industry. The fourth year of the war saw the addition of a million women, many of them married, to the full-time labor force waging the production war. Mobile recruiting vans toured towns and cities to draw in another quarter-million mothers for part-time work. Women played a direct role in the shipbuilding effort that contributed to the defeat of the U-boats in the decisive Battle of the Atlantic. The wartime peak of seven and a quarter million women in full-time work was reached by the middle of the year, and combined with those in part-time occupations represented over half the total female population. At the National Conference of Women sponsored in 1943 by the government, Prime Minister Winston Churchill paid tribute to the part that British women were playing toward the achievement of final victory:

This war effort could not have been achieved if the women had not marched forward in millions and undertaken all kinds of tasks and work for which any other generation but our own — unless you go back to the Stone Age — would have considered them unfitted: work in the fields, heavy work in the foundaries and in the shops, very refined work on radio and precision instruments, work in the hospitals, responsible clerical work of all kinds, work throughout the munitions factories, work in the mixed batteries.

★ 〚11〛 ★

The Girls Behind the Guys
Behind the Guns

Whatever the degree of adjustment, whatever the outward
appearance of harmony, the ancient doctrine was never wholly
abandoned — that the real and only power of women was the
power of sex and that their sole possible contribution to the
field of masculine endeavor was one of negative distraction
and disturbance rather than positive aid.

— A "ROSIE THE RIVETER"

It is our inescapable conclusion that most of these men have
never in all their lives thought of a woman as anything but
something that you go to bed with.

— JOSEPHINE VON MIKLOS, PRECISION GRINDER

After her 1942 fact-finding tour of British wartime factories, Eleanor Roosevelt returned to America mightily impressed by "the completeness with which the British have disre-
garded their prejudice against women workers." Everywhere she
found "women at work, many on highly skilled industrial production jobs that are ordinarily held only by men."

Total war had apparently submerged traditional male resentment toward women who did "men's work" because of what Mrs.
Roosevelt termed the "obligation to produce." But it did not escape the notice of America's First Lady, who was an ardent campaigner for women's rights, that the "age-old fight for equal pay
is still going on." She noted, however, that "the principle is being
recognized more and more," which she believed foreshadowed

"a considerable movement toward its fulfillment before the war is over." She was also struck by the fact that every second person she met in the Ministry of Labor was a woman and noted that the "responsibility of women in these things has made a difference in the position of women."

A representative of the American War Manpower Administration's "Women's Advisory Committee" who had accompanied Mrs. Roosevelt confirmed that there was "very little complaint" among the British about the female work force. "Women are working at all kinds of jobs — in the navy yards, in the factories, on the land, and even on demolition squads in the bomb-devastated cities," she advised the American committee. "One hears much discussion of what will happen after the war and much speculation as to whether women will be willing to go back to their old place when the need for them is over," and she quoted the British Home Secretary Herbert Morrison, who although "very pro women" had remarked, "You can't help wondering if they are going to be a little bit hoity-toity after the war."

The thing that interested us, me particularly, was the fact that there are so many who are older women and women who have family responsibilities which they can't shake off and are still doing these jobs and doing them often ten and eleven hours a day. . . . I think the men still can't escape a little surprise, and I think one finds that a little annoying. You cannot discount the fact that these people went through that terrible experience of Dunkirk and the evacuation; followed by that terrible winter of bombing — it has given them the feeling that people have if some member of the family has been desperately sick and just pulled through, or the people in the family sort of walk on eggs and are very kind and good to each other; very careful; very thoughtful and very thankful that they are there at all. They are much more ready to accept certain things than would be comparable in this country.

Although Britain's female mobilization had been authorized under the dire threat of a national emergency, it had been closely studied by the American administration's labor agency as the "arsenal of democracy" geared up for its own war effort during 1941. The accelerating draft had mopped up much of the male unemployment hanging over from the Depression years, but employers in the United States still were very reluctant to hire women outside their traditional jobs in retailing and light factory work. For every woman taken on in industry during the latter half of 1941, twenty men were hired by firms which kept 81 percent of their production work closed to females. They protested that women did not have the necessary skills, but at the same time females occupied fewer than 5 percent of the places available in the government-sponsored training schemes — and almost a third of these were in sewing and typing courses.

Yet the mounting enthusiasm of American women to play a part in the national emergency that President Roosevelt had declared in 1941 was evident in the numbers who volunteered for national defense. "Give the women something to keep their hands busy as we did in the last war — then maybe they won't bother us" was the attitude expressed by one government official responsible for channeling this fervor into voluntary civil defense efforts. It was an attitude that was remarkably slow to change even after the United States was actually at war with Germany and Japan.

Many women came forward after the president had put Mrs. Roosevelt and New York's feisty mayor Fiorello H. La Guardia in charge of coordinating the nation's air raid and blackout precautions in the weeks following Pearl Harbor. When the enemy bombers failed to appear, many women like Josephine von Miklos grew disenchanted with pointless duty as volunteer wardens. "Poking with a flashlight into your neighbor's closet in the course of your duties as an air raid warden didn't seem to me a contribution to the war effort," she concluded, before deciding to become one of the first to trade in her fashion designer's drawing board for an oily lathe in a New England factory turning out shell fuses:

Working in munitions, as it is turning out, isn't very exciting, if you want the truth. Most of it is filthy and grimy, much of it is a very boring job. I can't say that I love it. I wasn't sure that this kind of life was going to work for me — me, the irrational, the spoiled and the individualistic, the so-called artistic, intellectual kind of person that I am. And I *hated* the grime and filth and getting up at five-fifteen in the morning and using an open latrine for a ladies room. But neither did the men of Bataan like their grime and filth. The Chinese and Russian and Australian soldiers haven't any fun fighting, nor do the men at sea.

Even the disastrous American defeats in the Philippines that marked the lowest ebb of Allied fortunes in the gloomy spring months of 1942 did not generate a sense of national peril that would have allowed the president and his newly appointed War Manpower Commission to persuade Congress to agree to a conscription of the female population. It was estimated that only 29 percent of the fifty-two million adult women in the United States were already employed in full-time work and it was decided that the drive to mobilize a large part of the thirty-seven million still tied to their homes was to be effected through advertising and public relations campaigns.

The president rejected as politically inexpedient the War Manpower Commission's plan for a national registration of women like the one Britain had instituted a year earlier. Instead it was left to local state and city authorities to begin "enrollment drives" with mail and house-to-house canvasses. The first state to launch an enrollment drive was Oregon, and the February 1942 canvass revealed that 302,000 women were ready and willing to seek war work. Michigan and Connecticut followed suit, as did Ohio. America's automobile manufacturing plants were then being rapidly transformed into tank and aircraft production plants. Ford was pouring millions of federal war dollars into the vast Willow Run complex, which would eventually become the largest employer of women in the area. Detroit reported that 180,000 women had registered for war work and female employment was to rocket from 44,000 to 107,000 by August 1942.

That same month the Women's Bureau of the Department of Labor reported that its latest survey showed that "the war industries expansion has permitted women to work side by side with men on the same jobs without taking over the jobs held by men." It was anticipated that as "more and more men go into the specific war services actual substitution of women on men's jobs in war industries are likely to increase." Government training centers were providing more women with technical courses, and it was envisaged that the increasing skills of the female factory worker would allow her to take over such jobs as lathe operator and precision grinder when the men were drafted. The biggest expansion had so far been in assembly work on aircraft production lines, where 34,000 females were now employed — a seventeenfold increase in less than nine months.

Women were also helping to expand technical services as flying instructors and ground mechanics, but the biggest influx of female labor during the first months had been in services related to civilian rather than war needs:

In large and small places Women's Bureau agents find women at work as elevator operators in hotels, stores and office buildings; as telegraph messengers and in other messenger services; as clerks, cashiers, soda-fountain girls, and pharmacists in drug stores. Women are serving as taxi drivers and filling station attendants. They are being hired as men are drafted from shoe, electrical-supply and food plants. They are replacing men as finger-print technicians in their laboratories, a type of work women have formerly done elsewhere. Women are serving at airports as registration supervisors, dieticians, passenger-service superintendents, and dispatch clerks. Women are reported as machine-shop instructors, as mechanics, and mechanics' helpers. They service typewriters, act as bank tellers and assistants, and are reported at work in brokerage offices, and as stock-exchange floor employees. They are serving as guards in industrial plants, with police power.

Just as in Britain, after an initial rush to do their patriotic duty, American women who put their name to enrollment registers then failed to volunteer. Few women had been employed in the four hundred sixty jobs in heavy industry that the Labor Department had decreed could be performed by females because half required "some rearrangement" of processes to take account of the limitations of physical strength. There was also the traditional resistance to women performing heavy work, especially if they were married. The general male reaction to their spouses doing any kind of factory work was revealed by a *Ladies' Home Journal* poll of wives which indicated that one in five did *not* have her husband's approval. Fewer than 30 percent of men answered yes to a 1943 Gallup survey question: "Would you be willing for your wife to take a full-time job running a machine in a war plant?" Notwithstanding, over half the women questioned in the same poll said they would be willing to take such a job. That the average American male still rejected the idea of working married women was evident from a typical protest letter published by a Seattle newspaper in the fall of 1942: "I never let my wife work, and I know she is a far sweeter woman than many women who have been coarsened by having to get out in the business world. I say, let's keep women out of industry and out of the war."

The administration took a different view. The War Manpower Commission estimated that at least two million more women had to be recruited into the work force in 1943. The shortage of male labor was quickly forcing employers to abandon their traditional attitudes, and the president had set seemingly impossible production targets for aircraft, tanks, and shipping during that critical year when the Allies hoped to turn the tide of battle.

"The Fortresses and the men who fly them — are fighting for you — your home — all the things you hold dear" was how the Boeing aircraft company launched its recruiting drive in the Seattle area, where women were bluntly asked: "Are You Doing Your Part?" The press cooperated with stories celebrating the heroic production efforts of individual women war workers who were portrayed as the "girls behind the guys behind the guns."

"We do feel that we are doing something for the war effort," commented a female bus driver. "Besides that, it's thrilling work, and exciting, and something women have never been allowed to do before." Job advertisements and newspaper stories emphasized the excitement and opportunities that war work opened for women in heavy industry. As a woman working in a navy yard told a reporter, "Somehow the kitchen lacks the glamour of a bustling shipyard."

Yet the excitement of heavy industrial work quickly wore off for those already in the labor force like Josephine von Miklos:

Maybe they read of so many bombers made each month, or production goals passed by eight percent or short by fourteen. They are proud if the numbers are great; they get sore when production isn't up to what it should be. But there isn't any glamour in *making* bombers and shells. That is just a job, a job to be done day after day, carefully and deliberately, with every person doing a certain thing, doing it exactly the same way, maybe a hundred thousand times, or five thousand times a day. The average man thinks, "25,000 time fuses," and it's just a number. But that is the number which an average shift turns out in an average eight-hour day, in just one little department of The Company, day after day.

"In the next twelve months, the American housewife must show that she can keep her head and her temper and roll up her sleeves

at one and the same time," observed a newspaper commentator
who minced no words in spelling out the choice facing the country's womenfolk in the summer of 1942. "If she can't, the menfolk fighting on distant atolls are likely to get slaughtered in the
hot sun for lack of ammunition."

The Women's Bureau had set the priorities to its recruiting drive
to attract two million more workers:

First, women with factory experience who have lost their employment
because of priorities in materials and plant adjustments to war
production.

Second, other unemployed women who are registered with the Employment Service seeking work.

Next, if necessary, the more than 800,000 girls coming from high
schools and colleges.

Last, women caring for their homes, particularly with small children,
should not be asked to go into factories and workshops until it is absolutely necessary. They can be much more helpful to the Nation by staying at home and taking care of the children, though it is recognized
that in some cases these women find it necessary to work.

The War Manpower Commission then turned to Hollywood,
as well as Madison Avenue, to boost its national campaign to attract first-time women workers. The emphasis was placed on patriotism, glamour, and the economic advantages. The heroines
of *Women on the Warpath* were flag-waving female war workers
charged with doing their feminine patriotic duty in a script that
steamed with the heady rhetoric of a Hollywood epic.

Staunchly have the women of America stood shoulder to shoulder with
their men in the pioneering past. Today they take up a new burden as
the nation calls for five million . . . a women's army trained and ready
to help save the homes it has been their duty to adorn. . . . Gone is the
day of the remote battlefield, a day when war is strictly a man's job. At
hand is the opportunity for women to assume a new responsibility. And
so on they come, these homekeeping, home defending soldiers of
America to put the feminine torch to the fuse of an almighty explosion
of tyranny.

Not that every appeal was directed to inspiring women to tie
up their hair, put on dungarees, and march into the war plants.

Wives who were also mothers of young children had to be reminded that they were contributing to the war by staying at home. This was the rationale behind *Women at Arms,* which was hastily cranked out by RKO pictures to tell the story of Mrs. Larkin — "just a plain housewife" — who was prevented by her two children from joining the WAACs or going into a factory. "She's the keeper of the Home, the thing we're all fighting for," the synopsis explained; "she's among the strongest, bravest and most valuable of America's women at arms."

"In 1943 America will have to produce more war materials than any country has ever been called upon to produce in the history of the world," announced a cheery U.S. employment leaflet to support the slogan "The More Women at Work the Sooner We'll Win the War." It listed the jobs a woman was now considered able to perform as part of the government's bid to raise the national female work force to eighteen million. "To win the war, we must meet these tremendous production quotas, we must release able-bodied men for fighting and for heavy industrial jobs. . . . This means about 2,000,000 *more* women working than worked in 1942. Every skill must be put to patriotic use immediately to help save *lives*."

Financial, rather than patriotic, considerations often counted more with women, especially servicemen's wives who received a minimum of $50 a month — $28 provided by the government and $22 from their pay. Economic necessity obliged Mrs. Amelia Bondelid, like many GI brides, to take a war job in San Diego, where she first worked in a dime store before joining the tool department of the Convair aircraft factory. She became a draftsman designing tool jigs for B-24 bomber wings and hulls:

Women couldn't work overtime beyond six days a week. The only other day I had off in two years was Christmas Day. The pay was better than anything else in town, but naturally women weren't paid as well as men. Other than that, I really liked the work. I took a course that lasted three months in drafting for aircraft, and they took us women and put us in tool design. You should have seen the looks on the men's faces when they saw Jackie and me walk in there. "The women are taking over," they said. We were teased a lot, and some asked us for dates or propositioned us. The whole bit. . . . Sometimes a group of us women would come out of Convair and we'd see army trucks or navy trucks full of guys in their combat gear going down to the ships, those big gray ships, and the guys would whistle at us and we'd wave back at them. But we knew where they were going and we practically cried for them.

Women workers in the heavy industries, such as Mrs. Rosair Earley, who became a shipyard coppersmith, discovered that some areas of so-called heavy industrial work were not as physically demanding as they were made out to be:

It wasn't heavy work at all, and that is where I found out a little about men's work. I thought men did a lot of heavy work, but I found that they have a pretty soft deal. That was rough on a lot of men after shipyard work because we found out that they didn't have to work so hard after all. But we worked six days a week and got time and a half for Saturday. They treated us pretty well. In fact, there was too much help. People were falling all over each other. So far as I was able to make out, it was the same in all the shipyards. I don't think it was that way in some of the aircraft plants; they worked harder.

"It was interesting how fast these plants converted to an all-female crew, except foremen and the older 4F types," recalled Mary Dandouveris, a student from the University of Wisconsin, who spent her summer vacations working in an aircraft assembly plant:

I worked on the swing shift as a riveter, and I didn't like the shift — 3:00 P.M. to 11:00 P.M. — it was cutting into my social life too much, so I asked to be transferred to a later shift, and then I did the filing. It was on the graveyard shift. We were filing the metal for the leading and trailing edge, which is the outer edge of the plane. You had only one-one-thousandth-of-an-inch error, and there were gauges and inspectors who came around to make sure that you didn't go beyond that. Women were particularly careful, you see, and light fingered enough, so that, working the files, you didn't make heavy dents or go beyond the minimum tolerance.

Nowhere was the wartime shift of American production to female hands more evident than in these vast aircraft factories. At Boeing's sprawling plant outside Seattle, over half the work force was eventually made up of women.

"That American women should take an active part in the man's job of building and repairing ships was almost inconceivable," pointed out a 1943 Women's Bureau pamphlet on "Employing Women in Shipyards." Just two years earlier, the most publicized women-employing shipyard had refused to hire female secretaries, and their lone telephone switchboard operator was "kept under lock and key." But the 200 percent growth in the American shipbuilding industry since 1941 — some shipyards employing forty thousand workers had been marshy flats only eighteen months earlier — could have been achieved only by relying heavily on the input of female labor. There had been tremendous opposition from the unions, and the International Brotherhood of Boilermakers and Iron Shipbuilders referendum on women workers brought strong protests that made fun of the whole idea, as typified by the strong negative views of one Seattle local:

Some of them want the silliest jobs. At the aircraft factories they use the Buck Rogers' riveter, driving 3/16th rivets. They don't understand that in the yards they'd be using an outfit that drives rivets 10 to 20 times bigger. If one of these girls pressed the trigger of the yard rivet guns, she'd be going one way and the rivet the other.

Union protests notwithstanding, the hiring and training of large numbers of women by the shipyards began in the fall of 1942 as the draft drained men into the armed services. Within the year, a third of the work force in some West Coast yards was female, and their welders and riveters became the headline-making heroines of the "Ships for Victory" program. A national recruiting campaign flooded the East and West Coasts with posters proclaiming that female shipyard workers were "Soldiers Without Guns" as the press ran accounts of prodigious feats of welding performed by women. The competition to build a Liberty ship in the fastest time reached a climax in November 1942 when the *Robert E. Peary* was launched by Henry Kaiser's Richmond yard in the never-to-be-beaten record time of four days, fifteen hours.

"Rosie the Riveter" became the symbolic incarnation of the World War II heroine of heavy industry. Radio stations across America blared with a popular recording of the song celebrating how patriotic Rosie was "making history working for victory," complete with the sound effects of the production battle:

> *Rose (brrrr—rrrr) the riveter*
> *Rosie's got a boyfriend Charlie:*

Charlie, he's a marine.
Rosie is protecting Charlie
Working overtime on a riveting machine.

Norman Rockwell immortalized a muscularly defiant Rosie with dungarees and rivet gun on a May 1943 *Saturday Evening Post* cover. But that same month a shipyard foreman was quoted: "The clamor was for big, husky women with the accent on youth. Yet slender, deft handed women of all ages are our best welders and ship-fitters. A Danish woman welder of 53 can match the best record of our best man." There were actually many more "Wanda the Welders" than "Rosie the Riveters" laboring in the shipyards and aircraft factories. But "Wanda" found no artist of Rockwell's caliber to popularize her, although welder's chrome-tanned leather outfits were featured in *Harper's Bazaar,* whose fashion artist designed as "a thoughtful touch" matching leather spats and a "tab stitched over the heart to hold identification badge."

Some women found they just did not have the stature or strength to manhandle heavy rivet guns or welding torches:

My first job was as an operator of a turret lathe and I was a little scrawny teenager at the time. It took my whole weight just to open the chuck. . . . It definitely was not woman's work, so I quit after three days. Then I went to work at the Liberty Tool and Lathe where they were making bullet dies. I operated drills and reamers to bring the metal up to the shape of a bullet. But after a while they put me in the office, where I stayed all during the war. I was sort of glad to get into the office because I rode the bus to work with a bunch of "Rosie the Riveter" types, and boy, were they a tough crew. Really tough customers.

Women in shipyards quickly learned that psychological resilience was just as important as brute strength for surviving in the male ritual of shipyard work. Many "Rosies" shared the apprehension that Lili Solomon felt on her first day at the yard:

Maybe you think it didn't take nerve for a woman to make that first break into the yards. . . . I never walked a longer road in my life than to the tool room. The battery of men's eyes that turned on my jittery physique, and a chorus of "Hi, sisters" and "tsk-tsk" soon had me thinking "Maybe I'm wrong. Maybe I'm just not another human. Maybe I am from Mars."

When she transferred from factory work into an East Coast shipyard, Josephine von Miklos encountered a far fiercer resentment from the men who regarded the female invasion as "a huge joke" — but one which had unpleasant sexual overtones for many women:

The truth of the matter is that we live among a legion of waterfront Casanovas. Now, you'd think that at least some of these ten thousand guys would have seen women before. We have reason to assume that these men were bred by mothers, that they have wives and daughters and sisters and sweethearts. But that's where we evidently are wrong. These fellows, most of them, have not been bred by mothers, they have *no* wives and daughters and sisters and sweethearts. They have, in fact, never before seen or heard or touched or spoken to anything remotely resembling a female. We haven't the faintest idea whether they have ever been told that the world is inhabited by anything but men in shipyards. Nor do they show the slightest sign of knowing that women are people too. Well it is pretty funny. It is funny when a few of us walk through the yard and they whistle and hoot at us. We have discovered that the only way to stop them is to whistle back at them and hoot louder than they do. It is funny when they yell, half in astonishment, and half derision: "There's women in the yard!"

Sociologist Katherine Archibald recorded at first hand in the Moore Dry Dock Company in Oakland the rampant male sexism that plagued the wartime shipyards:

Sex attitudes made up the tangled background of the male worker's point of view. Sex was his greatest avocational interest. Whether bounded by the proprieties of marriage or unconstrained in the reaches of bachelor fancy, it was the spice of his existence, the principal joy of his social life. The largest part of shipyard conversation, beyond the routine of the day's necessities, was occupied with some aspect of the pleasures or the problems of sex; and shipyard jokes were broad and racy in the extreme. . . . The emphasis upon sex, moreover, as it evoked the biological distinctions between men and women, also reinforced the lines of social demarcation. Traditions supposedly governing the proper division of labor between men and women were linked with even more profoundly rooted traditions concerning divisions in the biological function, and change in the structure of the former might seem to imply a threat in the latter's sacrosanct stability.

Women were more often than not denied the opportunity to work together as a team; instead, they were divided up in mixed groups. Virginia Wilson, a housewife turned wartime welder, discovered the reason for this the morning that her yard foreman assigned a three-woman team to take sole charge of constructing a prefabricated keel section:

For once we had been given responsibility, for once we had been put on our own, for once we had enough to do. "When we finish we'll hold open house and invite you in to tea," we told our leadermen. Our enjoyment was such that we did not notice that something was amiss until late in the afternoon. Then we became gradually aware of the hostility of the men. Our woman burner reported they were "seething with resentment" that women should be given a unit to construct. The women checkers said, "You should just hear what we hear outside our checking shed, my dears." This was the first time I had come up against the hostility of one sex toward another and I could not believe it.

The wolf-whistles and the lascivious gestures were taken in good humor until they were translated into direct sexual harassment. But the grabbing and pinching, although resented, often went unreported by the women "when, for instance, the man is your boss, and you depend on him and his good will to help you learn about the new machines around you." This continual pestering was regarded by Josephine von Miklos as a juvenile attempt by males to protect their territory, which also included silly attempts to make the women's work more difficult:

They're just like schoolboys who think that bathroom jokes make them sound grown-up. If a guy shows us a job, and tightens the machine just before we take over, the screw or nut or bolt or handle will invariably be so tight that it takes an enormous amount of extra strength to undo it. When we tighten the stuff, the machine works just as well. But they seem to love to see us pull and push and puff, and then maybe have to ask for help. We haven't quite decided yet whether they do it to prove to us that we can't do the work, at least not as well as they can, or because they want to exhibit some more of the superior and boundless strength of the male animal.

The management of some war plants banned women from wearing makeup in an attempt to contain the temptation to male sexual harassment. When the Boeing Aircraft Corporation sent home fifty-three women for wearing tight sweaters, it became a cause célèbre. Their union objected that what was considered perfectly moral attire in the office should not be considered immoral on the shop floor. Management brought the National Safety Council into the dispute by claiming that sweaters caught fire, attracted static electricity, and were a dangerous hazard because they might snag in rapidly turning machinery.

Ann Sheridan, whose ample bosoms had made her popular as the "Ommph girl," entered the fray by declaring that while a small figure in a large sweater might be a threat to safety, a big girl in a tight sweater was only a moral hazard to men. Controversy also erupted over the much-copied "peekaboo" long hair of Paramount star Veronica Lake, which was held to be a hazard near machinery. Patriotically she sheared off her locks, thereby sending her film career into a decline from which it never recovered.

Bundling their hair in the approved wartime factory turban and concealing their "oomph" in loose-fitting dungarees or thick welding leathers did not unsex women — or prevent the sparks of sexual attraction taking fire in the most inhospitable of environments in a shipyard. According to Katherine Archibald, passion always found its own opportunity for fulfillment:

In the shipyards, rumor was continually busy with suspicions and reports of salacious activities in the obscurer parts of ships or in some vaguely identified warehouse. Like evil-smelling breezes, tales of scandal floated from group to group: of a stolen kiss or an amusing infatuation; even of the ultimate sin, with or without price, in the fantastic discomfort of the double bottoms. One persistent report concerned the activities of enterprising professionals for whom a shipyard job was said merely to provide opportunity for pursuit of a yet more lucrative career. The end result of all such talk, of course, was to deny the possibility of the establishment of businesslike relationships between men and women on the job and to discredit women as effective workers.

The feminine figure in male garb working in an industrial environment had a unique sex appeal that the advertising industry was not slow in exploiting. The wartime sales pitch for everything feminine, from cigarettes to face cream, soft drinks to soap, was given a patriotic slant by featuring glamorous crane operators pouring steel, pretty girls behind plows, earnest housewives assembling aircraft. The stereotype "Rosies" and women welders populated the pages of the wartime magazines; and their characters, popular romantic fiction. Pond's Cold Cream ran a series of ads featuring women in a variety of war jobs with the copy line "We like to feel we *look* feminine even if we are doing a man-size job . . . so we tuck flowers and ribbons in our hair and try to keep our faces looking pretty as you please." Pacquin's Hand Cream reminded women in war plants that "hands that do a man's work can still enchant a man."

It was not just the advertisements that attempted to preserve the socially acceptable feminine image of women war workers. Magazine articles focused female war workers' attention on the need to keep their FQ (Femininity Quotient) high. A *Life* feature on a pretty "Rosie" from a Boeing bomber factory revealed the secret beauty tips that enabled her to look like a "Hollywood factory girl":

Now at day's end, her hands may be bruised, there's grease under her nails, her makeup is smudged and her curls are out of place. When she checks in the next morning at 6:30 A.M. her hands will be smooth, her nails polished, her makeup and curls in order, for Marguerite is neither drudge nor slave but the heroine of a new order.

While women were publicly urged to preserve their femininity in a man's world, their employers showed little patience in meeting their special needs. A Woman's Bureau survey of three thousand female workers in thirteen factories revealed that more than half were married, widowed, or divorced, with the responsibility for running the home as well as their job. But when the high rate of female absenteeism became a major issue during the peak of the war production drive in 1943, women were bombarded by literature and posters accusing them of "throwing a monkey wrench in the war effort" and being a "boon and ally to the Axis."

Women AWOL, as it was called, made newspaper headlines and the Labor Department proclaimed "ABSENTEEISM IS SABOTAGE." "The workers not producing all they can are denying our men in the South Pacific the right to live, because they are keeping from them materials that they need to live by" was the blunt message in the War Manpower Commission's drive to bring more female labor for the factories with a recruiting booklet "This Soldier May Die — Unless You Man This Idle Machine."

The provision of child-care facilities became a major issue in the United States in 1943, just as it did in Britain, when the labor crisis forced industry to bring in more and more married women with young children. President Roosevelt ordered the Federal Works Administration to build nursery schools, but Congress held up funding in response to the popular belief that it was a bad thing for mothers of infants to be at work. The Federal Works Administration's child-care director protested. "Whether we like it or not, mothers of young children *are* at work. So we do need day-care centers." In the end only three thousand nurseries were built during the war to care for one hundred thirty thousand children. Staffing problems and the relatively high fees charged made them unpopular with working mothers.

Providing shopping facilities to cut absenteeism was solved by the enterprise of American retailers. The lead was taken by New York's Bloomingdale's department store, which set up a pioneering branch at the Sperry plant on Long Island. "It's no slap-dash affair, either," enthused a press reporter, explaining that the connection between a "lipstick and bombing raid over Germany" was that women no longer had to take shopping days off that harmed the war effort. Other large American department stores were quick to recognize the business opportunity that was opening up for selling direct through their own branches at the major war plants. Surveys confirmed that most interviewees gave "high pay" as their reason for working after the more patriotic response "to help win the war." "They're here to make money" was the frank assessment of a New England war plant manager who criticized the amount that his machine-shop women spent on clothes: "When they come to work, before they change to slacks, you'd think they were going to the opera." In the East many female office workers deserted their desks to make twenty cents an hour more at the factory bench. The highest rates of pay were earned by women who did "men's work" for the first time in the shipyards, steel plants, and aircraft factories.

Typical of thousands of high school girls who abandoned further education for the duration, Corinne Aldridge worked at the Emerson gun-turret plant outside St. Louis:

I used to earn $15 a month at college baking biscuits. Then when I got my first pay check here — $32.60 all in one week — I tell you. But somehow when you get working it's more than money. You learn about the war and you feel different about a lot of things.

American women also learned during World War II about the importance of organizing to press their demands for equal pay. In 1940, fewer than eight hundred thousand wage-earning women were unionized, representing less than 10 percent of organized labor. Four years later, this had more than doubled to three million women, representing 22 percent of the total unionized labor force. The activity and success of union campaigns for equal pay for equal work by women was in direct proportion to their female representation. Discriminatory pay differentials were eliminated entirely by 1945 by the United Electrical, Radio and Machine Workers, a union in which women represented more than a third of its membership. Similarly the United Rubber Workers, which represented a large proportion of women, negotiated an equal pay clause for many of its contracts; and the United Auto Workers union, with over a third of a million female workers, was a powerful voice arguing for maternity leave and other special benefits for women.

The Roosevelt administration had supported the principle of equal pay for equal work from the outset, but the male-dominated unions and management claimed that women were to be paid less since they did not have the men's skills or seniority. Hundreds of thousands of "Rosie the Riveters" and "Wanda the Welders" might have stormed the bastions of traditional male dominance, but when it came to such crucial issues as pay and job security, it was the men who had the political power. Sexual discrimination continued in much of the wartime workplace because union leaders and management regarded much of their female work force to be "hostilities only." Even before the war had been won, American and British industries were preparing to stick by the principle of "last in first out" to lay off women workers.

★ [12] ★

The Girls They Left Behind

Hasty war marriages, on embarkation leave, sometimes between comparative strangers, with a few days or weeks of married life, have left both parties with little sense of responsibility or obligation towards one an other.

— LONDON PROBATION OFFICER, 1945

From Buffalo to Wichita it is the children who are suffering most from mass migration, easy money, unaccustomed hours of work, and the fact that mama has become a welder on the graveyard shift.

— *WASHINGTON POST*, 1944

"I n wartime there is a decay of all the established moralities, which tend to be replaced by hedonistic life adjustments on a short-time basis," observed an American sociologist of the changes in social behavior that were reflected in the soaring marriage and birth rates during the war. The keepers of the American national moral conscience applauded the judge who condemned the "breaking down of moral fibers," the loss of a national "sense of decency and respect for young girls and marriage." But there was another side to the story, as one British woman explained:

They were wonderful days, during the war, despite its dangers, the bombs falling, the nervous tension and the appalling damage and loss of life. When one was young, it was possible to gloss over much of that and concentrate on the glamour and excitement. We got what we could out of life, for we never knew which day might be our last. We were all changed by the war — a lot. And I think that the uncertainty of living was one of the main reasons.

The opening years of the war brought a dramatic rise in the British marriage rates. Young couples clutching at the stability offered by matrimony resulted in an additional quarter-million weddings. By 1940, almost half the female population in the twenty- to twenty-four-year age group were married, a 20 percent rise over the prewar figure. In the final two years of the war, a million more marriages took place than would otherwise have been anticipated. The same wartime stampede to the altar was observed in the United States, where the annual marriage rate also increased 20 percent in the two years after Pearl Harbor.

Many couples who might otherwise have delayed tying the conjugal knot married rather than risk the uncertainties of a long separation. Those who did wait often found, as one American put it: "War, however, is a notable breeder of personality and physical changes and many of those engaged couples who had been compatible before the war were so changed physically and psychologically, that there was no longer any compatibility. And yet because they felt bound by their previous betrothals they entered into unsatisfactory connubial relationships."

In the first year of the war it is clear that many young American men married to escape the draft, since fathers with young children had a lower rating under the 1940 Selective Service Act. An official was quoted as estimating that up to December 1941 "about half the increase in marriages must be traced to barefaced draft evasion." Other couples cut short traditionally long engagements and moved up their wedding dates to enjoy some married life together before the husband joined the military. Many succumbed to a "last fling" fever, which sociologists blamed for the 1941 epidemic of "military weddings."

A War Department bulletin proposed that, while there was no question of an official moratorium on marriages, drafted men should be discouraged from hasty marriages because up till then only 6 percent of enlisted men had wives. Matrimonial entanglements were not considered good for morale, because a worried GI was an inefficient soldier: "And what boy can help worrying if he is trying to support himself and a family on $30 a month." This should not be the sole criterion, according to Eleanor Roosevelt's "Ask Me" column in The Ladies' Home Journal of March 1942. In answer to a reader's request for advice on whether "young engaged couples should marry or wait until the war is over, if the man is called to active duty," the First Lady suggested this must be "a personal question." But in the urgent atmosphere of war, the heart more often than not ruled a draftee's head. "It was a very emotional time and so many of them got married on leaves to total strangers," recalled an American woman. "Some of the guys used the line that it would be their last leave, and then got carried away by it and got married."

Women were also "carried away" because they wanted to be sure of their man during a long separation. Some girls felt they had to legitimize a physical relationship, as did an American college girl who married her soldier on his first leave after basic training:

We were both emotionally tense after months of separation. I don't know just how it happened, but suddenly I realized that I was no longer vir-ginal. The seven-day furlough was almost over and the pressure to get married was now greater than ever. . . . We were married on the sixth day of the furlough. Then I received a letter from him stating that he had found a room for me near the camp and that he had made ar-rangements with his commanding officer to have his weekends free. I could surely find a job there. So overnight I packed a few belongings and boarded a train for another part of America where I had never been before. One and a half days each week were deliriously happy; five and a half were dismally lonely, like a prisoner in a foreign land. . . . Then he received orders to move and I went back to my home community.

In the United States many teenage girls married their high-school boyfriends as they were drafted. Thousands of young brides followed their new spouses to rural towns near army training camps. This put a severe strain on housing and medical facilities. "When the troops came, right on their trail would come the little war brides, fifteen- and sixteen-year-old kids from every corner of the nation," recalled Dr. Thomas J. Taylor, whose small Mid-west practice was swamped by young mothers-to-be from the ad-joining army transit camp. "They'd just be dumped off in our little town, and of course every one of them was pregnant and ready to deliver." Apart from the obstetric complications, the consequent welfare problems of caring for his patients was enormous:

I vividly recall when a second-class rooming house was jammed with war brides and babies and I was called there because of a rather severe flu epidemic. I remember walking through that rooming house and each room had three or four mothers with babies, all of them, and they all had the flu. A bathroom down the hall, no money, desperate. I tried to do right and called the Salvation Army. In that particular case they did a heroic job clearing up that mess. This was repeated over and over in staging areas throughout the country until finally, late in the war, the message got through to most of these kids and they didn't follow their husbands out.

An unfortunate aspect of the "war-bride" phenomenon were the notorious "Allotment Annies" who hustled departing soldiers into marriage to collect the $28 a month the U.S. government automatically allotted to servicemen's wives. With a private's pay rising to $50 a month for overseas service, some greedy "Annies" took on four, five, and even six husbands. These unscrupulous women made bigamy a business, and in return for V-mail letters to GIs overseas they lived very well off the pale blue-green government checks. Some, with the financial acumen of actuaries, specialized in airmen, anticipating that their higher mortality rates increased their chances of collecting the $10,000 jackpot government insurance check if their husband was killed in action. Elvira Taylor achieved national notoriety as the "Allotment Annie" who operated out of Norfolk, Virginia. She managed to snare six sailors and was about to hook a seventh before she was arrested as a result of two of her "husbands" starting a fight in an English pub when each showed her picture as his "wife." When they had been cooled off by the military police, they joined forces to expose the duplicitous Elvira, who was discovered by checking the navy pay records to have contracted four other bigamous marriages.

The 20 percent leap in the American marriage rate after Pearl Harbor resulted in a baby boom. A similar celebratory jump became apparent nine months after the tide-turning victory won by the navy at the Battle of Midway in June 1942, and through to the end of the war the American birthrate continued to peak nine months after such Allied triumphs as El Alamein, D-Day, and the fall of Berlin. This natal phenomenon reflects not only victory euphoria but also confidence in a stable future. In Britain, by contrast, the birthrate actually declined between 1939 and 1941, in spite of the record number of marriages recorded in the first two years of the war, probably an indication of instinctive parental apprehension about the nation's chances of survival. The Allied victories in 1943 and 1944, however, appear to have been celebrated in similar fashion as in the United States, as births in those years were pushed up 10 percent and 25 percent over 1939.

The "friendly invasion" of the Yanks satisfied the sexual hunger of some British women who found the pangs of the long wartime separation from their husbands unendurable. One of these was a Birmingham nurse who fell in love with a curly-haired American lieutenant:

We met often and began to like each other a lot. One night, as we were all having a drink, Curly said: "Let's go on our own tonight." We did — and landed up in a deserted air raid shelter where we made love. We did this several nights. Curly said he loved me and I said I did too. I was worried, as there was one thing I had not told him. I was already married. I used to take my wedding ring off and put it in my purse — then put it back on again when I got back to the hospital. I did this every time I met him. Then one night in "our" shelter, he asked me to marry him. I did not know what to say, being already married. I wanted to say "yes" so much, but somehow I knew that I had to keep putting him off. When the war came to an end, Curly went back to America. We wrote often to each other and he sent me gifts. But then my husband came home, so I stopped writing to him as I was so afraid that my husband would find his letters. When I had a son, I kept wishing it was Curly's.

Like many others, Ivy of Bristol remained dutifully faithful as she kept her love alive for the four years that her husband was in the Middle East. She read his farewell letter "over and over again and cried buckets every time." To alleviate the long days of waiting and wondering, she took a wartime job in a munitions company making magazines for Spitfire fighters:

When the sirens went off, we were supposed to run to the shelters, but most of us stayed at our workbenches. I told myself that every rivet I hammered home was a nail in Hitler's coffin — and consequently I broke three hammers in one week, much to the amusement of my foreman.

Every night after I got home and had done my housework and put my child to bed, I would sit down and write to my husband. I would start a letter one night and finish it off the next night, which meant that he was getting three or four letters a week from me. I never told him worrying things. If either of us was ill, I kept it from him and told him after we had recovered. He had enough to be worried about out there in the thick of the fighting.

In the United States a Vassar graduate provided moving testimony of why so many women took a war job to relieve the anxiety of worrying alone at home about soldier husbands at the front:

We must learn to wait. To endure the slow trickle of time from hour to hour, from day to day, for weeks, in anguish and suspense. And wait for some message, a letter from far off — a small scrap that tells something of how he was — some time ago — when it was sent. . . . The war work we can do is more than welcome — we work hard to put off the next returning cycle of thought — is he safe, is he well, will I hear from him soon? We learn to crowd a lifetime of living into one week — or a few days — or hours. War brides, married while he was on furlough, we wait for the next leave when we can get back. In those brief days, the joy is desperate, underlain with the knowledge of certain separation again — the clock ticks off numbered moments gone. And the train takes him off again — off to unknown places where our love cannot follow. . . .

The strain of separation made even the most devoted serviceman's wife susceptible to the chance of temporary emotional solace with other men. And as many were to discover, the wagging tongues of neighbors could spread unpleasant rumors to the most distant of battlefronts. Gossip may have been unfounded and malicious, but distance magnified the suspicions of soldiers enormously. As a 1943 survey of GIs' opinions revealed, there was overwhelming disapproval of wives and girlfriends wearing slacks in the street, although a three to two majority favored girlfriends back home dating *provided* they were not married. One or two husbands interviewed felt it was "all right" for their wives to go out "occasionally" with "mutual friends." One soldier responded, "Depends on WHOSE girl," and the consensus was: "All right if she keeps her mind on HER man."

Keeping her mind on her distant partner was not always easy

during those times. One American wife who had no intention of being unfaithful nevertheless found that her wartime dating placed her marriage under considerable strain. She faced what must have been a dilemma that confronted many:

One day someone suggested I go on a date — a purely platonic date, of course — with a fraternity brother of my husband. And the date was platonic to the point of brutality. . . . Gradually I began to realize that I was falling in love with this man and he with me. And accordingly we broke off the relationship, abruptly. Soon thereafter I discovered I was pregnant — by my husband of course. (The other affair had never gone that far.) When I wrote the news to my husband he was very disturbed. Though solicitous of my welfare he couldn't help revealing the fact that the role of father was incomprehensible to him under the circumstances. I could understand him because I felt the same way. We had never been truly married and both of us knew it . . . the sum total of our married life was seven weekends. . . . I was haunted by my recently discovered relationship with the second man. . . . I learned that my husband has gone overseas. I shall not see him now for the duration at least. The second man, like me, finds it difficult to call our relationship off, even though he knows I am pregnant and I strongly wish to remain loyal to my husband. . . . I haven't the slightest idea how it will all turn out, but I must confess, being as rational as I am, that I can see many possible outcomes — but none is satisfactory.

Wartime wives were haunted by fears about how the war would affect their particular marriage. "I think that as well as the fear of death, one realized that things might never be the same again," recalled one British wife; "I remember praying that my husband would never have to kill another man, how could anyone have to face that experience and remain the same person?"

An American girl who had been going steady with a soldier posted overseas in 1943 jilted him after being shocked to receive a letter from him telling of the emotional strain of life at the front:

He was sent to Italy where the fighting was very intense for a long time, and he wrote to me whenever he could. Then, in one of those V-mail letters he told me he cried many nights during the heavy fighting. In my sheltered life with my stereotyped notions of what a man constituted, the thought of his crying turned my stomach. I was convinced I had loved a coward. I never wrote to him again.

There were just as many heartaches at the other end of these V-mail relationships. One GI even resorted to writing painfully to the secretary of war in 1945 when his wife refused to answer charges made by a friend back home that she was "running around" with other people:

So at this time I am writing to you people and seeing if you can help me out in any way and if you can I would sure be glad if you could. My age is 25 years and I think I ought to know what I am doing, anyway before I have to live with my wife I stay in the Army the rest of my life and I come in the Army in Oct 1941. So I close now and I hope you can help me out with getting my divorce.

A GI stationed in Persia in 1943 received what GIs came to fear as the "Dear John" letter asking for a divorce:

The time has come to clear things between us. You will have realized, before now, that our marriage was a mistake. I beg of you to put an end to this mistake and get a divorce. I left your house this morning, because I didn't want to saddle you with the role of a betrayed husband. As a matter of fact, I have never been yours, but now I belong to someone else, and this finishes things between us. . . . Elaine

In anger and desperation this particular man passed his wife's brushoff letter to *Yank* magazine, asking if his faithless wife could still go on receiving his monthly allotment. He was advised to apply to a legal assistance officer for a divorce: "Yours is the classic version of a common problem. All the proof in the world that a soldier's wife is faithless does not change the fact that a family allowance is given her regularly as long as she remains legally married to the soldier."

Even stable marriages contracted long before the war would break up under its stress. A welfare counselor to a large Midwest army base cited the case of a sergeant with a son of fifteen and a daughter of twelve, whose wife dutifully corresponded with him two or three times a week throughout the war, and who had survived the bitter fighting in the Ardennes. "Two weeks before he sailed for America and was separated from the service, he received a letter from his wife stating she did not desire to see him and wanted a divorce. She believed that she had managed better without him!"

That war jobs and long periods of separation gave many wartime wives a new sense of independence was indisputable. "The more money, the less family life, is an established pattern in the United States which war psychology has merely emphasized," wrote an American sociologist of the new mood of the sixteen million working women — of whom six million were married *and* continued to rear children under fourteen years of age. Fired by this new sense of financial independence, some women abandoned their husbands and families without even the formality of divorce. In the cities of the Northeast it was not infrequent for nursery school teachers to question whether the children of deserted fathers were as eligible for relief as those of deserted working mothers.

"For most soldiers, the obligations of husband and father are unknown — wives become the dominant members of family during the war . . . and have shown marked reluctance to give up their authority and freedom when the family is to be united again," wrote the counselor of the Separation Center at Fort Leavenworth. Men returned home to be disillusioned by wives who not only "wore the trousers" but also had aged during the years of separation and were not beautiful dreamgirls on a par with their wartime diet of glamorous Hollywood pinups.

Many marriages survived while the war was on because the separated partners needed the emotional reassurance and a romantic idealization that made divorce unthinkable. Only when the servicemen returned to reunite the threads did they discover that the romantic aura was gone and little remained except a personal incompatibility. Inherently unstable unions quickly came apart under the tensions of two strangers actually having to live together for the first time.

One out of every three American servicemen was married by the end of the war. There was a doubling of petitions for divorce by 1945 when, for every hundred couples getting married that year, thirty-one were legally separating. In Britain the comparable figure was five divorces for a hundred marriages, but this was up from the one-in-a-hundred level of 1939. Under wartime law GIs overseas had been given the option of not answering a divorce summons by their wife, so this had had the effect of depressing the wartime divorce rates. If her husband refused to consent to proceedings, a woman often found it impossible to obtain a legal separation as long as he was in uniform because many American judges regarded it as their sacred duty to try to preserve the sanctity of the family while the war was on. After VJ-Day this restraint was removed, and the number of divorce petitions shot up.

In Britain, the number of adultery petitions filed after 1942 rose by 100 percent *each year*. The final twelve months of the war also saw a spectacular eightfold jump in the number of husbands who were suing for divorce on the grounds of adultery, suggesting there had been a dramatic national increase in infidelity, since by 1945 two out of every three petitions were being filed by men, whereas until 1940 female petitions had been in the majority.

"Separation was intolerable for some wives and sweethearts," was the rationalization that one British wife gave for the epidemic of wartime adultery. According to her view, the pressures that led many wives into extramarital affairs were compounded by a measure of social tolerance; "although promiscuity was not as widely publicized as it is today, nevertheless living from day to day, encouraged it."

Barbara Cartland, who acted as a voluntary welfare officer attached to Britain's women's auxiliaries, related in her war memoir *The Years of Opportunity:*

Men came home and found their wives had been unfaithful; women who wanted a divorce after a few months of marriage; girls who were pregnant; soldiers who arrived home to their wives ill and no-one to look after the children; children with a bad mother and a father overseas — there was no end to them.

Cartland relates how she was able to dissuade one young WAAF bride of six months from divorcing her husband on the grounds of sexual incompatibility with an explanation of how the necessity to "keep a stiff upper lip" and repress emotion in the face of danger often made a serviceman "an indifferent lover." As a wartime counselor, she admitted that it was hard to condemn the girls for succumbing to the temptations of wartime promiscuity:

It is not very easy to say what a woman should do or should not do when she hasn't seen her husband for four years. . . . They were young, their husbands were not fluent letter-writers — they started by not meaning any harm, just desiring a little change from the monotony of

looking after their children, queuing for food and cleaning house with
no man to appreciate them or their cooking. Another man would come
along — perhaps an American or an RAF pilot. Girls were very scarce
in some parts of the country and who could blame a man who is cooped
up in a camp all day or risking his life over Germany, for smiling at a
pretty girl when he's off duty? He is lonely, she is lonely, he smiles at
her, she smiles back, and it's an introduction. It is bad luck that she is
married, but he means no harm, nor does it cross her mind at first that
she could ever be unfaithful to Bill overseas. When human nature takes
its course and they fall in love, the home is broken up and maybe another baby is on the way, there are plenty of people ready to say it's
disgusting and disgraceful. But they hadn't meant to be like that, they
hadn't really.

In her wartime welfare work Miss Cartland adopted a down-
to-earth practicality when dealing with a husband who had faced
death and danger on the battlefield unflinchingly but who was
"white-faced and shaken" when he returned to find that his wife
was expecting another man's child. She counseled that, but for
the war, the worried and lonely spouse might have resisted the
temptation of what had probably started out as an innocent
friendship. "Sometimes there were tragedies and crimes," she
wrote, noting that she admired those who adjusted to the situation. "At first they swore that as soon as it was born it would have
to be adopted — then sometimes they would say, half-shame-
faced at their own generosity, 'The poor little devil can't help itself and after all it's one of hers, isn't it?' "

Of the 5.3 million British infants delivered between 1939 and
1945, over a third of a million were born illegitimate — and this
wartime phenomenon was not confined to any one section of society. The babies that were born out of wedlock belonged to every
age group of mothers, concluded one social researcher:

Some were adolescent girls who had drifted away from homes which
offered neither guidance nor warmth and security. Still others were
women with husbands on war service, who had been unable to bear the
loneliness of separation. There were decent and serious, superficial and
flighty, irresponsible and incorrigible girls among them. There were some
who had formed serious attachments and had hoped to marry. There
were others who had a single lapse, often under the influence of drink.
There were, too, the "good time girls" who thrived on the presence of

well-paid servicemen from overseas, and semi-prostitutes with little moral restraint. But for the war many of these girls, whatever their type, would never have had illegitimate children.

Illegitimate births increased from an annual prewar 5.5 average per thousand births to 10.5 over the six wartime years, with a 1945 peak of 16.1 But analysis of the United Kingdom statistical records indicates that wartime conditions brought a decline of at least a third in the "shotgun weddings" that prompted a couple to marry before the birth of their "irregularly conceived" child. Such a proportion indicates more than a hundred thousand babies would not have been born illegitimate but for the dislocations that war brought to people's lives. The upswing in the illegitimacy rate was almost as great in the United States, rising from 7.0 per thousand in 1939 to a peak of 10.0 in 1945, which averaged out at a wartime rate of 8.3 illegitimate births per thousand. Some 650,000 wartime babies were officially estimated to have been born out of wedlock in America.

Contrary to the expectation of the U.S. Census Bureau, it was the latter part of the war that brought the biggest increase in the illegitimate birthrate. It seemed that in the aftermath of Pearl Harbor marriage preceded pregnancies, and as the 1943 official report stated, "It is somewhat surprising that the ratio of illegitimate live births to total births has not increased but actually declined in the first year of the war." The fall-off in the illegitimacy rates during the first part of the war was also apparent in the British illegitimacy records through to 1943, after which they climbed steadily through 1945.

The rate of illegitimate births was *not* highest among teenage girls, as might have been expected. Both the British and American records indicate that the biggest percentage increase was the virtual doubling of the illegitimacy rates for mothers between twenty and thirty. It appears that the more mature women were the ones most affected by the relaxed morals of wartime, and that traditional considerations of fidelity were not the great restraint on married women that they had been in the past. Although the children born to married women were regarded as legitimate unless registered otherwise, that many British mothers of illegitimate children were married to servicemen is confirmed by the detailed investigation conducted by some of the larger municipal authorities. The records kept by Birmingham, for example, indicate that almost a third of all recorded illegitimate births were to married women, and that the rate had trebled by 1945. Although this level was elevated by the large number of American service camps around the urban area, a similar rise was observed in other large cities.

The wartime rise in illegitimacy rates put pressure on the public welfare authorities in Britain and the United States to assume the burden of a growing social problem that wartime conditions had greatly accelerated. During World War II, the unmarried mother became a candidate for social welfare rather than a target for society's collective moral outrage. The demand for female factory workers had encouraged many young women to leave rural areas and sheltered homes, and the draft of many women into the armed forces exposed them to increased sexual temptation and opportunity. The government, therefore, could hardly turn its back on them. Before the war an unmarried mother who was cast out by her straitlaced parents would probably turn to a religious charity, making the churches, as one authority aptly put it, "the main driving force in tackling the problem of illegitimacy and the greatest obstacle in the way of its solution." But this was to change as the number of unmarried mothers outstripped the resources of voluntary organizations like the Salvation Army. Many of the wartime unmarried mothers were also wage earners, independent of parent or husband, who resented being branded as sinners and objected to the atmosphere of reproach and moral censure that pervaded the church-run homes, whose austerity was a hangover from the old poor-laws.

The British government groped toward a solution that would be politically acceptable to conservative religious opinion, which was already alarmed at the perceived national moral decline. But by 1945, guidelines had been set by the Ministry of Health, and funding was being made available to local authorities and the voluntary societies for the provision of maternity homes and services. The most significant change was that unmarried mothers were enabled to collect child allowances and maternity grants that assisted the increasing number of women who were determined to raise their infant rather than resorting to the traditional solution of adoption.

"Total war is the most catastrophic instigator of social change the world has ever seen, with the possible exception of violent revolution," was how a leading American sociologist put it. Francis E. Merrill, a professor at Dartmouth College, observed in his 1946 study that wartime duty had transformed the American nation into a "people doing new things — grimly, protestingly, gladly, semihysterically — but all changing the pattern of their lives to some extent under the vast impersonality of total war." This analysis was a measure of the impact of the war on the social structure of every belligerent nation:

Millions of families work out new adjustments, as the wife and mother plays the roles of the absent husband and father. Millions of women go to work for the first time in their lives, often at hard and exacting manual labor in shipyard and aircraft factory. Millions of their children somehow learn to fend for themselves and come home from school to an empty and motherless house. Millions of wives, sweethearts, mothers and fathers are under constant nervous tension with their loved ones in active theaters of operations. Millions of wives learn to live without their husbands, mothers without their sons, children without their fathers, girls without their beaux.

The American National Conference on Family Relations warned that "In every war, the family is the first and greatest casualty." The universal wartime disruption of family life would have its most profound effect on adolescents, who by the final years of World War II were creating a major juvenile delinquency problem in every warring nation. Arrests of teenagers were up, no matter whether it was Munich, Manchester, England, or Milwaukee. The files of the German SD security police, British probation officers, and juvenile courts across the United States attest that sex offenses among teenagers were among the most widespread social problems of the war.

Britain was the first nation to be afflicted with high wartime arrest rates for teenage girls. There was a 100 percent increase in the first three years after 1939, and large numbers of them were judged in "need of care and attention" — indicating that they were morally "at risk." The supervisor of an East London reformatory asserted that the "earlier maturity" and the "jungle rhythms heard by juveniles from morning until bedtime, and slushy movies are in part responsible for an increase in sex delinquency among youths." Another factor was the unsettling experience for city schoolchildren of the 1940 evacuation to the country and the government's mobilization of mothers of adolescents fourteen years and older.

Many girls left school early to take a war job, and there were plenty of servicemen to provide excitement as an escape from wartime deprivations. London and the other large cities were crowded with GIs, Canadians, and other foreign troops by 1943. In one London district the number of teenage girls judged "in need of care and attention" had multiplied sixfold in the year before the invasion of France. A probation officer from London's dockland area described the obvious fascination with soldiers from overseas:

All that seems to be necessary is for the girls to have a desire to please. . . . Those girls who are misfits at home or at work, or who feel inferior for some reason or another, have been very easy victims. Their lives were brightened by the attention . . . and they found that they had an outlet which was not only a contrast, but was a definite compensation for the dullness, poverty, and sometimes, unhappiness of their home life.

An emergency Home Office study commissioned that year found that American GIs were particularly seductive:

To girls brought up on the cinema, who copied the dress, hair styles and manners of Hollywood stars, the sudden influx of Americans, speaking like the films, who actually lived in the magic country, and who had plenty of money, at once went to the girls' heads. The American attitude to women, their proneness to spoil a girl, to build up, exaggerate, talk big, and to act with generosity and flamboyance, helped to make them the most attractive boy friends. In addition, they "picked-up" easily, and even a comparatively plain and unattractive girl stood a chance.

If it was the glamour of the GIs' Hollywood image that thrilled British teenage girls, their counterparts across the Atlantic were stirred by a misguided adolescent patriotism. While their brothers participated in the national war fervor by joining up, thereby assuming the trappings of manhood, adolescent American girls had no such outlet. Psychologists surmised that the "Victory Girls" or "cuddle bunnies," as they were called, went "uniform-hunting" at railroad stations and bus terminals as a way of sharing in the wartime adventure. When detained by the police they would often claim that they were sexually promiscuous "because it's my patriotic duty to comfort the poor boys who may go overseas and get killed." Most of the young servicemen picked up by these girls were lonely and not averse to accepting the sexual invitations they were offered. The "patriotutes," as they were dubbed in the American press, often dispensed their favors for a Coca-Cola, a meal, or the price of a movie.

Though branded as semi-prostitutes, few actually sought sexual relationships with the cold commercialism of "the world's oldest profession." The American Social Hygiene Association held a conference in the fall of 1942, which concluded this type of girl was involved in "sexual delinquency of a non-commercial character," and that a "basic motive in her sex hunger is adventure and sociability, but she does not confine her attention to one or two male friends." These teenagers were often flotsam of hasty marriages contracted at the last minute by soldiers looking for emotional security before going overseas. One young woman picked up in Times Square in New York told a magazine reporter:

I've only gone with three or four men a week since I've been here. I didn't take money from any of them. I'm not bad, but a girl who's been married gets lonely. I couldn't go back to a small town life after Broadway. It's so quiet at home, no place to go, nothing to do.

"Goodtime girls of high-school age are the army's biggest problem today as a potential source of disease," according to a 1943 report from the base surgeon of a large Midwestern army airfield. "While mothers are winning the war in the factories, their daughters are losing it on the streets." Well over half of all the women arrested for sexual offenses in the United States by the end of the war were under twenty-one. FBI statistics show that there had been a 70 percent increase in teenage prostitutes, and in cities like San Diego with a large transient service population, the number of girls arrested had increased threefold. According to U.S. army records, nearly half of the soldiers who contracted VD blamed girls under nineteen years of age.

"From one end of the country to the other, it is the children who are paying the price for uncontrolled mass migrations, easy money and the unaccustomed bouts of war work, and the fact that 'Ma' is a welder on the graveyard shift," wrote Agnes Meyer in a series of reports filed from across the United States for the *Washington Post*. A million American children were estimated to have dropped out of high school to participate in the war effort. In the gypsylike encampments around the new plane factories in Wichita, Kansas, and the unplumbed and overcrowded frame houses for workers from Detroit's sixty-seven-acre Willow Run bomber factory, she found the disruptive social conditions that bred juvenile delinquency: "Many of them under crowded living conditions are witnesses of parental immorality. . . . In fact, parental behavior is the cause of much delinquency everywhere. Marital upsets and promiscuity among the workers are increasing. Women who earn money for the first time after a lifetime of being home slaveys acquire a defiant psychology."

From Los Angeles in 1943 came reports of "zoot-suit" riots by teenage gangs sporting over-large jackets and pegged pants, and from Washington State the press headlined "Wolf Packs," hard-drinking urban teenagers who assaulted girls and tore up cinema seats. Former President Herbert Hoover sternly reminded American mothers who might be failing to provide "watchful care" over their children that they were losing the battle against immorality on the home front even as their soldiers defeated the Axis powers overseas.

Press and public concern stirred Congress into action. Early in 1944 Senator Claude Pepper's Committee on Wartime Health and Education held five days of hearings on the "#1 wartime social problem in America." It concluded that "absentee parents" and homes upset by the war, along with substandard educational facilities in many of the wartime boom-towns, were to blame. While not disagreeing with the cause, *Time*'s comment on the 592-page Pepper Report was that its remedies for the problem were "a dime a dozen." Some of the committee members wanted to set up "Parents' Courts" to fine and imprison mothers and fathers who could be proved guilty of excessive neglect. Youth centers with chaperoned dances were favored by many communities. New Jersey passed a law forbidding soldiers to date girls under sixteen, and New York set up a "Wayward Minors Court" to deal with the large number of girls arrested for not being "properly escorted" after the 10 P.M. curfew in the Times Square area.

The chief of the U.S. Children's Bureau, writing in May 1944, delivered a telling indictment of the lot of the wartime American teenager:

War situations may intensify adolescent unhappiness and insecurity, and lessen the possibilities of satisfaction within normal family and community relationships of the basic need for affection and attention. Earlier feeling of unhappiness and rejection may be intensified by absence of the father from the home; absorption of the mother in gainful employment, voluntary war service, or the difficulties of home making; deprivation of companionship of elder brothers, sisters and companions. . . . Yet the consequences of delinquency press far more heavily upon girls, and intensify their need for social guidance and protection.

★ [13] ★

The Girls They Met "Over There"

The type of woman who approaches you in the street in Italy
and says "Please give me a cigarette" isn't looking for a smoke.

— *GI HANDBOOK,* 1943

Lust, bargaining, exploitation, the trading of a quid pro quo
disguised as a pretense of affection in some transitory relationship — such is sexuality in wartime.

— WILLARD WALLER, 1944

P rostitution, together with armaments manufacture, shares
the dubious distinction of the business that has been the
principal commercial beneficiary of twentieth-century warfare. In
common with the "merchants of death," the women who pursued "the lively commerce" discovered that fear generated by war
was a potent stimulant to their business. Long lines of soldiers
formed up outside the French military brothels that catered to
the sexual needs of the Allied armies on the Western Front according to the dictates of good discipline: officers' houses were
indicated by blue lights and other ranks by red lamps. For those
who preferred to risk infection rather than to copulate under
military supervision, there was always a willing "mademoiselle"
to be found in staging towns like the one in Armentières who
was the subject of the popular war song.

These female camp followers had always been part of the bag-
gage-train of European armies. During the Thirty Years War it
was recorded that one forty-thousand-strong army that devas-
tated the Rhineland in the 1620s was accompanied by "100,000
soldiers' wives, whores, servants, maids and other camp followers." The practice had spread to the United States during the Civil

War, when the regiments of women who followed General Joseph Hooker's Army of the Potomac became known as "Hooker's girls," coining the popular term for prostitutes.

Nell Kimball, the celebrated New Orleans madam, ascribed the increased trade that World War I brought her famous whorehouse to the epidemic of anxiety that gripped the male population after the United States entered the war in the spring of 1917:

> Every man and boy wanted to have one last fling before the real war got him. One shot at it in a real house before he went off and maybe was killed. I've noticed it before, the way the idea of war and dying makes a man raunchy, and wanting to have it as much as he could. It wasn't really pleasure at times, but a kind of nervous breakdown that could only be treated with a girl and a set to.

The same "nervous breakdown" in European soldiers brought the "red-light regiments" out into the streets of Berlin, Paris, and London — leading to the 1917 music-hall quip that the American doughboys were "Over here to make the underworld safe for democracy." London was so notorious that the New Zealand Red Cross dispensed prophylactic kits to protect the health — if not the morals — of their native sons whose six-shillings-a-day pay made them targets for streetwalkers used to British soldiers who had only their daily sixpence to offer.

Nor was it just in Piccadilly Circus that avarice was stirred by the foreign military uniforms in World War I. A Canadian major was invited by a titled lady to spend the weekend at her country estate. "You men in the army lead such dangerous lives, and may never return from the next offensive," announced his hostess over dinner, explaining that her husband had recently been killed in action. "It is our duty to make your leave enjoyable, so here I am." It was impossible for the major to resist such an invitation, but he was to be nonplussed the next morning when the butler confidentially advised him: "Her ladyship has the greatest difficulty maintaining this estate. It would be helpful if you would leave a contribution of a hundred pounds."

It is a reflection on the social transformation that followed in the wake of World War I that when the Wehrmacht goose-stepped into Paris in July 1940, one of the Reich military governor's first acts was to issue a decree making the city's most select brothels in rue Chabanais and rue des Moulins "Lodgings for German Officers in Transit." What offended the staff was not the prospect of their conquerors bathing in the copper tub in which Edward VII, as Prince of Wales, had doused the prettiest girls in champagne, but the leaflet that advertised their services and gave the address of the nearest Métro station. For the female staff who were accustomed to receiving only "carriage trade" clients, this was insult enough, but the German leaflet advised all visitors to the two houses to immediately visit the nearest army prophylactic clinic because "99.5 percent of all venerally infected cases have caught their disease from uncontrolled prostitutes."

Prostitutes *were* made synonymous with venereal disease, not just by the Germans, but also by the British and United States armies' commands, who declared war on the women blamed for the million and a half syphilis and gonorrhea casualties suffered by the Allied armies in World War I. The Wehrmacht applied the lessons learned twenty years earlier when the kaiser's army strictly regulated the "sexual logistics" of the troops and thereby cut its VD casualty rate to half that of the French army by 1918. Corpsmen collected the fees at the medically supervised military brothels behind the front lines, imposing a strict ten-minute time limit per man during the evening "rush" hour and providing prophylactic treatments as well as keeping a detailed log of the visitors' ranks and regiments so that fines could be levied on those who contracted and failed to report venereal infections.

In World War I the venereal infection rates of the British army were seven times higher than the Germans, principally because national prudery prevented the high command from acknowledging that there was any problem at all until 1915, when the Canadian and New Zealand prime ministers forced the chiefs of staff to issue free contraceptives to the troops. The American forces would follow suit, but the controversy over birth control required official statements that the policy was adopted to prevent the spread of disease abroad, rather than interfere with natural procreation at home. After the war the American government's efforts to control the unmentionable "social diseases" had fallen far short of the Roosevelt administration's "National Social Hygiene Policy." So when the Selective Service Act of 1940 drafted millions of young American men into military uniform, Congress was soon being pressed to pass laws to protect the health of soldiers and sailors from the prostitution rackets sure to spring up around the new military bases.

"Blitz the Brothels" became the national war cry that led off the attack on commercialized prostitution in the United States. Launched in 1940 by the armed forces, the U.S. Public Health Service, the Federal Security Agency, and the American Social Health Association "For the Control of Venereal Diseases in Areas Where Armed Forces or National Defense Employees Are Concentrated," it was given the authority of federal law by the so-called May Act of 11 July 1941, with a call for "a united effort for total physical fitness."

The May Act restored the provisions of Section 17 of the 1917 Draft Act, which prohibited "prostitution within such reasonable distance of military and/or naval establishments . . . needful to the efficiency, health and welfare of the army or navy" and frightened off many of the would-be brothel racketeers. Its provisions also alarmed some senior American army commanders, who regarded Senator May's political handiwork as a potential threat to morale — and many base commanders hesitated to use the powers they had been granted. It was only invoked on two occasions in 1942 before the implicit threat of joint FBI and military action was sufficient to bring about the closure of most overt red-light districts. At the end of the year a survey revealed that commercialized prostitution, while not eliminated, had been dramatically reduced in 526 of 680 local communities.

Blitzing the brothels might have been successful in checking what could have been a wartime explosion of organized vice in the United States, but it simultaneously created a new phenomenon, according to Dr. John H. Stokes of Philadelphia, writing in the *American Medical Journal:* "The oldtime prostitute in a house or formal prostitute on the street is sinking into second place. The new type is the young girl in her late teens and early twenties . . . who is determined to have one fling or better. . . . The carrier and disseminator of venereal disease today is just one of us, so to speak."

Free-lance prostitution in the United States was soon providing spicy copy for the press as reports flooded in from major navy bases and army camps. Cab drivers serving the U.S. navy's large base on the Virginia coast were reported to have been threatened with losing their licenses for graft they received by ferrying customers to and from illicit destinations. Even *Time* magazine ran a piece on the social problems of the U.S. navy's principal East Coast port:

Whereas before Pearl Harbor, the majority of Norfolk's prostitutes were professionals, today probably 85% to 90% are amateurs. Many are young girls lured to Norfolk by the promises of big paying jobs. Hundreds of these girls arrive every week. They hang around bus terminals while phoning for a room somewhere. . . . Farm girls and clerks from small towns find it easy to have all the men they want . . . many do not charge for their services.

In San Antonio, Texas, one out of every four "car-hops" — as the streetwalkers were called — was reportedly infected with VD, causing the "professional prostitutes" to blame the amateurs: "They say the young chippies who work for a beer and a sandwich are cramping their style." In New York State, Canadian girls crossed the border on evening trips into Plattsburgh, and the community pleaded for action to seal off the frontier to them. "We've got the finest beach in the country; the biggest naval air station in the world and the hottest red-light district this side of New Orleans," was the wartime boast of cab drivers in Pensacola, Florida, whose fares were quoted as: "A dollar to the beach, half a buck to the Air Station, and a dime to the District!"

On the other side of the country, at the nation's notorious "divorce capital," Reno's famous "Stockade" red-light district was shut at the army's request, but as one girl who was then resident in a city college remembered:

When they closed down prostitution, you know what happened. They just spread all over the area. They had guest homes where the divorcees could come and live for their six weeks, and a lot of prostitution was in the guest homes throughout the area. What they accomplished by closing it down was to lose control of it. Some air corps guys came into town looking for whores and saw some girls going into our fraternity houses on Greek Row. So two or three of them came to our house and asked one of the girls if they could see the madam. These were freshman girls, and one of them said, "Oh, you must mean the housemother." . . . Rather than embarrass the housemother and the boys, one of the seniors said, "Fellas, you've got the wrong house!"

By 1943 the army and navy were so concerned about complaints of girls and women roaming the streets of Miami that a
special directive was issued to military police to stop men soliciting these "women of easy virtue." But they were soon reporting
failure to curb "soliciting of women in the streets" because "the
females in question often take the initiative in making the ac-
quaintance of a soldier or sailor." Offduty servicemen flocked into
Miami every night from the large number of navy and army bases
at the outskirts of the resort, so the women's search, according
to the report, was "usually crowned with success because of the
large number (about 50,000) of young and virile soldiers and
sailors stationed or visiting that area, a larger number of whom,
likewise, appear to be primarily interested when off duty in seeking the companionship of the opposite sex."

A special army report on vice in Miami surveyed the extent of
the problem on an average Thursday night. Cruising in an un-
marked car, two officers visited the bars, dance-halls, and parks
in search of promiscuity. They found many "well dressed, unat-
tached women sitting at bars and tables in saloons and night clubs"
whose apparent intent was "picking up a soldier or sailor, which
they usually succeeded in doing before the saloon or night club
was closed at midnight." At the Tatem Hotel in Miami Beach,
they stopped at the popular 534 Club and Charlie's, which chaplains had condemned for immoral excess in their burlesque and
strip-tease shows. Members of the audience were quizzed "but no
grown person interviewed considered them to be lewd or obscene" in spite of "poorly done murals of the Vargas type."

The Servicemen's Recreation Center at Pier 42 had closed early:
the colonel and captain noted, tactfully, that it was "well managed but not well patronized." The Frolic, Bali Night Club, Club
600, Bowery, and the Spur Bar were packed, and in most of the
bars it was very noticeable that the female population considerably exceeded the male — and that whenever a man came in the
women went to the powder room for an excuse to come back and
sit with newcomers. At the Bali, "petting" was going on at the
tables, which included many uniformed WAVES, "one of whom
was observed to be 'petting' with an Ensign." The United States
uniform was being treated even more disrespectfully at the "rough
and tumble" Spur Bar, which was packed with a crowd of semi-

intoxicated sailors — one drunken CPO had already passed out on a bench.

In the early hours of the morning, the investigators found that the prophylactic station near the navy sub-chaser school was crowded with sailors who had presumably already found sexual satisfaction. Signs of promiscuous behavior were evident at every corner; "many enlisted personnel and their girls, when not in sight of the shore patrol, were observed locked in each other's arms, petting and kissing as they moved down the streets. As they progressed farther from the middle of town, these couples were observed disappearing in the alleyways, yards, parks and shrubbery." Petting went on openly in "practically all the cars even though the lights around were bright enough to make the performance easily visible from almost every direction." But although the survey concluded "no actual immoral acts were observed," the inescapable impression was "one of great immorality with no effective means being taken to prevent it. Even in instances where there were no immoral intentions, the fact that the men were up and out in the streets until all hours of the morning would appear to leave them ill-fitted for a strenuous training program the following day."

Honolulu, because it served the fleet naval base at Pearl Harbor, boasted the liveliest commercial prostitution center of the war. It escaped the "Brothel Blitz" until 1944 because Oahu was a military area. The commanding general and admirals knew the contribution it was making to the morale of thousands of sailors, marines, and soldiers en route to the Pacific battlefields, so no attempt was made to interrupt its very lively commerce until the tide of war had been turned against the Japanese.

The Oahu brothels were reputed to be a ten-million-dollar-a-year business — and the average fifty thousand prophylactic treatments administered each month during 1942 is indicative of the extent of their use. Unofficial inspections and adequate prophylaxis kept the VD rate down, as did the forced hospitalization of all girls found to be infected. The local communities — unlike those in mainland America — did not want the Hawaii brothels blitzed, because they believed that it protected their daughters and wives from the huge transient male service population.

A daily ritual that took place on Waikiki beach until the summer of 1944 was a vivid illustration of how sex had become an intimate partner in the war. A lithe six-foot woman in her mid-twenties, seductively draped in a diaphanous Hawaiian muumuu with her immaculate hair crowned by dark glasses and a broad sun-hat would parade provocatively through the ranks of sun-bathing American servicemen. She never failed to stir the men to the rhythmic chant of a marching cadence:

> One . . . Two . . . Three . . . Four
> Mamie's . . . What . . . We're Fighting . . . For.

For many GIs, Mamie Stover was the "Mademoiselle from Armentières" of World War II, the archetype soldier's girl who offered sexual consolation from the mechanical inhumanity of war. Unlike the ubiquitous pinups of Hollywood sex goddesses, Mamie's charms were available to any GI who paid for them. Business acumen, rather than social conscience, was what motivated the legendary Mamie Stover, the uncrowned Queen of the Pacific. "I think it's immoral for a woman not to accumulate money during a war," she explained in a famous aside. "When men are throwing twenty-dollar bills away like empty beer cans, a woman ought to be busy with a basket."

The war made Miss Stover not only famous, but very rich. Thousands of GIs willingly forked out for their never-to-be-forgotten visit to "Mamie's House" with its specially constructed "Bull Ring" in the middle of an empty room. This device, which maximized her profits and time, comprised "four Pullman-size adjacent compartments with a red couch — and she moved determinedly from couch to couch while her servants shuttled men in and out." When she retired from active duty, a half-millionaire, in 1944, the joke went round the enlisted men of the Pacific fleet that "never had so many men paid so much for so little."

Mamie, whose figure decorated many a bulkhead in the U.S. navy, demanded the highest rates of return for her favors. Her competitors who had less to offer tried doubling their rates in 1942 when U.S. army pay was increased — until their customers threatened a boycott to keep the average price down to three dollars a session. But even at less inflationary rates than the legendary Mamie's, many of the Honolulu prostitutes made enough to move out of the red-light district to smart houses in uptown Honolulu. Protests from the affronted residents brought a police crackdown — and the first recorded prostitutes' strike.

In August 1942, the staff of the brothels took to the streets with a shrill protest against police harassment, claiming they were "essential to the welfare of U.S. armed forces." All except three of the downtown bordellos closed their bedrooms. The lines that formed up outside these were so long that by the normal closing hour of three o'clock one afternoon, military police had to be called to control one hundred eighty-five angry men who were lined up to visit the five girls still on duty. When the police agreed to end their campaign, the girls went back to work in September and it was "business as usual" for the next two years. The "Close them" order was finally given in 1944 by a commanding general who enlisted the support of the Honolulu Council. That September the red lights went out for the final time as Mamie Stover and her regiment of competitors "officially" closed their front doors.

The German decision to leave much of Europe's most sophisticated brothel system intact may have made collaborators of some *"sous maîtresses,"* but it also provided many with the chance to serve the Allied cause with the aid of the French underground resistance movement. The *"sous maîtresses"* of the French "Closed Houses" were usually former prostitutes whose motherly solicitude for their girls was combined with the business acumen and toughness of a man. From long experience of the male they acquired a canny sixth sense, which enabled them to spot members of the Gestapo or Vichy's provocateurs from the desk where they dealt with clients. Each girl's bedroom, into which she always locked herself and her temporary lover, was regarded as sacrosanct by the police, who subscribed to the view of the Gallic male that "to interrupt a man in the course of his amours may do him psychological damage." Since the "Closed Houses" as their name implied were close-shuttered to deny prying eyes, they were ideal hiding places for fugitive Allied airmen, and with their secret exits and passages through to adjacent buildings they were well equipped for a fast escape in the event of a raid.

Because the Germans required that the prostitutes be registered with the local gendarmerie, any Gestapo suspicion about a brothel was passed on to the resistance by sympathizers on the police grapevine if requests were made for the papers of a particular girl or "Closed House." Scores of Allied flyers who came down over France or other occupied countries made their way through brothels on the escape pipeline to the Spanish border. Roxanne Pitt, who helped run one of the successful escape routes, recalled that not every flyer could feign sexual interest when the Gestapo was expected to call:

One day I escorted to a brothel in Montmartre a shy young English pilot who looked such an innocent Mummy's Darling that it seemed immoral to leave him there. As I heard later, he was so bashful that when *la sous maîtresse* showed him into the salon he caused some innocent merriment among the visitors. One of them must have described his behavior as a good story, for it came to the ears of the Gestapo, a member of which visited the brothel a few days later posing as a Frenchman. The manageress saw through him at once but concealed the fact. It seemed likely that a Gestapo raid was imminent. In such cases the usual procedure was to pair off the refugee with one of the girls, but this young man had been brought up so strictly that he seemed incapable of playing his part; and so he was dressed up as a prostitute instead.

Brothel girls in the French ports of Lorient, Brest, and La Pallice from which the submarine wolf-packs sailed to ravage the Atlantic convoys were also suspected of spying for the Allies and passing on the names of U-boats about to put to sea. Some German commanders quarantined their crews for three weeks before a patrol to protect their health and the disclosure of their missions, since their men always went on a spree before sailing. To avoid the disease and security hazard posed by the seaport brothels, the Todt Organization built "rest-camps" as well as the mighty concrete pens. Equipped with beer- and dance-halls, the camps were staffed with plenty of imported German females, who with the German Red Cross nurses could be persuaded to share the comfortable hotel-like accommodation provided for the crewmen.

The wartime report of an English army physician had observed that there was a "well known relationship between the distance from home and VD incidence," with length of individual service abroad the chief factor:

Among other ranks, with their more limited resources for sublimation through social and intellectual interests, the effect of long continued service overseas is seen in the increase in the venereal disease rate and, perhaps, in the type of commerce from which infection results. The sense of guilt lessens and the proportion of cases of the more sordid form of prostitution seems to increase.

The same memorandum advised that army VD rates could be cut by a third if home leave could be arranged every third year of overseas service. Such measures were clearly out of the question in wartime — and by shouldering the "white man's burden" the British soldier on long spells of overseas garrison duty had become accustomed to patronizing the "more sordid forms of prostitution" offered by the more exotic cities from Cairo to Calcutta. Although native red-light districts were officially condemned by the military authorities with "out of bounds" notices, resort to them was condoned even though the risk of disease was high.

Bombay and Calcutta became the main disembarkation ports for the influx of Allied troops on their way to the distant battle-fronts in Burma and China. In advance of the arrival of the first GIs, the American consul in Bombay reported to Washington that native brothels were certainly cheap — the usual fee was five rupees (a dollar and a half, less than ten shillings at contemporary exchange rates), which increased four- or fivefold at weekends, with "call time" limited to ten minutes. Long "working hours" and entertaining up to ten men a night were not unusual because British military doctors charged a steep one hundred fifty rupees (forty-five dollars) for the regular medical examinations and prophylactic treatments.

The principal Bombay brothel district was nominally "out of bounds" to British military personnel, but in accordance with the principles of good order and discipline, the better houses in Grant Road were regarded by some British officers — and not always the junior ones — "as a sort of club." It was in one of these that a *Newsweek* reporter found "Molly." She wore a thin crepe de chine evening dress to work, and was typical of the women who staffed the low-rise houses in Bombay's red-light district in World War II. "Darkly slim," her dusky Mongoloid features, flashing eyes, and pearly teeth caught the attention of the American reporter, who was intrigued to discover she wore "a delicate necklace with a gold pendant emblem of Queen Victoria" in recognition of her

Anglo-Indian heritage. "Molly" was a twenty-rupee girl in the prostitute house run by a "Madame Marcel," a thirty-eight-year-old Detroit woman who claimed she had "been in the game" ever since her husband deserted her. She boasted "how she had educated two daughters at a distance from New York, putting one in hospital as a nurse and the other in a bank" on the earnings of her "family" of seven Indian girls.

In Karaya Road, one of the better streets of Calcutta's notorious brothel district, girls cost thirty rupees (nine dollars) and business was brisk for the rickshaws, taxis, and horse-drawn gharries drawn up outside the stucco houses with fake pillars and ornate grills.

The queen of the Karaya Road is a girl men begin to hear about when they reach Cairo or Karachi or on ships crossing the Indian Ocean. Her name is Margot. She is fair, although not blonde, wears her hair brushed hastily back, shoulder length. Unexpectedly fresh-looking, with clear gray-green eyes, a profile that looks as though always held against a strong breeze on grassy hilltop, and a figure that can be described as voluptuous. She wears a blue halter, a flowing skirt of figured silk, and sandals on her bare feet. All in all, I think Margot has been to a lot of movies. . . . Margot's fee is 85 rupees for the shortest possible visits and at this rate — with her parlor always full of patient men of rank and determination — she is reputed to make somewhere in the neighborhood of $1,500–$2,000 a week. Nobody seems to know exactly where she comes from. I heard her nationality given as English, Anglo-Indian, Anglo-Burmese and French. . . . There is nothing else remotely like Margot in Calcutta. There are only some 30 odd of the plush-seat houses on the Karaya Road, with fewer than 100 prostitutes at rates up to 50 rupees — and beyond that are Calcutta's miserable 40,000 slaves.

For the sheer variety of its sexual diversions, few red-light districts in the world during World War II could match Cairo. The pleasures offered reached something of a peak of sexual exoticism in the frenzied year before the Battle of El Alamein, when British and Australian troops poured in on their way to halt Rommel's advance across the Western Desert.

"Give Us the Tools and We Will Finish the Job" was the cheeky sign that one Cairo brothel keeper hung out after Churchill's famous 1942 appeal to the United States. In the back alleys of the ancient city of the pyramids, there was no shortage of servicemen who obliged. The incidence of murders and rapes, however, prompted the British military police to embark upon one of their periodic efforts to put the worst districts of the city out of bounds. But policing the squalid streets, even in the name of King Farouk, proved impractical as the legend of wild sexual practices continued to lure the hard-bitten soldier and curious journalist. A British war correspondent, however, recalled that not all the sights in the notorious Wagh El Birkhet were depraved: "the only significant thing in a boring, rather nauseating hour — a fellah bowing in prayer to Mecca on the roof of a brothel, through the lit windows of which we could see Baudelaire's 'affreuse juive.' "

While Rommel's Afrika Korps was still advancing on Cairo, one prudent Cairo madam who evacuated her girls to what she hoped would be the safety of Alexandria was doomed to disappointment when a lost Italian pilot dropped a single bomb and demolished her house of ill repute. The incident also faced the British army authorities with a dilemma after Cairo GHQ was told that the corpses of six British officers had been dug out of the rubble. It was decided to spare their next of kin painful embarrassment by camouflaging the true circumstances of the deaths. Accordingly, the three officers who had been upstairs "on the job" were posted as "killed in action," and the three waiting downstairs for their turn were listed as "killed on active duty."

The landings at Casablanca, Algiers, and Oran in November 1942 confronted the American military authorities and servicemen for the first time with North African brothels. Unable to "blitz the brothels" overseas, the Congress-ordained American military policy of suppressing prostitution was forced into uncomfortable compromises. Field commanders adopted a pragmatic "off limits" strategy, which designated supervised brothels for the use of their officers and men while their headquarters and the War Department denied such a policy existed. The army corps of chaplains knew only too well that it did, but many chose to turn a blind eye rather than make themselves unpopular with their commands and men. Those who were more concerned for morals than morale risked confrontations by penning protest letters to the chaplain general in Washington, while preaching to remind GIs of responsibility to the women they had left behind. "Do you see that sunset?" was a favorite theme of one chaplain. "Over westward beyond that sunset lies America, and in my hometown in one of its cottages lives the girl I love. I'm keeping myself clean for her!"

In the Medina quarter of Casablanca, glass-topped walls surrounded an estimated twelve thousand prostitutes. It was not glass shards, but the armed guards, that General Eisenhower ordered to enforce strictly the "off limits" notices pasted on Medina's walls. On December 10 the military police were removed and GIs stormed through the single gate for three days of hedonistic explorations, which came to an end when "disturbances" were given as the official reason for reimposing the ban called for by the chaplains and the medical corps. In Algiers the Casbah was also put "off limits," although four large brothels outside were taken over by the army. The largest was the Sphinx, which observed a strict shift system — enlisted men and civilians during the daytime, with evening hours reserved for officers.

Monsignor Arnold, chaplain general of the U.S. army, was bombarded with letters from chaplains in North Africa charging that "a number of houses of prostitution formerly operated by the French have been taken over by military authorities of the army of the U.S. and are now operated and managed by military personnel." Prophylaxis stations had been set up adjacent to, and in some cases inside, the brothels, which one Catholic chaplain claimed, with some justification, were "operating under the VERBAL but not written orders of his commanding officer." In Oran the army doctors demanded the military brothel there be shut after they were threatened with a VD epidemic because French physicians had issued false health reports for the prostitutes "unofficially" working for the U.S. army. Mounting protests and the forthcoming invasion of Sicily were instrumental in General Eisenhower's decision to order the unofficial whorehouses shut down in July 1943, when a strict off-limits policy was reimposed in the theater.

A survey of GIs' sexual habits in Italy, taken two years later, concluded: "Army life overseas wrecks these old emotional ties when it takes a man away from his wife and sweetheart, and leaves him a set of memories and occasional letters. In its place, he has new dangers and lots of frustration and uncertainties. . . . There is a new set of accepted 'rights' and 'wrongs' in this overseas situation."

224 ★ Virtue Under Fire

A foretaste of the problem that was to confront them in Italy was given by British medical officers in Sicily, who were treating forty thousand VD cases a month, a rate twenty times higher than that of soldiers stationed in England. As one report advised, "Prostitution is almost universal among all but the highest class of Sicilian women. Government regulated brothels also existed in all of the large towns." Control had broken down, although General Patton wasted no time trying to restore it by installing U.S. army medical teams in Palermo's six large houses of prostitution. This did not endear him to General Montgomery, his archrival, whose pride as well as his puritanism were offended when it was announced that they were open for business again under U.S. army management.

The invasion of Italy proper magnified the scale of the problem, but it was the capture of Naples in October 1943 that pitched the American and British commands into a two-year-long battle with prostitution that Allied chaplains and doctors of both armies would later concede they lost.

Naples became the main staging port for the grueling Italian campaign as well as the principal rest and recreation center for thousands of Allied troops. Wine and girls were as plentiful as food was scarce for its inhabitants, who were packed into what one British officer called "its human rookeries." K-rations became the passport to the discovery made by GIs of Latin passion. "Even when they aren't in love the Italians ape the mannerisms of the lover. Thus they can be joyous at eighty. Italian love is both articulate and silent. The lovers quickly knock down any barrier between them."

In Naples, as one official American report put it, "Women of all classes turned to prostitution as a means of support for themselves and their families." A British officer recorded his surprise that Prince A. and his twenty-four-year-old sister came down from their palace to his office. "The purpose of the visit was to inquire if we could arrange for his sister to enter an army brothel. We explained that there was no such institution in the British Army. 'A pity,' the Prince said. Both of them speak excellent English, learned from an English governess. 'Ah, well, Luisa, I suppose if it can't be helped, it can't be.' They thanked us with polite calm, and departed."

There was an estimated female population in Naples of over a hundred and fifty thousand, of which an estimated fifty thousand were regular prostitutes in the "undetermined number of brothels which had previously been regulated by the civilian government and used by the German and Italian Armies." A month after Naples had been liberated the U.S. Fifth Army headquarters quarantined a large bordello outside the city and placed the other brothels off limits to American troops. But the strategy that had failed in North Africa was even less effective in Naples. Prostitutes refused to work in army brothels for twenty to fifty lira (fifty cents) per man when they could command ten dollars, fifteen, or even twenty outside. Uncontrolled prostitution sent VD rates rocketing to over one hundred per thousand men by the end of the year, and almost every affected GI gave Naples as the source of infection.

The British army, which had no clear strategy other than the ineffective one of placing sections of Naples out of bounds, reacted to the soaring VD rates by blaming it on the Germans. A circular that arrived in all units by Christmas warned:

From reports that have been received it is apparent that prostitution in occupied Italy, and Naples in particular, has reached a pitch greater than has ever been witnessed in Italy before. So much is this so that it has led to a suggestion that the encouragement of prostitution is part of a formulated plan arranged by the pro-Axis elements, primarily to spread venereal disease among Allied troops.

British military intelligence might have believed in a sinister Nazi plot, but a U.S. army doctor discerned that the dramatic rise in venereal disease was not a product of the Germans' corruption of Italian womanhood. "It was not lust, but necessity, not depravity of the soul but the urge of instinct to survive which led numerous women into the ranks of the amateur prostitute on whom regulatory legislation had little or no effect."

The magnitude of the sexual problems that confronted the Allies in Italy was put into sharp focus when a U.S. army medical officer conceded victory in the battle against venereal disease in Naples to the prostitutes: "Women of all classes turned to prostitution as a means of support for themselves and their families. Small boys, little girls and old men solicited on every street for their sisters, mother, and daughters and escorted prospective customers to their homes." When the casualties of sexual infection exceeded those from the battlefront, special "Casanova Camp" treatment centers were set up, surrounded by barbed wire to keep the men in and the Italian women out.

The indignity of being processed through one of these American VD treatment centers was vividly described by army veteran John H. Burns:

On the back of the jacket and on the trouser leg were painted these large and smeary letters: V D. . . . Finally it came his turn at the end of the file to enter the dispensary. Inside the screen door the line forked into two prongs and was being funnelled past two GIs each with a hypodermic in his hand. Along the walls of the room were electric ice-boxes. And many little glass ampoules of an amber liquid. Ahead of him were men with either arm bared or with their buttocks offered like steak to the needle. "They give ya a choice on where ya want ya shot," the blond boy said. "If ya take it in the ass, they'll use a longer needle ta get through the fat. My advice is ta take ya shots round the clock. Then none of ya four parts gets too sore. Ya'll be hurtin anyhow." Then . . . he felt already the stinging in his other shoulder. All his life telescoped down to three hour periods and a hypodermic needle with yellow drops dribbling out of it. What was it called. Pncilin? Penissiclin? Pencillin?

Nor was it solely the economic facts of life in war-shattered Italy that worked to afflict so many Allied soldiers with venereal disease, as Burns explained:

To us GIs the girls of southern Italy fell into two tight classes only. That's where we got stymied. There were the girls of via Roma, whom the Neapolitans, mincing no words, called *puttane*. These girls asked fixed prices either in lira or PX rations. They satisfied us for a while as long as we had the money, but their fee was steep for a GI unless he was a big operator in the black market. And then too something in a man's vanity craves something other than a girl who's shacking up with Tom, Dick and Harry. American men are so sentimental that they refuse to have a whore for their girl — if they can help it. That's the schizophrenia of our civilization with its sharp distinction between the Good Girl and the Bad Girl. Consequently after a few tries, with the fear of VD always suspended over our heads, we began to look at the Good women of Naples. And here entered the problem of the GI Italian Bride. I remember that Italian girls began to look sweet to us early . . . perhaps because their virginity was put on such a pedestal.

Italian women of every sort proved irresistible to Allied soldiers. "When ya walk down the via Roma," as one corporal observed, "ya can tell by their eyes whether they will or won't. They make no bones about it over here. . . . Christ, what eyes they give ya!" Confidential questionnaires that investigated what the U.S. army called its "most persistent problems" revealed that while 72 percent of GIs paid cash for their sex, "27 percent pay nothing (but perhaps give gifts of rationed goods), and only 1 percent say they pay with cigarettes, food and clothing." Contrary to the popular belief, the survey found "no observable relationship between a previous record of combat and frequency of sexual contact." The most sexually active were the supply soldiers of the Quartermaster's Corps, many of whom were black. Most worrisome of all was the discovery that there was "no evidence that VD talks or movies cuts down the exposure of men to VD overseas."

British and American officers had their pick of Italian women who were willing to express their gratitude for liberation by shacking up with them in their comfortable billets. This made the lower ranks bitter, and one private complained:

There are plenty of prostitutes hanging around where I work to satisfy me. Our organization has fought an officers war for twenty-eight months. They [officers] have a fine club, whiskey, dances with civilians and U.S. women from Rome, with nurses, with native girls. We've had nothing. I don't blame the officers as a whole. Only the organization leaders. We've had no wholesome contact with women since we've been overseas. All our relations with women we have to sneak. Naturally we aren't thrown into contact with the better females. The only women I've talked to for two years have been whores. Occasionally we see a Red Cross girl, but that doesn't ease the longing for female companionship. With a better chance at mild flirtations, a little necking possibly, I think the disease rate would fall. So far, if we want female companionship we have to resort to prostitutes. And it's rough to hear a good orchestra, laughter from the officer's club. They seem to think we can remain celibates while they bask in feminine company.

The root cause of the medical defeat that the Allied military command suffered during the Italian campaign was pinpointed by one of the army psychologists who conducted the U.S. army's 1945 survey into the sexual habits and attitudes of GIs:

Should a soldier merely want female companionship this may be easily had if companionship means merely being with a woman. Many write that they just want to dance and talk to, or be with a woman or change from the eternal male society of the Army. Here again, he is almost completely frustrated for a variety of reasons. British or American Army girls are so few in number that he cannot hope to win one of them as a companion, if even for one night a week. Also, it may become an entangling alliance in which case he is one of the 30% who are married, or of the 20% who have "loyal" sweethearts waiting at home. If he turns to an Italian girl for companionship, he generally finds himself unable to talk to her beyond a few simple expressions. If he maintains the companionate non-intercourse approach to the relationship, he is almost surely a frustrated man, and if he is tempted to shift the relationship to a sexual one, he probably finds less resistance than he was accustomed to in his pre-Army experience. None of this is written in terms of "guilt" or "propriety"; those seem to be the *facts* of the situation.

★ 〔14〕 ★

Oversexed, Overpaid,
and Over Here!

Americans were "cheeky" compared to our usual "Mr. Frigidaire Englishman," but what a boost to the ego when one is greeted with "Hello, Duchess" (and you were treated like one!) or "Hi, Beautiful!" That was so GOOD! As we got to know these boys, how generous they were; we never lacked for chocolate or cigarettes and even precious luxuries like nylons they could get for us.

— BRITISH GIRL

The million and a half GIs who "invaded" Britain before D-Day faced neither the hazards of language nor the army of prostitutes encountered in Italy. Instead the American command had to overcome traditional reserve and downright prudery. "The British consider sex behavior as entirely a personal matter not subject to legislation and regulation," reported the U.S. army's chief of preventative medicine. "Public opinion frowns on brothels and so very few are known to exist, and outside London there was very little commercialized prostitution."

But the average GI had very little difficulty in satisfying a hunger for female companionship.

To British women, the arrival of the Americans was a bright flash of excitement after nearly three years of blackouts and Blitz. It seemed to many that these strapping, well-fed, and confident young men has stepped straight out of a Hollywood movie. "Suddenly the GIs were there," recalled a Derby woman. "If they'd dropped from Mars we couldn't have been more surprised." A shy Preston girl remembered blushing when a smiling-faced GI told her, "Gee, you've got lovely eyes," and his partner called out, "She's just like a baby Betty Grable!" Another woman from Birmingham, who was a teenager at the time and described herself as "fancy free," was more explicit about the instant sexual attraction that drew British women to American soldiers:

We were half starved and drably clothed, but the GIs said we looked good anyway. A lot was said about them being oversexed, overpaid and over here; maybe it applied to a few, but it was mainly a myth which was put over by Lord Haw Haw in his Nazi propaganda broadcasts from Germany to upset British soldiers overseas and try to split the Allies. That's my story anyway — and I'm sticking to it! It was just the case that the British women and the American GIs were in the same place at the same time — it was rather pleasant, really!

Myth or not, the glamour of the American serviceman presented an implicit sexual rivalry to British husbands and older brothers, who resented the fascination that the "Yanks" held for their wives and girlfriends. It was the British male who coined and gave lip service to the wartime anti-American epithet that the only thing wrong with their Allies was that they were "overpaid, oversexed, and over here!" The reputation of "Yanks" was encouraged by wild press reports and letters from reactionary matrons like (Mrs. SPECTATOR) who expressed outrage that "girls of thirteen and fourteen have attached themselves to coloured soldiers and others and been able to see films that only have the effect of arousing in them instincts that ought to be unknown to them for many years."

It was not just the physical exuberance of the smartly turned-out American serviceman, touched with the aura of Hollywood extra, that provoked suspicion and hostility in the native male population. It was also a question of hard cash. British soldiers found themselves at a huge financial disadvantage when it came to competing for the entertainment of their own womenfolk. Even a lowly American private with his $3,000 average annual paycheck was a big spender by comparison with the 100 pounds received by his British ally. With 50 percent extra pay for flying duty and 20 percent extra for overseas and sea duty, nine out of ten GIs were above the $50 a month averaged in civilian life, and those who were single never had as much money in their lives —

and the only thing to spend it on was entertaining British girls! They were also prodigal with gifts of luxury foods passed on from their military supplies.

Even the way the Americans spoke marked them out as different and glamorous, often provoking naughty giggles from English girls when they used the GI slang expressions such as "bum" for a layabout and "rubbers" — the native word for erasers — when they referred to contraceptive sheaths. The prudish Hollywood Hays office censors had unwittingly protected movie audiences from many of the coarse expressions that were common parlance among American soldiers. "Holy Cow!" "Jeez!" and "Goddamn!" upset the girls who operated the telephone exchanges, who complained about the "blasphemous language" used by GIs. British teenagers, however, relished the new oaths that so upset their parents' sensibilities. A boy recalled the adolescent enthusiasm with which he and his friends bandied about their favorite GI expletives: "And I ain't a-shitting, boy!" or "You ain't a-tooting, boy!"

The British military authorities soon found it necessary to prepare a pamphlet for the female staff of the NAAFI military canteens advising them that the language and apparent freshness of the GIs should not always be taken at face value:

The first time that an American soldier approaches the counter and says, "Hiya, Baby!" you will probably think he is being impudent. By the time several dozen men have said it, you may have come to the conclusion that all Americans are "fresh." Yet to them it will be merely the normal conversational opening, just as you might say, "Lovely day, isn't it?" Remember that most Americans think that English people are "stand-offish." If you snub them you will merely confirm this impression.

Eisenhower's headquarters had also prepared a handbook that advised American soldiers of the more staid British customs and habits. At the same time the U.S. provost marshal had issued a leaflet "How to Stay Out of Trouble," which contained stern warnings about the "females of questionable character" who were eagerly awaiting them to get Yankee dollars. These were the very women that many GIs were hoping to encounter, of course — and they were not to be disappointed. "Their main aim in life," recalled a British wartime taxi driver, quoting the American vernacular, "seemed to be to get something to drink and 'a cute piece of ass.' "

Too young to be called up himself, John Lazenby spent the year before D-Day driving carloads of offduty GIs through picturesque Cotswold villages in pursuit of drink and girls. He learned all about their "camp-followers secreted in cottage attics" and "illicit trysts with local ladies." Their sexual banter and adventures with women resulted in his "rapid education in varied directions," like his "dreadfully innocent consternation one evening hearing a bunch of them yelling 'Just you look at Red's broad's tits like two goddamn milk bottles!' "

American servicemen deserved their reputation of being "wolves in wolves' clothing" when it came to making passes, but not all the English girls surrendered to their assaults. One ATS corporal recalled the evening she and two companions were trudging in pouring rain back to their barracks along a lonely road:

Along came a jeep with four Yanks in it. They stopped and offered us a ride. Although there were three of us, we just didn't trust them and turned the offer down. When I tell you that we had to walk the whole five miles back to camp, and preferred this to the lift, you will appreciate just how strongly we felt. I knew quite a few civvy girls who were "loved and left" — literally holding the baby.

The refusal of many predatory American soldiers to take no for an answer from a pretty girl, led to frequent complaints of sexual molestation. According to Mrs. Anne F., the mothers on a Birmingham housing estate near a U.S. army base protested that they had to use physical force to fend off the GIs. She soon developed her own technique of repulsing unwanted advances:

Almost every evening, I among others, would hear a knock on the front door and on opening it would find a GI who stated that a Greg So-and-So had sent him. When one flatly denied knowing his friend, he would calmly say, "Come on, baby, I know your husband is away in the forces." One would have to slam the door in their faces to keep them out. I remember one afternoon and evening the local camp was invaded by teenage girls and women from miles around. There were hundreds of them looking for Yanks. Next day the woods behind our estate were put "Out of Bounds" to the GIs. But the things we found in our front gardens were unbelievable! Some of the women had a "good time" with

Americans, others just did their washing for them, while others completely ignored them. The pubs made a packet out of them and the kids went a bundle on them as they were very generous with chocolate and sweets.

In London, the assault was more likely to be made first by the free-lance prostitutes known as "Piccadilly Commandos." These most brazen of wartime British tarts swarmed around the entrance to the Rainbow Club that was opened for Americans in 1942 in the old Del Monico's on the corner of Shaftesbury Avenue. The sign over the reception desk indicated "New York — 3,271 Miles," but the club promised a taste of home with its canteens, jukeboxes, and pool tables. "Rainbow Corner" became a magnet not only for homesick GIs in the London blackout, but also the regiments of streetwalkers whose opening "Hello, Yank, looking for a good time?" became a much parodied wartime joke.

Piccadilly *was* wartime London for American servicemen. Former Staff Sergeant Robert Arib recalled the standing joke in the Rainbow Club that it was "suicide" for a GI to go out into the blacked-out streets without his buddy:

The girls were there — everywhere. They walked along Shaftesbury Avenue and past the Rainbow Corner, pausing only when there was no policeman watching. Down at the Lyons Corner House on Coventry Street they came up to soldiers waiting in doorways and whispered the age-old questions. At the underground entrance they were thickest, and as the evening grew dark, they shone torches on their ankles as they walked and bumped into the soldiers murmuring "Hello, Yank," "Hello, soldier," "Hello, dearie!" Around the dark estuaries of the Circus the more elegantly clad of them would stand quietly and wait — expensive and aloof. No privates or corporals for these haughty demoiselles. They had furs and silks to pay for.

Betty Knox, a former dance-hall singer turned breezy columnist for the *London Evening Standard,* related a story that was supposedly typical of the GIs' attitude to London: "One night, as Ambassador John G. Winant left the American embassy he met two soldiers. Could he do anything for them, Winant enquired. 'Are there any dames in this joint?' one soldier asked. 'This is the American embassy, and I am the Ambassador,' Winant replied. 'Say, those Limies must have been pulling our legs,' the soldier stammered, backing off into the blackout."

"There is absolutely no end to the vulgar business of soldiers making love — or should I say lust — in public places; many cases are reported of the immoral act of intercourse going on in view of the public," complained Chaplain Frith in 1944 to his superiors in Washington about soldiers' behavior in London. "During morality lectures, the soldiers confessed to me, in a general way, that the reason they had thrown away all propriety was that they were away from home where no one knew them, and no one seemed to interfere to prohibit their freedom of action." The blackout, it appears, made the British policeman even more of a "friendly bobby" who could be relied on to turn a blind eye to couples making out in the dark sanctuary of a convenient telephone box or doorstep — and U.S. military police were more concerned with rowdy drunken GIs than with breaking up the trysting couples.

American soldiers were often surprised at the apparent lack of jealousy displayed by English males even when they flirted openly with their womenfolk. "Most of my friends had one particular GI Joe — and so did I," admitted one woman, who confessed that she was a "grass widow and a pretty young miss" who enjoyed the "parties galore" at the American bases. "My husband came home occasionally, and he was always welcomed; I'm sure he regarded himself more or less as 'just one of the boys.' " According to some women, other husbands serving overseas openly encouraged their wives not to be lonely. She cited the example of her friend: "One day I caught her crying and she let me read the letter from her husband. In it he said he was having a good time with the opposite sex and she should do likewise."

Not all husbands were as tolerant of their spouse's infidelities with their American allies. A GI who was stationed in Norfolk remembers how they lost one of his company, not to the enemy but to a British soldier who returned unexpectedly to the family home and "found one of our men in bed with his wife and threw the GI out of a second-story window and killed him. He was sent to prison."

The main sexually motivated wartime violence in Britain, however, arose not from clashes of GIs and resentful British husbands, but between white American soldiers and their black comrades over English women who refused to subscribe to the color bar that was enforced in the U.S. army.

The first serious clash between black and white GIs occurred in September 1943 in the sleepy Cornish town of Launceston. It resulted in two MPs being wounded in what came to be called "the Battle of Launceston." In Manchester the next year, the sight of a black sailor kissing a white English girl in a railway station sparked a series of race riots that brought a call for the city councillors to ban all GIs from places of entertainment for a fortnight. The censored wartime British press played down such incidents, including the fight that broke out in a pub near Kingsclere, Newbury, in December 1944. After the blacks were driven out of the bar by white GIs, they returned with rifles to shoot their way in, killing the publican's wife in the process.

Complaints about the bigotry and feuding between the black and white American soldiers resulted in the prime minister's being asked in the Commons to "make friendly representations to the American military authorities asking them to instruct their men that the colour bar is not the custom in this country." A Home Office letter of September 1942 made this official policy clear in a circular sent to all chief constables. But the secretary of war found himself on a "razor's edge" over the issue after a U.S. general issued orders that "white women should not associate with colored men. They should not walk out, dance or drink with them."

Many British women objected strongly to the discrimination. A NAAFI counter lady explained, "We find the coloured troops are much nicer to deal with in canteen life and such, we like serving them, they're always so courteous and have a very natural charm that most of the whites miss. Candidly, I'd rather serve a regiment of the dusky lads than a couple of whites."

"Some British women appear to find a peculiar fascination in associating with men of colour," noted a Home Office circular in 1943, giving voice to deeply rooted racial fears; "the morale of British troops is likely to be upset by rumours that their wives and daughters are being debauched by American coloured troops." Barbara Cartland wrote from her experience as a WAAF moral welfare adviser that the black soldiers had a powerful attraction for many girls:

It was the white women who ran after the black troops, not vice versa. Approximately 1,500 coloured babies were born in Britain during the war, but I am prepared to bet that if the truth were known it would prove in nearly every case the woman's fault. Women would queue outside the camps, they would not be turned away, they would come down from London by train, and they defeated the Military Police by sheer numbers.

Popular sympathy remained steadfastly on the side of the black regiments, even when the victim was a British woman. In May 1944 when a U.S. army court-martial sentenced to death a black GI for allegedly raping a housewife in a village near Bath, his case was taken up by the *Daily Mirror,* which exposed the conflict in the woman's testimony. She claimed she had been dragged out and assaulted after answering the door to the soldier who asked directions to Bristol. His defense was that he had already paid her a pound on two previous occasions to have intercourse and that it was only when he refused her demand of double that sum that she vowed to make trouble for him. The *Mirror* campaign sent a thirty-thousand-signature petition to General Eisenhower, who finally set aside the conviction in July for "lack of evidence."

"A new aspect of sex opened before us," wrote one respectable unmarried English woman then living at Tidworth near the large American encampments on Salisbury Plain:

It was not wrong to indulge, and right and proper if you were in love. We pooh-poohed these arguments at first, but we were all worn down in the end. I stuck to my principle for ages, even refusing an invitation to a cottage which someone had let to Larry, a tall and handsome West Point beau from the 2nd Armored Division, for a week. I spent a weekend in Bournemouth with him, without anything untoward happening. Then his roommate at Tidworth went off for the weekend and I madly and irresponsibly joined him there — and that was it. Fortunately his boast that American contraceptives were the best in the world turned out to be a fact. Larry whimsically kept his in a small cocoa tin.

"But we were not just 'an easy lay' although many of us were depressed by the war and the grayness of life in blacked out England," insisted one twenty-five-year-old English housewife, whose husband had been away three years fighting in North Africa. "We were bruised by such accusations." She wrote with feeling about her own wartime affair with an American army lieutenant:

My romantic memories are far too precious to go into print, but they gave me love of America I shall take to my grave. It was as lasting and sincere as many of the wartime loves were. In fact our "swop loves" in wartime as husbands or lovers were away, were often very innocent. But as sexual appetites vary, so it was in wartime — and my only near rape was as a result of two British servicemen, not Americans. Perhaps all Yanks were not after all so "oversexed" as the popular saying because our attitudes to women's behavior and couples' courting was still rather Victorian.

Margaret Mead, the celebrated anthropologist, observed in her contemporary study *The American Troops and the British Community* that the amatory success of the GIs with British girls had much to do with the differences in dating behavior on the other side of the Atlantic:

American men and boys enjoy the company of girls and women more than the British do. British boys don't go out with girls unless they have what one British boy described to me as "an ulterior purpose, good or bad." . . . To an American eye, the absence of flirting and backchat among secondary school boys and girls is astonishing. American boys and girls start having dates with each other in their early teens, long before they are emotionally mature enough for anything really connected with sex. . . . Of course this is very confusing to British girls who haven't had any practice.

The American servicemen had become so "practiced" in the arts of seduction that a popular joke that swept wartime Britain was "Heard about the new utility knickers? One Yank — and they're off." To get them off, however, more than one GI had to resort to the plea, "Gee, honey, I bin walking round the minefield, now when do I get the Purple Heart?"

By no means every American serviceman succeeded as readily as many boasted. An upper-class English lady insisted, "By and large, the Yanks all had beautiful manners, apologizing if one trod on *their* toes, but all ranks appeared to drink and get drunk. Middle-class people would be no more likely to have mixed with coarse Yanks as coarse Englishmen — and I saw no Lady Chatterley stuff!"

One woman who did worked in a munitions plant at Thatcham, near the airfield at Greenham Common from where the

American 82nd Airborne Division was flown to Normandy on the eve of D-Day. She volunteered to staff a GI tea-bar in Newbury, and from her factory windows the girls "could see Thatcham Station on payday when there were queues of GIs, billfolds bulging, waiting for the train to London."

The soldiers used to line up outside a hut by the railway line where the local "street ladies" lurked while officers and the MPs "turned blind eyes" to the goings-on. Lorryloads of GIs would often toss out chocolate bars or VD kits containing contraceptive rubbers as they roared through the Berkshire lanes. They blew them up like balloons and would festoon their lorries with them. Officers kerb-crawled for girls, three to a jeep. I loved their parties and found Americans such good dancers. There was much jealousy by British men and their memories have not dimmed as to what English women were "supposed to have got up to" while they were serving abroad. The Americans were so very trusting of us, wanting to be liked and be our guests. The pity of it was that enemy propaganda blew up the horrific stories of what we were up to "in bed with GI Joe" and encouraged the men overseas to think that they were being kept away until the Yanks were safely home again in the States.

An anonymous British versifier wrote "The Lament of the Limey Lass," two of whose bittersweet stanzas summed up the wistful sentiments of many of the women and girls who had fallen for brief affairs with Americans:

> They tell us we have teeth like pearls,
> They love our hair the way it curls,
> Our eyes could dim the brightest stars,
> Our figures beat Hedy Lamarr's.
>
> And then he leaves you broken hearted,
> The camp has moved — your love departed.
> You wait for mail that doesn't come,
> Then you realize you're awful dumb.

In answer to this resentful lament, a GI composed a retaliatory song that unromantically stated their predicament:

> With Yankee girls you can't compare —
> The difference is, You're here! They're there!

Yet many of the relationships were deep and romantic. After the American troops had departed for D-Day, a tent painted with the white message "Sorry, Jean, Had to Go — Johnny" was a poignant reminder of one broken heart they left behind. The U.S. army postal service recorded that over a quarter of the letters mailed by GIs from France during the first four weeks after 6 June 1944 were posted to addresses in the British Isles. Although scores of love affairs were to die on the battlefields of France, Belgium, and Germany, the fact that twenty thousand English girls applied to become the wives of American soldiers was testimony that a proportion of these romances endured the final year of the war.

The ubiquitous U.S. army jeep gave the American serviceman an advantage in the offduty pursuit of local women that was officially dignified as "rest and relaxation." It was not only a war-winning weapon, but a machine that helped to make the military alliance between the English-speaking powers into a romantic union when the American troops launched their "friendly" invasion of Australia in the spring of 1942. "It was rather fun finding ourselves comrades in arms with some of the flower of Australian womanhood," wrote one GI of his first encounter with their uniformed women. "For downright friendliness, Mom, the Aussies are the tops and that includes us Americans," another GI wrote home after landing in Sydney. The arrival of the jitterbugging Yanks blew a gale of fresh air in stuffy Australian dance-halls, where even the beer was rationed and the girls waltzed at arm's length. "Like South Dakota by the Sea" was another American's view of Melbourne and Townesville, where the arrival of the U.S. army swamped the female population with a thousand male escorts for every available local girl.

The warm welcome given the Yanks by the womenfolk was resented by Australia's male population. This anger flared into bar brawls that "made John Wayne fights look like high school picnics." The most celebrated series of pitched battles erupted in Sydney during the summer of 1942, when the Australian 1st Army Division arrived home. The troops were tempted to use some of the skills they had learned from battling against Rommel's troops against GIs accused of "stealing" their girls. But as usual, it took two to tango. An American sailor recalls being in a Sydney bar "full of soldiers, sailors and a few civilians and their women, all making love with almost no attempt at privacy. It reminded me of paintings by Breughel the Elder."

Many women looked back on their romantic encounters — chaste and unchaste — with Americans as one of World War II's uplifting experiences. "I'm sure they helped to bring us out of our insular shells," one British housewife observed. "My girlfriend and I often went out with them. They were great company and there was an awful anticlimax when they all went home."

The GI invasion did indeed shake some of the British out of their insular attitudes to sex. The American military obliged their hosts to educate the public to an awareness of venereal disease, which produced a healthier attitude to sex and a healthier postwar generation. The alarming consequences of the prodigious sexual activity of GIs in Britain was revealed by the VD statistics that tripled from twenty cases per thousand to almost sixty per thousand by the first months of 1943. This was nearly three times the rate of troops in the United States and six times higher than the average level reported by the British army for soldiers on home duty. The chief of preventative medicine of the U.S. army called for action at the highest governmental level, endorsing the findings of the American Social Hygiene Association fact-finding mission:

There does not exist in British law a basis for venereal disease control and prostitution of the sort that we have in this country. . . . The attitude of the British public towards venereal disease and prostitution is quite dissimilar to the attitude in this country. Nothing like the public education carried on in this country has been experienced by the British public.

The first year of the American "occupation" of Britain brought frustration to the U.S. army medical staff because their attempts to establish prophylactic treatment centers and contact-tracing for suspected carriers were blocked by the 1916 Venereal Diseases Act, which made it libelous to imply inaccurately that someone carried the disease. Condoms were also in critically short supply because of the scarcity of latex in the wake of the Japanese takeover of Malaya, and those that were available in Britain were of a particularly uncomfortable design, which many GIs complained was "too small."

Prophylactic posts, under American Red Cross supervision, were permitted to be set up near the famed Rainbow Corner and at accessible locations throughout London including each main railway station. But as long as civilian health education lagged far behind that of the United States, the only source of information about the "unmentionable" social disease was "discreet little advertisements announcing the location of treatment centers in public latrines." Complained a U.S. army wartime report:

British sensibilities forbade the display of prominent signs and the rigid requirements of the total blackout forbade the use of the conventional green light. Perhaps the most important reason for the small use of station prophylaxis arose from the fact that the vast majority of the sexual exposures were wholly uncommercial and on a friendly basis. Surveys among soldiers revealed that under these circumstances they were much less impressed with the desirability or necessity of prophylaxis after exposure.

A high-ranking Joint Committee on Venereal Diseases was set up under Ministry of Health auspices to consult the American and Canadian military authorities. Under American pressure it met in the summer of 1943, but it "bogged down in a discussion of prostitution and was never revived." But it was months before the Ministry of Health could persuade a reluctant government to reinstitute the anti-VD measures that had been used in World War I. The new regulations did go part of the way to meeting the American proposals for establishing a system to trace civilian women who were suspected of being infected. Contacts could be followed up only after being named by two separate individuals — and after the case had been given the go-ahead by the Ministry of Health. Investigations were to be hampered by the desperate shortage of trained civilian medical staff, but more were recruited when it was found that fewer than 15 percent of the women who were suspected carriers had actually applied for treatment.

One enterprising Norfolk prostitute, who had been named by no fewer than five GIs as a source of venereal infection, went so far as requesting that the Ministry of Health help her get the American bomber station at Shipham to post on the camp bulletin board her notice and medical certificate announcing that she had been successfully treated. "Request Refused" was the terse answer from the commanding officer.

Even the most straitlaced of Britain's town councils had been sufficiently alarmed at the rising VD rate to agree to cooperate with the crash advertising and public education program launched by the Ministry of Health in 1943. After some heated debate in Parliament and racy speculation in the press, the chief medical officer of the Ministry of Health announced the launching of "the most intensive effort in the field of health education yet undertaken in this country." Its goal was "to try to break the taboo on the public mention of syphilis and gonorrhea and so dispel the secrecy which for generations has favoured the spread of venereal disease."

Labeled by fastidious civil servants as the "Let Knowledge Grow" campaign, its purpose was to make the public aware of the dangers and symptoms of the disease for which free treatment had already been available for a quarter-century. Initially it had been feared that the public would react squeamishly to words such as "intercourse" and "sexual organs" appearing in the press, on the radio, and in films and lectures that were shown in factories, clubs, and even some schools. Government surveys, contrary to anticipation, revealed that there was no squeamishness to the anti-VD campaign, which, by the end of the war, had made the public thoroughly familiar with the disease through artfully explicit posters, which 90 percent of the people interviewed approved. "It is hard to realize that even at the beginning of this war, the words syphilis and gonorrhea were taboo," noted the London correspondent of the *New York Herald-Tribune*.

The wartime VD campaign unleashed an enormous public response indicated by the eighty thousand letters received by the Ministry of Health, mostly from women. These revealed that VD was most prevalent in nineteen- to twenty-three-year-olds and that "infection often results from a romantic love affair or a single act of promiscuity with an apparently 'respectable' man." The success of the British "Let Knowledge Grow" campaign was due in large part to the shock value of the posters — one showed a woman's veiled hat jauntily perched atop a skull with the headline "Hello, boyfriend, coming MY way?" above a warning that "The 'easy' girlfriend spreads Syphilis and Gonorrhea, which *unless properly treated* may result in blindness, insanity, paralysis, premature death."

The wartime health education campaign was ultimately responsible for the erosion of the taboos against explicit public discussion of sex. In the military context it was responsible for the decline of VD cases both in the civilian population and among American troops pouring into England for the crucial cross-Channel assault. U.S. army statistics reveal that in the months leading up to May 1944, the rate of infections fell by nearly two-thirds — although sexual activity must certainly have not. The statistical data, moreover, indicates the health campaign spared around fifteen thousand GIs — or enough men to man a front-line infantry division — from falling casualty to syphilis or gonorrhea during the months before and after the invasion of France. The Allied ground forces proved to be only just sufficient to tip the military balance during the June battle for Normandy. It is therefore not difficult to appreciate an early concern of its planners that the greatest amphibious assault of the war might have been threatened by a pre-invasion VD-Day.

★ ⟦ 15 ⟧ ★

Yielding to the Conquerors

The average soldier who landed at Utah Beach and survived to take Germany, the man who was neither stud nor sissy, probably slept with something like twenty-five women during the war — and few of them were, I might add, prostitutes."

— GI WITH 4TH ARMORED DIVISION, 1945

It seems to me that while the American Forces are doing their big part in the invasion of Europe in a temporal way, we are also invading other lands in a moral and spiritual way, and the imprint we are leaving on the invaded peoples is not too good a picture.

— U.S. ARMY CHAPLAIN, JUNE 1944

"Y ou will go there as liberating heroes and those women will be eager and urgent in the solicitation of you. Now bear these facts in mind," American troops embarking for the D-Day invasion were warned. "The women who will be soliciting your attentions are prostitutes of the most promiscuous type." Mindful of the degree to which the strength of the Allied armies in Italy had been sapped by VD, and fearful that medical services in France had been run down by the German occupation, Allied medical and military planners had taken unprecedented measures to keep the troops spearheading the liberation of Europe safe from disease.

A fleet of mobile VD treatment centers staffed by two medical officers and six orderlies had been mounted on three-ton trucks "to treat as far forward as possible all cases of primary and recurrent venereal diseases." Equipped with thousands of high-strength penicillin doses, they were to provide quick treatment injections to keep up strength at the fighting front. The hitherto limited supplies of the "wonder drug" had already saved thousands of battle casualties from serious infection. Some medical experts were against using the "magic bullet" of penicillin as a fast cure for venereal disease on the grounds that it would remove a powerful restraint on the troops. But strategic rather than moral considerations enabled the D-Day planners to overcome the objections that a "one-shot" treatment would encourage military promiscuity.

The easy availability of a quick cure was a comforting reassurance for those members of the Allied forces who were encouraged by the enthusiasm of the reception they received in the towns and villages of Normandy to celebrate the liberation. Nor did their commanders interfere. Within hours of the American capture of Cherbourg, two houses of prostitution were doing a roaring trade "run for, and indirectly by, American troops, with the familiar pattern of the designation of one brothel for Negro troops and the other for white, with a military patrol stationed at the doors to keep order in the queues which formed." The SHAEF medical inspectors might protest this infraction of military regulations, but they could do little but insist that "Off Limits" notices were pasted on the French-run "Closed Houses" that reopened for business even before the shelling had stopped. Battling the Germans was of more concern to the Allied commanders, and they regarded posting military guards outside the brothels as a waste of military manpower.

"Approximately 60 percent of my company had relations at one time or another with professional prostitutes or pick-up girls," noted a sociologist who fought in Normandy — and it was the same story for the British and Canadian troops. One English soldier recalled with amusement his first visit to a brothel shortly after D-Day:

We went in and there was a small bar full of ladies hanging about in their underwear and brassieres. "Act natural!" I said to Knobby, "pretend you have gone into one of these all your life." I went across to a beautiful blonde girl who was holding a poodle and boldly asked, "*Voulez-vous couchez avec moi et combien?*" I had 200 francs, which I reckoned to be more than enough, and to my delight and Knobby's surprise, she agreed and took us up to her room. To my dismay she insisted on get-

ting out a basin and washing my privates. In the cold water my anticipation withered so rapidly that she tickled it with her finger and said,
"*Alors, c'est un petit patron.*" I said, "Just you wait a moment!"

When the Germans were finally put to headlong flight across
the Seine in August, SHAEF's chief of preventative medicine acknowledged that because of some Allied generals' "firm conviction that the operation of brothels was a duty which the army
owed the individual soldier," they were losing the battle against
the French prostitutes:

The history of venereal disease control problems in France has been
largely one of difference of opinion between those who favored segre-
gation and licensing of prostitution and those who opposed it. Unfortunately the subject being what it is, it has never been possible to gain
a free and open discussion; it is generally accounted that since the War
Department policy is clearly stated and specifically directs the repression of prostitution, it is necessary to give apparent support to such a
policy, even while doing the contrary.

George S. Patton was one of the generals who persisted with
the "contrary policies" he had followed during the Sicily campaign. He infuriated the chaplains in his Third Army by encouraging the opening of a string of brothels that were supervised by
military medical personnel. "I realize that our Commanding
General is not a typical officer, and if I thought for a moment
that he was I would be tempted to reconsider my decision to stay
in the regular army," wrote Father H. F. Donovan of the 29th
Infantry Division to the War Department, and detailed the extent of Patton's transgressions:

After my last Mass yesterday I drove to the house of prostitution, received the information from the MP on duty that 44 men had made
use of the house between 2 P.M. (opening time) and 4:27 P.M., took a
picture of the sign "BLUE & GRAY CORRAL RIDING LESSONS —
100 FRANCS" and a picture of the 45th customer, whose name, rank
and number I have. . . . I passed by the House again and was present
when an MP officer closed it and put it "Off Limits" at 6:57 P.M. — 76
men had made use of the House.

American officers were not moral exemplars. Their activities brought charges from the French town council in Bayeux that they had made "a public pastime," according to another army chaplain:

German officers had run their brothels quietly. They did not demand that the owners of private billets *"couchez avec"* as American officers did. The French Welcome Societies stopped furnishing girls to American army camps for dances because of immoral treatment. I personally saw about a dozen officers taking French girls into their billets during the dance, turning off the lights and being there from one half to one hour at a time.

Even before the first Allied troops entered the French capital, it was appreciated that any attempt to put the hundreds of Parisian brothels off limits to Allied soldiers would have been doomed to futility. Accordingly, on 2 September 1944, the provost marshal of the Seine Section U.S. army toured the city brothels accompanied by a representative of the Brigade Mondaine "for the express purpose of selecting certain houses of prostitution to be set aside for officers, others for white enlisted men, and still others for colored enlisted men." American headquarters in France faced up to the reality of the situation even if their policy was "somewhat interfered with." Three days later the chief surgeon of the U.S. army ordered the French Ministry of the Interior to direct all prefects of police to exclude all U.S. military personnel from the brothels or close them! The "unofficial policy" nevertheless prevailed, in the face of repeated criticisms from the War Department, because the local military commanders were "unable or unwilling" to assist in policing the red-light areas which the French authorities regarded as a necessary social convenience.

The brothels of Paris enjoyed their second wartime boom as American and other Allied troops crowded into the narrow streets of Montmartre and the other red-light areas. The U.S. army headquarters at the Hotel Scribe, according to a *Newsweek* correspondent, "had all the better aspects of Custer's last stand" with the street lined with jeeps whose embattled drivers were assaulted by streetwalkers. "The women of Paris are still very smart.

They dress fit to kill and make up thickly but on the whole artistically. . . . but Chanel No. 5 doesn't smell the same as it did in 1940, although the 'feelthy picture man' is still there."

Paris became the mecca for "rest and recreation" during the final months of the war in Europe. The city became, in the words of an American colonel, "the natural objective of every soldier on pass or furlough; and countless numbers of soldiers in groups all the way from one or two to entire convoys 'got lost' on their way from hither to yon and would end up in Paris for a bit of sight-seeing. The German occupation had done nothing to improve the morals and behavior of the Parisian women of the brothels and boulevards and the lack of food, and later of fuel, gave the American soldier with a K-ration an unbeatable bargaining position."

One GI enthusiastically explained in a letter to his father back in San Francisco:

French girls are easy to get, what with American cigarettes and chocolate and us being heroes in their eyes, so I'm not going to be choosey from now on and get my fun where I can get it while I'm still alive. And to hell with tomorrow — it may never come. . . . I hear penicillin will cure 95% of VD cases in one day. Do any of your doctors use it yet? But don't worry about me, I'll try to be careful.

Graphs showing VD statistics, euphemistically referred to as the "Hit Parade," were posted in the regimental headquarters of every U.S. army unit. There was a sixfold increase in the fall of 1944, and two-thirds of all those troops who contracted sexual infections in France attributed it to their stay in Paris.

The British army suffered the same VD casualty rate in liberated Belgium. Ghent alone was reported to have two hundred registered and seven hundred unregistered prostitutes, and nearly all of its one hundred forty-eight small cafés functioned as brothels. Not every sexual encounter was with a prostitute, as one Scottish sergeant fondly recalled of his night of passion with a young girl called Janine just after Brussels was liberated:

A warmth and pleasurable joy swept over me as I lay in the arms of the loveliest girl in the world, her long hair falling like silken water over my shoulders. Her lips filled me with gasping urgency and my stroking hands reaching for some joy I never knew existed. The girl Janine, in

my arms, whispering to me, stroking my head, kissing my face and
reaching for the happiness that eludes men and women in time of war,
never knowing if this day is going to be your last on this earth. Her
insistent hushing as we made love lulled me into another sleep, till in a
rushing dream I was roused by her strident tones "*Allez Jock . . . Six
heures . . . Allez!*" All that day I was filled with one aim, to get off duty
as quickly as possible and return to the avenue du Canada. My heart
was thumping like a child at his first party as I jumped from the tram
at the terminus, my small pack bumping heavily on me with its load of
cigarettes and chocolate . . . then I saw the house . . . Janine's house.
. . . Its walls were now daubed with obscenities and rough painted
swastikas. Above the door were two large scrawls "TRAITEUR COL-
LABORATEUR." There was no movement within the silent rooms, only
the whispering of a torn curtain in the window of her bedroom. A tear
fell from my eye as I thought of Janine — then I walked into the war
once more.

In Brussels, it became impossible for a British soldier to walk
"more than ten to twenty yards" without being accosted by a fresh
streetwalker. By March 1945, the VD rate had climbed to such
an alarming level that SHAEF headquarters shipped penicillin
supplies to civilian hospitals in the Belgian cities to treat the
prostitutes who were suspected of harboring sexual infections.
With the push across the frontiers of the Third Reich now gathering pace, it had become essential to cut down the VD attrition
rate and maintain the strength of frontline units. When German
cities and towns began falling to the Allied advance, SHAEF
headquarters counted on Eisenhower's "nonfraternization" policy to check the epidemic of promiscuity which afflicted the
"Crusaders for Democracy."

The moral chaos into which the Thousand Year Reich crumbled during the final months of World War II defeated any strict
enforcement of "nonfraternization."

When the Allies fought their way through to the Rhineland
towns in the spring of 1945, they found bands of youngsters calling themselves Edelweiss gangs, who sported pink shirts and
bobby-sox. They roamed the rubble hurling insults and stones at
the Hitler Youth — when they were not trading sexual favors with
willing girls. "Nazism has so poisoned the nation that neither
marriage nor chastity is respected. Soldiers' wives have lovers.
Married women are unfaithful to their husbands. Husbands

openly sport mistresses" was the rationale offered by one gang leader in Düsseldorf for his group's sexual promiscuity. Parental as well as administrative discipline had collapsed under the Allied land and air assault, and by the time American forces reached Berlin, the problem was so pervasive that GIs were astonished to be accosted by young girls in the city's ruined streets.

When Germany surrendered on 7 May 1945, an estimated four million fathers and elder brothers of the defeated male population remained in Russian captivity. This contributed to the "unofficial polygamy" between German women and the men of the occupying armies — in 1945 one out of every five German births was estimated to be illegitimate. That a large percentage of these children were fathered by Allied soldiers was an indication of the rapid failure of General Eisenhower's original "nonfraternization" policy. The "liberation" of German women began despite a U.S. army decree that contracting VD inside the German frontier would be taken as "prima facie" evidence of fraternization, entailing a $65 fine. Neither the policy nor the penalty was effective. Officers and soldiers in every Allied army were soon fraternizing openly. As an American intelligence officer reported from Aachen, one of the first towns in the Third Reich to fall under Allied control, it was difficult for the average GI to regard the native women as hostile:

The essential kindness of the American soldier was in evidence. Soldiers helped German housewives with their chores, played with the children and through other small acts of friendship made living more tolerable through the creation of a friendly atmosphere. Conversation with some of those soldiers evoked such comments as: "These Germans aren't bad people. We get along with them OK. All you've got to do is to treat them good and you have no trouble."

Germany's female population did not resist the demands of the occupying soldiers; as one American report put it, "Women were told that it was right and patriotic to bear children for any soldiers desiring the same." They soon discovered that sex could be traded for food and cigarettes from the GIs, who unlike their British comrades in arms had not suffered the bombing of their homes by the Luftwaffe and found it easier to forgive the Germans. The average GI, it seemed, could identify with the cleanliness and domestic values espoused by the conquered, but still house-proud, German women. "Despite living in cellars and bombed buildings, the German civilians have kept clean," one U.S. army intelligence officer noted. "The girls, in particular, look out of place amid the debris. They wear bobby sox and pigtails with gay colored ribbons. They wear thin dresses, and they are fond of standing in the sun."

"We cannot expect the GI to behave differently," observed an American officer who urged the abandonment of the unworkable nonfraternization policy. "After all, he is human. He wants companionship — he's lonely, and the Germans are pastmasters at getting around men who feel that way." Physical and sexual hunger combined with a flourishing black market to make sex a commodity to be traded for the necessities of life. "In this economic setup, sex relations, which function like any other commodity, assume a very low value," explained one U.S. army survey. "Because of this situation, plus the fact that every American soldier is a relative millionaire by virtue of his access to PX rations, the average young man in the occupation army is afforded an unparalleled opportunity for sexual exposure." The unofficial "rate of exchange" in Berlin immediately after the end of the war was: "German girls consider four cigarettes good pay for all night. A can of corned beef means true love."

The lifting of censorship in the summer of 1945 encouraged newspapers in America and Britain to run sensational stories that ridiculed the failure of the nonfraternization policy. "Have six years of war not taught us to call a spade a spade rather than a digging implement?" an English army captain in Germany wrote anonymously to *The Spectator*. "It would be better to confess our sexual trespasses, as our European neighbors so blithely do theirs, than to risk alienating our friends by denying the true basis of 'Fraternization' which is primarily sexual and not a social impulse, a get-together with German womankind and not with the German race."

American war correspondent Julian Bach reported on what he called a "vast social, ideological and moral upheaval" that was taking place in the ruins of the Thousand Year Reich:

When a pack of king-size cigarettes brings $18.50 on the Berlin black market, then the economy is sick. When a buxom fraulein, taught by

Hitler to loathe and despise all "North American Apes," turns around, and, for the sake of a handful of Hersheys, cuddles up to a GI whose name she does not know (and probably could not conveniently pronounce), then moral values are in travail.

So much fraternization was taking place in Germany during the spring and summer of 1945 that GIs jokingly compared it to Prohibition. One staff sergeant in the 30th Infantry Division explained the difference: "In the old days a guy could hide a bottle inside his coat for days at a time, but it is hard to keep a German girl quiet in there for more than a couple of hours." A tank driver commented, "Fraternization? Yeah, I suppose it's all right. Anyway I've been doing it right along. But every now and then I wake up in a cold sweat. I dream that we are at war again and the German bastards I'm fighting this time are my own!"

The hostile press publicity brought an exchange of top-level communications between General Marshall and SHAEF headquarters, which was followed by an official relaxation in June 1945 that began with the directive that the nonfraternization order was "obviously not expected to be applied to small children." Social contact with women was soon allowed because of what Eisenhower assured correspondents was "the rapid progress which has been made in carrying out Allied de-nazification policies." As one philosophical American soldier/writer observed, "Women are always the first to un-make the conquest and betray the conqueror — and properly, else the males' preposterous wars would continue for ever, unrelieved by sanity."

A very different attitude was encountered in Japan, where, to the embarrassment of General MacArthur and the delight of the GIs, more than adequate provision had been made for the occupying soldiers. In accordance with the Oriental view of sex as a necessity uncomplicated by the taboos and inhibitions of Christian doctrine, the nation that had dispatched medically inspected prostitutes to army bordellos on the Pacific outposts of their empire also set up facilities to meet the "rest and recreation" requirements of the American army. To forestall a wholesale violation of Japanese women, plans had been made even before the first American soldier had set foot in Tokyo to build a $6 million bar and café complex to house "5,000 women entertainers" who, according to the coy announcement in the *Nippon Times*, "will entertain Allied troops."

When the first GIs arrived, they found temporary "Special Recreation Centers" had already been set up in the surviving unbombed factories because only nine of the three hundred ten brothels that had packed Tokyo's celebrated Yoshiwara red-light district had survived the American firestorm raids. Price lists for these "establishments" were posted on the quartermaster bulletin boards in all U.S. army camps — with the ever-present reminder about the need for prophylaxis to avoid infection:

20 yen — a buck and a quarter — for the first hour, 10 yen for each additional hour and all night for 50 yen. If you pay more, you spoil it for all the rest. The MP's will be stationed at the doors to enforce these prices. Trucks will leave here each hour, on the hour. NO MATTER HOW GOOD IT FEELS WITHOUT ONE, BE SURE TO WEAR ONE.

In addition to the "Special Recreation Centers," the street corners of the bombed-out Yoshiwara district were soon crowded with young Japanese girls sporting gaudy rayon pajamas and crude attempts at Western makeup and hairstyles.

Outraged chaplains protested that the U.S. army was sanctioning "licensed houses of prostitution" — and with VD rates at near epidemic levels in Europe, medical supervision was being unofficially supplied to the "recreation centers." Some Catholic officers made themselves unpopular with the GIs and MacArthur's staff by insisting on hewing to a stricter moral line. A veritable typhoon broke in the American press after a navy chaplain had complained to *Newsweek* magazine that the liberty men on his ship were directed to "houses of prostitution" in the Yokosuka where there was a separate "geisha house" for officers and chiefs. He had personally watched "a line of enlisted men, four abreast, almost a block long, waiting their turn," and his letter continued:

MPs kept the lines orderly. As the men were admitted into the lobby, they would select a prostitute (113 on duty that day), pay 10 yen to the Jap operator, then go with the girl to her room. When the men returned they were registered and administered prophylaxis by Navy corpsmen.

"The Navy neither authorizes nor forbids patronage of houses of prostitution, but takes all practical measures to safeguard the health of personnel" was the equivocal denial issued by Admiral Nimitz. The commander in chief of the U.S. Navy Pacific was obliged to publicly acknowledge for the first time the hypocrisy of the Allied military policy, which provided discreet medical supervision for the local prostitutes while turning deaf ears to the protests of zealous chaplains.

As one service chaplain spelled out:

We have won the victory of arms. We believed that the civilization for which we fought was immensely superior to the KULTUR of the German, who under Hitler's leadership, placed boys and girls camps near together, with obvious expectation. We have read with horror the Japanese concept of women as men's playthings. But will the parents and families to whom American servicemen return, their thinking warped by "take-a-pro" morality, will these families be convinced that the better civilization has won? Or that we lost our civilization in winning the war?

Many European women who thought they were going to marry a Yank would never see the promised land. "There were, I remember, American GIs and officers who most cruelly betrayed and seduced Neapolitan girls, concealing from them and their families that back in the United States they'd a wife and kids," wrote Sergeant John H. Burns. Yet many GIs did make good on their matrimonial promises. By the end of the war some sixty thousand immigration applications had been filed by British war brides and another eight thousand by French, Italian, and Dutch women, with four thousand from Australian and New Zealand women.

One English girl's GI boyfriend, who had promised to come back and marry her, was wounded and shipped back to the United States. He mailed the engagement ring, and to speed her application for a visa, she agreed to go through a proxy marriage. "It was held in a Roman Catholic church where all the family worshipped and was heard over the American radio network and reported in all the local papers. I listened in over the transatlantic telephone and could even hear the organ playing in the church and the giving of their vows." But after all the publicity the newly "wedded" couple were disappointed to find that the state of North Carolina did not recognize the legality of her proxy marriage and this particular GI bride never saw the United States.

Such was the appeal of America as the land of every British girl's wartime dreams that many of them married on trust. A transit camp had to be set up in the south of England to process the migration that the War Department called "Operation War Bride." Early in 1946 the first six hundred sailed for the United States aboard the steamship *Argentina,* which had been specially fitted out as a nursery ship. Many of the women in the "bride ships" crossed the Atlantic with a sense of apprehension that was heightened by having to nurse seasick infants. But the fate that awaited them in booming postwar America was bright, compared to the bleak future that faced the thousands of displaced families jamming the refugee camps in war-shattered Europe. One British war bride recalled:

My first impression of America was all food. It was absolutely sickening to see the amount of food. We went out to dinner the first night I arrived in New York and I remember a steak that was the size of my plate, it was more than I had had in England during the entire war! Anybody who had come out at that point was overwhelmed by the amount of food, we had been hungry for a long time. Everybody there was so tired by the end of the war, but here was a country teeming with vitality. It took me a time to catch my breath and become part of it.

America proved to be the promised land for many of these new immigrants. One English woman married a U.S. army sergeant despite her parents' objects that her future husband was a fisherman. She went to the United States after the war expecting to have to work as a secretary in hard times. When she arrived at Redondo Beach, California, however, she discovered that he "owned a fleet of five boats and was in a very good line of business."

But not every GI bride found the glamour and excitement that her wartime romance had led her to expect. Peggy was one of the unfortunate ones who realized, too late, that she had made a terrible mistake. When she came to the end of her long journey she found herself and her two children face to face with her husband, out of uniform for the first time, and not in glamorous Hollywood or exciting New York, but in a grimy town in Pennsylvania:

It was getting dark when I got off the train. He was wearing one of those long overcoats like I'd seen people wearing in the old movies. He looked like Himmler. I stared at him and thought, "Lord! What have you married?" And his mother! I was shocked to find that she was German to the hilt. The first thing she said was "Ach die Lebersehen!" when she saw the two children. I looked at him and said, "Am I really in America?" I woke up next morning and I told him, "I'm going home. I don't like it here."

"Like many young girls at that time, they were infatuated with the GIs and who could blame them?" observed a British woman whose best friend had married an American soldier, only to return.

It was not just the women that the GIs married and brought back who made an impact on the American male. "My husband says the girls in Europe aren't like us. They're more human and understanding" became a common complaint of the wives of veterans in the year after the war ended. *The Ladies' Home Journal* went to one of the new arrivals for an answer:

I am surprised in this country, where you put so much emphasis on all the surface aspects of sex, that you shy away from the real meaning behind them. Your movies, your ads, your magazine illustrations, are full of allure and romance. Yet you shy away from the real relationship between men and women, which can be the richest, finest experience of your life. You make jokes about it instead. Like the European girls, all your young girls want to get married. But when they do, so many of them act as though they'd achieved their goal and finished a job. They seem to think everything should now come their way. I'd say European women don't feel this way about marriage. They feel it's the beginning of a job, at which they must keep working. They're happy to work at it, because they know it can be the most rewarding job in the world.

This was perhaps one of the lessons that the "girls they met over there" during World War II sent back from the Old World to the New.

The Seeds of Sexual Revolution

World War II affected women profoundly. Before the war, unless the job was something very special, married women left work and the man was expected to provide. All that changed with the war — so did women's attitudes. Many of us were earning almost as much as the men and we learned to be not so dependent. Life spent sweating over a hot stove became a thing of the past for many.

— A BRITISH HOUSEWIFE

Like you, Mrs. America, Eureka will put aside its uniform and return to the ways of peace . . . building household appliances.

— EUREKA VACUUM CLEANER ADVERTISEMENT, 1943

"Was the permissive society set at this time?" mused one of the first British war brides of 1939. On reflection she agreed the collective wartime experience of her generation played its part in shaping the "sexual revolution" two decades later:

It was all there then, not quite so obvious as now. Whenever young vital people meet in unusual and unsettling circumstances, there will always be a permissive group. Togetherness in the blackout was the car seat or doorway. We were brought together that way by the pressures of time and shortage of accommodation and a sense of unsettling uncertainty, in fact nothing was positive. Our generation, through sex education in the forces and all the "free talk," learnt a thing or two about birth control. Few of us lived mentally or physically for tomorrow — or even next week. Many relationships were set for as long as war lasted — or the posting arrived for elsewhere. A free and easy — in some ways a slightly mad style of living took over. Many girls were married or spoken for, but husbands and boyfriends were not there. Company relieved the tension of what was about to happen. In the background a slight fear hid behind the bravado. The then current saying — given with a grin — was "Don't worry, it may never happen." It often did! Many girls were left pregnant with no hope of marriage because of death, overseas posting or denial. Wartime work was plentiful for us and men were there for the taking. Girls were now able to walk into a public house and order their own drinks and buy cigarettes. We paid for our own cinema tickets and the days of sharing costs had begun. No one would have thought of a date paying her own way before the war. But we didn't feel obliged to allow favours, if we didn't fancy the escort in "that" way.

The lives and moral attitudes of many millions of people had undergone an extensive emotional trauma, and in the unsettled conditions of wartime many social inhibitions had lost their restraining force. Making the best of the present without thinking about the future had led to pleasure-seeking and increased promiscuity. A British woman summed up in 1945 the personal impact that the war had on her life and that of her contemporaries:

We have known terror and heartbreak, frustration, strain, the unbearable joy which unexpected happiness amid war can mean, in all a worldwide testing of limb and spirit which has never been imposed on any earlier generation. We have matured more rapidly, emotionally, than any previous generation — excluding even the last war's, for then war was localised and women did not play a direct part in it.

Even before World War II had ended its social costs were being measured not just in the lives lost and the destruction of homes, but by the continued upswing in the barometer of illegitimacy, venereal disease, and divorce rates. This was taken as an indication that there had been a wartime breakdown in public and private sexual conduct, and something approaching a moral panic overtook church and lay organizations on both sides of the Atlantic. They began calling for firm and fast action to restore the old moral values of "The Married Way" and sexual continence. Indeed, so many marriages were threatened by wartime adulteries that one English bishop proposed a blanket indulgence for war-separated couples who went through another religious ceremony to renew their marriage vows.

This was too radical a proposal to be taken seriously even by the Church of England, whose spiritual head, the Archbishop of Canterbury, had launched a crusade of moral reconstruction two months after the death of Hitler had signaled the final destruction of the Nazi evil. Addressing the nation from the pulpit of his ancient cathedral on Sunday, 12 July 1945, the archbishop called upon people to reject "wartime morality" and return to living Christian lives. "People are not conscious of injuring the war effort by dishonest or sexual indulgence," he warned, "and as the war effort is the one regulating factor of their lives, this part of their lives remains unregulated."

There was general public agreement that the archbishop was right in denouncing the "breakdown in morals." Another ranking British clergyman even gave a catalogue of what he described as "the grim facts" of a national malaise, citing:

the increase in divorce, the declining birthrate, the spread of venereal disease, and the number of young couples who, as always in wartime, wed in haste without any intention of fulfilling the primary purposes of marriage. This is partly due to the influence of wartime conditions, and partly to the flaunting sale of contraceptives. Life is so uncertain that young people are apt at the same time to snatch at the immediate satisfaction of sex, and also be unduly cautious as to taking any risks in life. The throwing together of men and women in close proximity in war work has created a whole host of new problems. . . . It is to be feared that promiscuous sex is on the increase. Here the alarming factor is the growth of amateur prostitution, especially among younger girls.

"Are We Facing a Moral Breakdown?" also became the subject of national concern in America, where the divorce and juvenile delinquency rates made it the hot topic of WOR radio station's popular "Forum of the Air." The debate, which was aired within weeks of Japan's formal surrender, reflected a significant difference in the moral climate of the victorious Anglo-Saxon powers. In Britain the decline in national mores was equated with doom-laden prophecy that unless it was arrested the British Empire would crash like Imperial Rome, while in the United States the moral aftermath of the war was regarded as part of the ongoing process of social evolution. A consensus of American church leaders, educators, and labor officials was that while there had been a "loss of moral tone," the war had only "accelerated changes already taking place in courtship, marriage, family life and the interrelationship of the sexes. These changes, though rapid and disrupting, do not necessarily mean 'breakdown.' "

Even the French, who had prided themselves on their country's liberality in sexual affairs, succumbed to postwar moral fervor. With impeccable Gallic logic, the forces of reaction set about changing the law, to make brothels illegal. Led by the formidable campaigner Madame Marthe Richard, the challenge to the "*maisons tolerées*" quickly drew public support with charges that the brothelkeepers had profited from collaboration during the German occupation. By 1946, the ancient trade that had helped make Paris the erotic capital of Europe was proscribed, and the brothels were obliged to close their doors forever.

The call to put back the moral clock had been started in the United States a full year earlier when ex-President Herbert Hoover had warned that "the moral life of America is in danger," in April 1944. "We must accept the fact that total war relaxes moral standards on the home front and that this imperils the whole front of human decency," he wrote in a magazine article that drew attention to the emptiness of a military victory if not accompanied by a "moral victory."

Military victory, however, had been won only by millions of American and British citizens sacrificing the trappings of a civilized morality. Moral and social taboos, once broken, were not too easily restored, especially when the traditional patterns of life had been disrupted for so many for so long. It was beyond even the propaganda resources of governments to recondition the wartime mass psychology overnight. The brutalizing and dislocative effects of war had left many individuals reacting to the cessation of hostilities as another interruption in the transient pattern of existence to which they had become accustomed. Millions of demobilized servicemen had grown used to an adventurous existence that did not reach beyond tomorrow. It took months and even years for many of them to accustom themselves again to a routine civilian existence — this was especially hard for those who had entered the services straight from school and to whom the mundane world of everyday work was as much of a shock as joining the army had been.

The extent to which the attitudes of servicemen had been deeply affected by the war was to become apparent only in the decade

after 1945, when a new generation of American writers, led by
Norman Mailer, James Jones, and Irwin Shaw, began chroni-
cling their experiences with a force and conviction that shocked
the literary establishment. Unlike the English war novelists who
tended to romanticize the rather more genteel experience of the
officer, *The Naked and the Dead, From Here to Eternity,* and *The Young
Lions* were drawn with the brutally honest and often sexually explicit language of the enlisted man. The instant success and huge
sales achieved by these semiautobiographical chronicles of World
War II were in no small measure because they found a huge
market among the millions of servicemen who could identify with
the experience.

It was not just the immediacy of the war experience that made
these books — and their subsequent imitators — perennial best-
sellers, but also the way in which their authors had boldly portrayed the relationship between violence, sex, and the role of the
individual in a mechanistic war. Combat was presented, according to the author's viewpoint, as either the sublimation of sexual
energy or as direct sexual release. The characters battled their
way through the pages of these books in search of an emotional
catharsis on the field of battle, making their choices between heroism, wanton butchery, or cowardice. Homosexuality was dealt
with both candidly and unsympathetically in what was a reflection of the not insignificant part that it had played in their respective author's military life. In another echo of their military
conditioning, male potency was usually equated with an individual's prowess as a warrior — and comparisons were frequently
drawn between a soldier's ungovernable sexual impulse and the
war itself.

The pattern for World War II fiction became established with
the 1948 publication of *The Naked and the Dead.* Despite the protests of the moral reformers, there were sufficient readers who
believed that modern warfare was not to be romanticized as it
had been in the past. Not only did these books play an important
part in preparing the public for a more open and explicit discussion, but one of their main themes — the confrontation between
the final human citadel of sexuality and man's technological capacity for self-destruction — was to become the focus of much
contemporary literature.

Many wives, mothers, and girlfriends were to discover that the experience of battle left mental scars that often took longer to heal than physical wounds. Marriage counselors advised American women anticipating the return of veterans to "let him know you are tired of living alone, that you want him to take charge." A sociologist suggested they give "more than the wife's usual responsibility for her marriage," by offering husbands "lavish — and undemanding — affection." It was not just the coarse language that shocked some wives but also the sexual adjustment of many men was disturbed by bouts of impotence or aggression.

For most wives and sweethearts, World War II did not end when the shooting stopped. Not only was it many months before the majority of troops could be brought home and demobbed, but even before they had arrived to rebuild old relationships, the press had revealed the extent to which Allied troops had fraternized with the Italian, German, and Japanese women. Although the military authorities in both Britain and America took care to issue strong official denials, the secret U.S. army survey of 1945 indicated that three out of four veterans returned from overseas service more sexually experienced than they had left.

For many war-brides there was also the shock of discovering that the man who returned was not the romantic hero of a hasty embarkation wedding. One American observer concluded that as many as one in three war marriages were not worth saving: "We may as well reconcile ourselves to that fact, and accept a thumping increase in the divorce rate as one of the costs of war." Many of these marriages were quickly dissolved in the twelve months after 1945, which brought over half a million divorces in the United States and thirty-four thousand in Britain. But by no means all wartime brides resorted to legal process. It was a reflection on the hold that traditional moral standards reexerted once peace came that Phyllis — and many others like her — decided that for better or worse she had no choice but to learn to live with her mistakes:

When my husband finally came home we discovered we were two different people, so much had happened in those years apart. My husband, older than myself, was time-conscious, critical and came back with the attitude of an army regimental sergeant major; I am sure he expected me to jump up and salute on entering a room. We had to take it that the men were faithful while away, but my in-laws were very quick to tell tales of my friendships with the opposite sex. My husband later threw this at me when I complained of the years I had spent alone. I realized that settling down was going to be hard, but by this time I had two babies, quickly, and I was stuck. In a strange area, strange faces and hours on my own. He was finding it hard to get a civilian job and having to take orders, after having had some measure of authority. I missed going to work and the companionship and intelligent conversation. After a while we settled to some sort of married life, but there were times when I thought that if there was a hell on earth, I was living it. I did not want a divorce, I could never have left the children.

If the postwar divorce rates became one of the most debated manifestations of the "sexual fallout" of the war, the impact of female mobilization proved to be another more permanent catalyst in the postwar equation. Women's production had made a critical contribution to the Allied war effort, but in the year after the war three million American women and over a million British women were laid off or voluntarily left their wartime jobs. Many women were forced out of work, while many more faced redistribution from highly paid wartime jobs where they had replaced men to lower jobs in textile manufacturing and food preparation, which had been the traditional female employers.

At the height of the manpower crisis in 1943, the percentage of women in Britain's engineering industry had risen to 31 percent, compared to less than 10 percent in 1939 — but this was to fall to 13 percent after the war. Similarly, American women's share of the lucrative jobs on Detroit assembly lines was to fall from a wartime high of 25 percent to only 7.5 percent. In the United States and Britain, although almost three-quarters of the wartime female labor force managed to stay in work, nine out of ten suffered a sharp decrease in earnings as weekly paychecks fell by as much as a fifth.

The post–World War II downgrading of the economic status of working women was a repeat of what had happened after World War I. In 1919, the leaders of the suffragette movement had tried to link voting rights to equal pay. "The time has come now when we women have a right to ask that we shall be free to labor where our labor is needed, that we shall be free to serve in the capacity for which we are fitted," declared the veteran American suffragist Anna Howard Shaw. But the right to vote was to prove an easier goal to achieve than the right to equal pay.

Only in Germany did World War I bring the issues of sexual discrimination and women's rights into the center of the political forum. The "New Woman" proposed by the radical feminists of the Weimar Republic was to be liberated from her traditional baby-bearing and infant-rearing role through state-funded contraception, abortion, and government-sponsored child-care programs. Equal employment opportunities in industry and the professions were to be guaranteed. Hitler's rise to power blocked the rise of the liberated "New Woman" as envisaged by the Weimar reformers, but she was to prove a far more enduring model for female liberation than the American flapper. It was to be one of the great ironies of history that the ultimate realization of the Weimar model of the liberated woman was the very one that the Nazis so successfully repressed. That she was to be revitalized and reborn through the wartime experience of the female populations of the United States and Britain was one legacy Hitler most certainly did not intend when he began his war in 1939.

The breakdown of the traditional sex roles of a large section of the Allied female population was the most profound sexual consequence of World War II — even though its full impact was to take two decades to manifest itself. The female labor force, in Britain and the United States, expanded by over 40 percent during the war years. Its significance was not so much that the industrial sex-segregation barriers had been breached by women who made ships and aircraft, but that by the final year of the war three-quarters of the new women workers were married. Many of these were mothers of young children who entered the workplace for the first time. In answering the urgent call to join the production battle demanded by a total war, this large section of the female population had finally broken down the resistance to employing wives and mothers. While almost 90 percent of women eventually married, 85 percent of prewar jobs were held by single women, whereas by 1944 a quarter of all female workers were wives and mothers.

It was a significant breakthrough that was celebrated in Hollywood movies like *Since You Went Away,* and posters that gave women a new sense of pride and identity. "Some just love their jobs," reported one American housewife. "I think they for the first time feel important." Another found "the companionship of working with others is vastly more stimulating and rewarding than housework." "Rosie the Riveter" and her British sister-workers who had made women "proud to have dirty hands" also brought about a minor revolution in production techniques in factories on both sides of the Atlantic. Jobs and equipment were modified so that they could be handled by women's muscles.

The wartime labor shortage that was instrumental in helping break down the reluctance of employers to hiring married and older women, and that brought a general extension of the economic contribution, did not change the attitudes of management and unions to "women's work." The wartime female labor force was paid far less than the male rate for the job. Women were paid on average only 60 percent of what men earned in the same job in the United States and 50 percent in Britain. This was in spite of a continuous campaign for equal pay. In the United States women's organizations had received the Roosevelt administration's support for the principle of equal pay for equal work. In 1941 the Supreme Court upheld federal nondiscriminatory legislation on wages and hours, but the male-dominated unions and management contrived artificial sex-related scales for women doing wartime "men's work" like welding. They justified the lower pay for women by asserting that the female workers had not served long apprenticeships and were therefore less skilled and productive than men.

In Britain barriers to equal pay for women proved just as rigid. While women were praised for doing "men's jobs" like crane driving and welding and it was agreed that they showed "they were capable of greater things than tradition put into their hands," they were employed as semiskilled workers — and paid accordingly low wages. Britain's restrictive craft unions only reluctantly admitted women to skilled trades on a temporary wartime basis, at a percentage of the normal rates unless they proved able to work "without special assistance and guidance." This left plenty of latitude for the shop stewards and employers to carefully regulate female pay scales well below those of men. The wartime Transport and General Workers Union organizer in Coventry, Jack Jones, was not alone in insisting that women were not in engineering "to cheapen the industry or to take the jobs of the men for the whole of the future, but just for the duration of the war." The unions therefore sided with the management in drawing up special "women's work" categories, which assigned them "work of a very light kind."

Many British women became union members under the naïve impression that organized labor was committed to the struggle for equal pay. One woman who had left her job in a food store to become a mechanic and who hoped to keep her wartime job finally realized that she had been trapped by the system:

If they hadn't let us in and didn't make a fuss to raise our wages, we'd be as skilled as the men by the end of the war and yet working for smaller wages. See? And the boss would want to keep us on after the war instead of taking the men back. If we get into the union and get the men's pay, the boss will prefer to take on the men after the war. There wouldn't be a proper reason to keep us on, now would there?

Such overt sexual discrimination in job classification generated resentment among the British workers, leading to disputes and strikes that threatened production in several vital war plants. The government Royal Ordnance Factories, which manufactured most of Britain's shells and bombs, eventually abandoned discriminatory pay rates because "they found this business of sorting out men's work from women's work quite impossible." But private industry proved more reactionary. At a Glasgow factory which built many of the Merlin engines for Spitfire fighters and Lancaster bombers, management's insistence on sticking to the inequitable dual rates resulted in a week-long strike in October 1943. But the compromise that settled one stoppage that could have threatened the war effort sidestepped the issue of equal pay by fixing a rate for individual machines regardless of the sex of the operator. Nor was the real issue mentioned in the strike announcement, which merely proclaimed that:

Rolls-Royce workers are determined to achieve their demands and in doing so realize they are defending the wages of their husbands, brothers and sweethearts and other workers in the armed forces.

Throughout the war Churchill resisted the growing demands from the female labor force for equal pay with the same stubbornness he had marshaled to defy Hitler in 1940. Since all able-bodied British women were conscripted into some form of war work, his coalition government saw no need to make any concessions. A Royal Commission on Equal Pay was set up only after a parliamentary impasse was reached over remuneration scales for male and female teachers proposed by the 1944 Education Bill — and its majority report two years later came down firmly against making equal pay a guideline of postwar British industrial policy.

While women workers had invaded wartime "men's" jobs as welders, riveters, and crane drivers in heavy industry, they lost them when the approach of the Allied victory brought a rapid return to the traditional sex discrimination. Long before the last shot had been fired, "Rosie the Riveter" had become an extinct species in the shipyards as production rapidly declined and veterans returned to reclaim their old jobs. Women were also forced to withdraw from the engineering and aircraft industries; those who needed to continue working had little choice but to accept lower-paid "women's work" in their traditional industries of textiles and food. Only in the electrical industries did the female work force hold on to their wartime gains as production geared up for the peacetime market.

In politics, as in industry, there was a growing postwar reassertion of deeply embedded social beliefs about gender roles. Symbolic of this backlash was the United States Congress's rejection in June 1944 of the WASP militarization bill, which barred female ferry pilots from the cockpits of army planes. It was as much an economic as a political reaction, a response to pessimistic predictions on both sides of the Atlantic that the end of the war would bring an end to full production and a return to the Depression, with men being thrown out of work in favor of lower-paid women. The economic incentive, which had been a strong recruiting incentive for the female work force, was now turned against them to persuade them to return to the kitchen sink. As one American war plant foreman expressed it: "When a girl under the policy of equal pay for equal work has an opportunity to get a man's rate, including time and a half for overtime, her pay check looks so big to her that she naturally thinks that noisy, oily work on a machine is easier than housework."

Lavish tributes continued to be paid by American and British government spokesmen for the magnificent job that women had done, but behind the scenes their male-dominated bureaucracies were casting their postwar plans on the assumption that most of the female work force would meekly return to their ageless mission as wives and mothers. It was an assumption shared by most male factory workers. "Women still enjoy raising families, and the way to a man's heart is still through cooking," one foreman insisted. "Most of our women war workers will want to get back to housework as soon as we win the war."

Not until American women were actually asked — by an official 1944 survey of the War Manpower Commission — did the policymakers in Washington realize how wrong their assumptions were. Many women certainly did not want to go back to housework after the war. "I'd stay if they want me without taking a man's place away from him," was the typical response heard from women, who were reluctant to deprive a returning veteran of his job, but who wanted to continue working. Surveys of thousands of female factory workers in the United States found that 61 to 85 percent of all women war workers wanted to continue their employment in peacetime and that more than half of all married women wanted to keep their jobs and newfound economic prosperity.

For many thousands of women, work was not a matter of choice, but of economic necessity, as one 1944 report by the U.S. Department of Labor indicated:

Rose Carson who used to work in a five-and-dime store got a war job as a riveter in an aircraft plant and says she expected to keep on working until her fiancé was out of the service, had completed his education and was able to marry. Mrs. Martin, a candy-store clerk, who had recently lost her husband, had to keep a job indefinitely to support herself and three children. Mrs. Simmons, a saleswoman in a department store, was supporting an invalid husband suffering from rheumatic heart disease. Caroline Smith, a single woman and a stenographer, said she would have to continue in her position as she was the only wage earner in the family which included a disabled father. Mrs. Cartwright had taken a war job as a machine operator to help her husband buy a home and would have to keep on working after the war to meet monthly payments. Another woman, a school teacher, was contributing to the support of her crippled brother's children.

"Will the Factory Girls Want to Stay Put or Go Home?" was the question that Britain's semiofficial Mass Observation survey attempted to answer in the final year of the war. In contrast to the United States, only a quarter of factory workers polled unequivocally answered yes to the question "Should women be allowed to go on doing men's jobs?" Another 28 percent said that it "depends on postwar conditions," leaving the pollsters to conclude: "The most general opinion seems to be that women will want to go back home, or take up jobs which were considered suitable for women before the war, while waiting for marriage."

The Ministry of Labor, unwilling to put its trust in opinion polls, began weighing introduction of legislation to force women out of their wartime jobs to forestall possible unemployment when four million servicemen were demobbed. This would have reneged on the pledge Labor Minister Ernest Bevin had given in 1942 when he proclaimed: "It will become the bounden duty of every one of us to arrive at proper conclusions as to the right use and place that women must find in the postwar world."

The British government did not interpret "bounden duty" to guarantee equal pay as part of the ambitious social engineering planned by Sir William Beveridge for the creation of a postwar welfare state. The Women's Advisory Committee on Postwar Reconstruction made its dissatisfaction felt by directing the greatly increased female union membership to persuade the Trades Union Congress and the Labour Party to support their resolution calling for the rate for the job: "Women have established their claim to a share in the economic life of the nation. By having shared equally with men the tremendous task of producing for the needs of war, they have an equal right to employment after the war."

In the United States equal rights was also a growing political issue. "The American people, therefore must demand consideration of the status of women in all postwar plans," insisted the chairman of the Women's Advisory Committee. Like British feminists' call for equal pay, the Americans' claim for equal employment opportunity was a measure of the extent to which women's participation in the war effort had provided them with a new sense of their economic importance and political force as well as justification for calling on the male legislatures to recognize their rights.

"Surely we will not refuse to our own that which we purchase for strangers with the blood of our sons," was a convincing argument used to persuade the wartime Congress to accept the 1923 Equal Rights Amendment, which proposed making all sexual discrimination constitutionally illegal. But not until 1945 did the supporters of the bill receive presidential encouragement after it was passed by Judiciary Committees of both houses. But it was a measure of the postwar antifeminist reaction that the following year the Senate passed it by only a three-vote majority, far short of the two-thirds necessary to submit a constitutional amendment to the individual states.

The congressional rebuff to ERA came within months of the British Parliamentary Commission coming out against equal pay for women workers. These defeats were a sharp setback to hopes that had acquired a new momentum and focus in the wartime workplace. The failure of both Congress and Parliament to vote the equal economic rights that many women felt they had fought for in World War II was only partly attributable to an antifeminist backlash whipped up by men. The majority of American and British women were also still ambivalent about claiming a new role in society. Most regarded their wartime gains as "time out" for the duration from their traditional role centered on marriage, home, and dependency on the male breadwinner.

"Americans may no longer believe that a woman's place *is* in the home," *Time* magazine had observed early in 1945, but it was soon to be apparent many women and the vast majority of men did. "There are two things I want to be sure of after the war," a typical soldier wrote from the South Pacific. "I want my wife waiting for me and I want my job waiting for me. I don't want to find my wife busy with a job that some returning soldier needs, and I don't want to find that some other man's wife has my job."

To counter fear that American soldiers would return to an employment market saturated by women in spite of the guarantees of their old jobs by the GI Bill of Rights, the U.S. army distributed a booklet entitled "Do You Want Your Wife To Work After The War?" In slick Madison Avenue style it employed cheerful cartoons to show that the war had not dramatically shifted the demarcation between the sexes in the workplace. The record indicated that the female share of the United States work force had been growing steadily from 13 percent to 34 percent since

1873. "The war has merely speeded up a march that has been under way for a century and a half." GIs were reminded that "women are not made only for having babies" as the Nazis had dogmatically insisted:

Women are not all alike, and there are many who have long felt restive and rebellious about housework to whom the war has brought the first opportunity for release. To them dishwashing and baby tending are dull drudgery compared with the interest and excitement and sociability of working in a war plant.

To explain why so many women opted for domestic drudgery in the aftermath of World War II, it became an article of faith, twenty years later, for militant apostles of women's liberation to subscribe to the "feminine mystique." This was the title of the influential book by Betty Friedan which expounded on the success of the 1945 version of the male confidence trick:

When the men came back, there was a headlong rush into marriage. The lonely years when husbands or husbands-to-be were away at war — or could be sent away at a bomb's fall — made women particularly vulnerable to the feminine mystique. They were told that the cold dimension of loneliness was the necessary price they had to pay for a career, for any interest outside the home. The mystique spelled out a choice — love, home, children, or other goals and purposes in life. Given such a choice, was it any wonder that so many American women chose love as their whole purpose?

It is certainly true that the images of female war workers projected by the propaganda that lured large numbers of American and British women from their homes into the war effort played on women's old-fashioned notions of femininity. By making jobs like welding seem glamorous, it fostered the impression that such wartime work increased the chances of finding a husband and becoming a better homekeeper in peacetime. The trend was particularly apparent in the American wartime media. Women's magazines, newspaper features on female war workers, and advertising for wartime housewives all stressed the feminine attributes. "She does a man's work in the ground crew servicing airplanes, but she hasn't lost any of her glamour, sweetness and charm," ran a *McCall's* headline. A cosmetic company advertised that the war could not be won by lipstick, "But it symbolizes one of the reasons why we are fighting . . . the precious right of women to be feminine and lovely."

Women were also lured away from the masculine clothes of wartime work with the "New Look," which promoted the return to a more traditional and restrictive style of female dressing. Its instigator was Christian Dior, who admitted that he had hated seeing women who "looked and dressed like Amazons. But I designed clothes for flowerlike women, clothes with rounded shoulders, full feminine busts, and willowy waists above enormous spreading skirts."

The fact that many women responded so rapidly and eagerly to the revival of the myth of fragile femininity may have been less to do with their seduction by the so-called feminine mystique than the exhaustion of a large percentage of the female population with their wartime burdens. Anxiety and deprivation made a retreat to postwar domesticity a very attractive option for many women. The notion that somehow they were tricked out of the freedom they had won during the war raises questions about just how "liberating" their wartime experience really had been, as well as the extent to which it had redefined individual women's attitudes to their unique role of wife and mother.

Social welfare workers and child-care experts, moreover, blamed the lack of parental supervision in wartime for the high levels of juvenile delinquency. These accusations stirred the collective guilt of a large number of working mothers. It was reinforced by the emphasis laid on maternal responsibilities by the fashionable postwar theories of educators like Dr. Benjamin Spock, whose hugely popular writings sought to put motherhood and child-rearing in a modern context. Women were advised to devote far more time and indulgence to their children.

The tremendous increase in the numbers of couples getting married was another factor that checked the move toward greater women's liberation in the immediate postwar years. Men and women were not only marrying at a younger age during the war and after, but the marriage rate jumped by nearly 50 percent in 1946 and remained over 20 percent above prewar levels throughout the decade. Two out of three men who returned from the war were still single, and those couples whose marriages had survived the test of war wanted to make up for lost time by starting or expanding their families. Child-rearing became a national preoccupation as homemaking became a feature of women's magazines. The pressures of the postwar consumer industry discouraged many mothers from seeking work at a time when both the American and British governments were cutting back on their wartime support of full-time child-care facilities.

That so many women responded to the postwar call to their ageless mission was in itself to produce a larger than expected generation of postwar children, who were to make a significant contribution to furthering the "sexual revolution" when they matured. The "baby boom" children who were raised to adolescence according to the permissive "Spock doctrine" were to become an integral element in the sexual liberation movements that emerged in the late 1960s in the United States and had spread by the early 1970s throughout the Western world.

After the immediate postwar reaction, the trend to permissiveness was firmly established with the commercialization of eroticism in film, television, and advertising, which had followed the lead of the wartime pinups and girlie magazines. Sex appeal was to become an important element in marketing during the consumer boom of the 1950s.

A generation after World War II had ended, the seal was to be set on the "Permissive Society" when the old definitions of obscenity were successfully challenged in Britain and the United States. Homosexuality was no longer a criminal offense in many areas, and the laws against prostitution were relaxed or less stringently enforced. Abortions became legal for the first time, representing a significant increase in the freedom of choice for the female population — although only in the face of vehement opposition by the churches and moral purity campaigners.

The women's movement that spread its influence across the Atlantic was to become one of the most important cultural and political events of the decade. Significantly, it drew part of its inspiration and inheritance from women who had experienced a transient liberation during World War II. Now that they had raised their families and become bored with the postwar ideal of suburban domesticity, they had the time and energy to march shoulder-to-shoulder with their daughters to campaign vociferously for equal pay and legal rights, free birth control, abortions, and adequate nursery care.

Many of these issues were familiar causes to the women of the war generation, who were more united and determined this time to press for the status and rights that had been denied the female population in 1945. Although the movement succeeded in closing wage rates and the gender gap, full equal rights and pay were still elusive. Nonetheless, another major step had been taken by the end of the 1970s to put men and women on a more equal social footing. This time there was could be no backsliding. The consumer economy had expanded to the point where it depended not only on women's spending power, but also the labor of married women, who were working in larger numbers than at any time since the war.

The steady advance of women toward full equal economic and social status with men may well prove to be the most significant social revolution of the twentieth century — a revolution that is far from over. World War I, because it came at the more critical point in social transition, may have produced the sharpest changes in the status of women, but it was World War II, because it mobilized a far greater percentage of the female population, that was eventually to bring about the greatest transformation in Western society.

While many of women's wartime economic gains were given up in the retreat to postwar domesticity after 1945, the seeds of a profound sexual revolution had already been sown. They were to germinate and flower two decades later into a movement for female liberation that won many of the rights for which many women in World War II had been fighting.

Source Notes

Introduction

Chapter I: Making Love and War

7 "We were not really immoral" Radio call-in show participant to author, London Broadcasting "Nightline," 11 August 1982.

7 "By most people's standards" Letter to the author.

7 "In a war one has to love" John Horn Burns, *The Gallery*, p. 307.

8 "It is difficult to write" Letter to the author.

8 "I don't love him" Willard Waller, *The Veteran Comes Back*, p. 138.

8 "There was never a shortage" Archie Satterfield, *The Home Front*, p. 57.

8 "It was here today" Letter to the author.

9 "Theirs was a quick rush" Barbara Cartland, *The Years of Opportunity*, p. 165.

9 "Life has suddenly taken" Maria Ginter, *Life in Both Hands*, p. 47.

10 "My war memories" Letter to the author.

10 "It really was" Letter to the author.

10 "The most wonderful" Letter to the author.

10 "Despite the danger" Letter to the author.

10 "Carl was serving" Letter to the author.

11 "My standards of morality" Letter to the author.

12 "There was plenty" Letter to the author.

12 "Personal relationships" Letter to the author.

12 "We lived in a world" Letter to the author.

14 "It's very easy for some" Letter to the author.

14 "Through all these" Letter to the author.

15 "Suspended thus between" Ils Garthaus, *The Way We Lived*, p. 34.

15 "At first nothing made sense" Jenane Patterson Binder, *One Crowded Hour*, p. 170.

15 "She was very pretty" Letter to the author.

16 "The whole episode" Letter to the author.

16 "Our own servicemen" Letter to the author.

16 "There's the young guy" Bill Mauldin, *Up Front*, p. 51.

16 "to jilt a soldier" Dixon Wechter, *When Johnny Comes Marching Home*, p. 499.

16 "Thus love in America" John Horn Burns, *The Gallery*, p. 103.

17 "In fact women were" James Jones, *WWII*, p. 31.

17 "I haven't got" Aramis Hovespin, *Your Son and Mine*, p. 78.

17 "It is my contention" Myles Babcock, *A Guy Who Knows*, p. 60–61.

17 "Our love will never die" C. L. Beck, *Fighter Pilot*, p. 156.

Chapter 2: Cinderella Legions

18 "When the barrage opens" Martin Page, *Songs and Ballads of World War II*, p. 156.

18 "The position of women" Report of the Committee on Amenities and Welfare Conditions in the Three Women's Services, HMSO CMMD 6384 (August 1942), p. 1.

19 "never forgot the respect" Contemporary account quoted in *The Westminster Review* (January 1909), pp. 31–32.

19 "a delicate and refined" Quoted in Rosalyn Baxandall, ed., *America's Working Women: A Documentary History 1600 to the Present*, p. 75.

21 "The first uniforms" Letter to the author.

22 "I can remember" Letter to the author.

23 "There was a Cambridge girl" Phyllis Castle, "A Week in the WAAF" from *Leaves in the Storm*, p. 27.

23 "I was very proud" Letter to the author.

23 "to be made into" Letter to the author.

23 "We were made to march" Phyllis Castle, op. cit., p. 27.

24 "Out of that dreadful" M. D. Cox, *British Women at War*, p. 51.

24 "We were often too tired" Letter to the author.

25 "Hello 226—" Letter to the author.

25 "You can't hit back" Raynes Minns, *Bombers & Mash*, p. 48.

26 "We do not" M. D. Cox, op. cit., p. 65.

26 "Anyway, a fit woman" Raynes Minns, op. cit., p. 48.

26 "The girls cannot" Ibid.

26 "In the beginning" Letter to the author.

26 "maintenance of a large" Raynes Minns, op. cit., p. 49.

27 "The standard reached" Ibid.

27 "if one miscounts" Letter to the author.

27 "rushing across the field" Letter to the author.

27 "We had to stay" Letter to the author.

27 "When you hear the boom" Martin Page, op. cit., p. 156.

28 "the greatest event" Quoted by Dr. Magnus Hirschfeld, *The Sexual History of the World War*, p. 113.

29 "The girls I do choose" Bruce Myles, *The Night Witches—The Untold Story of Soviet Women in Combat*, p. 12.

30 "We didn't know" Ibid., p. 15.

30 "The girls learned" Ibid., p. 27.

31 "retching as I taxied" Ibid., p. 41.

31 "I flicked the guard off" Ibid., p. 42.

31 "I could clearly see" Ibid., p. 62.

32 "We were to have equality" Ibid.

33 "I know it sounds crazy" Ibid., p. 51.

33 "Lily told me" Ibid., p. 115.

34 "The German's whole attitude" Ibid., p. 221.

34 "Battle life" Ibid., p. 234.

34 "The sky was so full" Ibid., p. 212.

37 "being in the WAAF" Letter to the author.

37 "Sometimes, on a dark night" Bruce Myles, op. cit., p. 274.

Chapter 3: "You're in the Army Now, Miss Jones!"

38 "Women made, in my opinion" Mattie Treadwell, *The U.S. Army in World War II*, p. 379.

38 "We want to help" National Archives, U.S. Army, Research Branch,

Special Service Division, Preliminary Report on Motivations in Joining the WAC, 26 January 1943.

38　"The military services"　Mildred MacAffee Horton, "Women in the United States Navy," *American Journal of Sociology,* vol. 11 (March 1946), p. 449.

39　"no furs shall be worn"　Mattie Treadwell, op. cit., p. 8.

39　"moral injury"　Ibid., p. 7.

40　"who can do anything"　Ibid., p. 16.

40　"General Marshall shook"　Ibid., p. 22.

41　"I think it is a reflection"　Ibid., p. 25.

41　"we would throw away"　National Archives RG 247, File 250.1, letter from GI dated 1 July 1943.

42　"Female Marines?"　*The Best of YANK,* p. 112.

43　"the naked Amazons"　*Miami News,* 20 May 1942.

43　"Give the rejected 4F men"　*Augusta Herald,* 20 May 1942.

44　"It will be no picnic"　Mattie Treadwell, op. cit., p. 60.

44　"The recruiting station"　Ibid., p. 56.

44　"It was in the post office"　Ibid.

44　"Are you one of them"　Ibid.

44　"You have just made"　Ibid., p. 66.

45　"They learn more"　Ibid., p. 70.

46　"A threat to their"　Mildred MacAffee Horton, op. cit., p. 448.

46　"have been in waacs"　Mattie Treadwell, op. cit., p. 116.

46　"Hats and shoes"　Ibid., p. 142.

47　"Feel I can do more"　Ibid., p. 227.

47　"now every man"　Ibid., pp. 200–218.

48　"We're the Luckiest"　Ibid., p. 188.

49　"the first American women's"　Ibid., p. 361.

50　"I greatly doubt"　Ibid., p. 370.

50　"They were the best"　Letter from Air C in C MAAF to Dir WAC, 27 January 1944.

50　"We were the first"　Charlotte Knight in James H. Straubel, ed., *Air Force Diary,* p. 335.

51　"Beauty parlors"　Ruth Cowan, *Deadline Delayed,* pp. 196–197.

51　"During the time"　Mattie Treadwell, op. cit., p. 408.

51　"hardships, isolation"　Ibid., p. 587.

52　"At the big Seabee dances"　William B. Huie, *From Omaha to Okinawa— The Story of the Seabees,* p. 200.

52　"Why we GIs"　U.S. Army Weekly Editors, *Yank,* pp. 222–223.

52　"Thanks for the bouquets"　Ibid.

53　"Perhaps the greatest"　Mattie Treadwell, op. cit., p. 724.

53　"I was sick and tired"　National Archives, U.S. Army, Research Branch, Special Service Division, Preliminary Report on Motivations in Joining the WAC, 26 January 1943.

54　"Nothing could be more"　*American Journal of Sociology,* vol. 51 (March 1946), p. 450.

54　"It is my impression"　Ibid.

Chapter 4: The Khaki Issue

55 "Vague and discreditable" Report of the Committee on Amenities and Welfare Conditions in the Three Women's Services, HMSO CMMD 6384, August 1942, p. 49.

55 "Men have for centuries" Mattie Treadwell, op. cit., p. 218.

55 "She'll be wearing khaki" Martin Page, op. cit., p. 154.

55 "Virtue has no gossip value" HMSO CMMD 6384, op. cit., p. 49.

55 "I don't think air force men" Letter to the author.

55 "There was the attitude" Letter to the author.

56 "An airman got very fresh" Letter to the author.

56 "doing physical education" Letter to the author.

56 "He just gave me" Letter to the author.

57 "The incident I recall" Letter to the author.

57 "We were examined" Interview with the author.

57 "There were men present" Letter to the author.

57 "maternity home for ATS" Mass Observation Reports.

58 "No justification" HMSO CMMD 6384, op. cit., p. 50.

58 "too much time" Ibid., pp. 10–50.

59 "The British, though" Ibid., p. 49.

59 "wild and fantastic tales" Ibid., p. 51.

59 "every German soldier" Jack Cassin-Scott, *Women at War*, p. 25.

60 "STORK PAYS VISIT" *Washington Times-Herald*, 1 May 1943.

61 "contraceptives and" *Washington Times-Herald*, 8 June 1943.

61 "Long distance calls" Mattie Treadwell, op. cit., p. 204.

61 "When I went through" Ibid.

62 "Americans fall for" Ibid.

62 "Army personnel" Ibid., p. 206.

62 "You join the WAVES" Ibid., pp. 212–213.

63 "parents concerned about" *Washington Post*, 11 June 1943.

63 "men have for centuries" Mattie Treadwell, op. cit., p. 218.

63 "a certain bravado" HMSO CMMD 6384, op. cit., p. 50.

63 "While in mixed company" Interview with the author.

64 "use of contraceptives" HMSO CMMD 6384, op. cit., p. 50.

64 " 'Twas all over my SOP" Letter to the author.

64 "You could get two months' " Letter to the author.

65 "Prevention of Venereal" National Archives RG 165, File 720, War Dept. WAAC Memo "For the Director," 27 July 1942.

65 "entirely inadequate" Confidential Memo for Capt. Stephenson, "Observation of VD in the ATS," 2 June 1942 from J. F. Shronts, NA RG 165, File 726.1.

66 "should be presented" Mattie Treadwell, op. cit., pp. 616–618.

66 "the character of the women" A Record Group 165 File 720, War Dept. Bureau of Public Relations, "Memo For Mrs. Hobby," 13 August 1942.

67 "Quite apart from" Interview with the author.

67 "She told us to call her" Burns, op. cit., p. 91.

68 "My life consists of" U.S. Army Weekly Editors, *The Best of YANK*, p. 156.

68 "The women who make up" National Archives RG 165, Decimal Section 250, Report on Board Proceedings Aux Agnes B———, 13 July 1943.

69 "potential problem" National Archives RG 165, Decimal Section 720, "Sex Hygiene Course — WAC," May 1945 — Lecture V: Homosexuality.

70 "to inform you" National Archives RG 159, Decimal Section 250.1, "Office of the Inspector General" Memo for Oglethorpe et al., for Colonel T. B. Turner — evidence, proceedings, transcript, 17 June 1943.

71 "In talking about" Ibid.

71 "I think it is a sort" Ibid.

72 "As I walked in" Allan Berube/San Francisco Lesbian and Gay History Project, as published in "Coming Out Under Fire," *Mother Jones* (February/March 1983).

72 "I was sitting" Ibid.

Chapter 5: Plaster Saints

73 "A soldier's the sort" U.S. Army Weekly Editors, *The Best of YANK*, p. 210.

73 "The Army does not" *U.S. Infantry Journal* (March 1943), p. 41.

73 "Men, being two-legged" "Psychology for the Fighting Man," *U.S. Infantry Journal* (January 1943), p. 56.

74 "He must make a compact" James Jones, *WWII*, p. 54.

74 "The psychological effect" Myles Babcock, op. cit., p. 58.

75 "the wonderful phrase" *U.S. Infantry Journal* (March 1943), p. 41.

75 "The soldier liked" Ibid.

75 "Living in herds" James Jones, op. cit., p. 31.

76 "Toilet taboos" Allan Sherman, *The Rape of the Ape*, pp. 81–82.

76 "strips us of the later" Sigmund Freud, *Reflections on War and Death*, p. 62.

76 "The men in a successfully" Joel T. Boone, "The Sexual Aspects of Military Personnel," *American Journal of Social Hygiene*, vol. 27 (March 1941).

77 "Your rifle" "How to Shoot the U.S. Army Rifle," *U.S. Infantry Journal*, (January 1943), p. 37.

77 "And, furthermore" Henry Elkin, "Aggressive and Erotic Tendencies in Army Life," *American Journal of Sociology*, vol. 55 (March 1946), p. 441.

77 "The profane term" Ibid.

78 "I don't want" Martin Page, op. cit., p. 21.

78 "Aside from the richness" Louis L. Snyder, ed., *Masterpieces of War Reporting*, p. 259.

79 "All GI talk" James M. Mead, *Tell the Folks Back Home,* p. 263.
79 "When the presence" Louis L. Snyder, op. cit., p. 55.
79 "They call me Venal Vera" Martin Page, op. cit., p. 134.
79 "Dirty Girtie" Ralph G. Martin, *The G.I. War,* p. 58.
80 "Browned-off with bints" Jocelyn Brooke, "A Soldier's Song" as quoted in Vernon Scannell, *Not Without Glory,* p. 159.
80 "And we talked of girls" Ibid., p. 58.
80 "I may say here" Charles Allen Smart, *The Long Watch,* p. 21.
81 "Drinking, like sex" Bill Mauldin, op. cit., p. 84.
81 "seen only one white" Dixon Wechter, *When Johnny Comes Marching Home,* p. 498.
81 "Sooner or later" John Horn Burns, op. cit., p. 217.
82 "action to protect" Public Records Office, Ministry of Health, Records MH 55, File 1339, Letter to Prime Minister from Women's Cooperative Guild, 13 May 1940.
82 "might reasonably be" Ibid., Memo 17 May 1940.
82 "Quite possibly" Ibid.
82 "It is well known" Ibid., File 1333, Provision for VD Treatment in Wartime and Ministry of Health Circular, September 1939.
82 "definite signs" Ibid., File 1334.
83 "There is good reason" Ibid., File 1377, Shipping Federation Circular.
84 "Pay day for soldiers" "The Prostitution Racket Today," *Journal of Social Hygiene* (March 1941), pp. 327–333.
85 "As to potentially" National Archives RG 407, Adjutant General's Office, Decimal File 726.1, "Excerpts of Statements Made at Joint Army/Navy Conference on VD," 28 February 1941.
85 "No. 1 Saboteur" *New York Times,* 23 November 1941.
86 "Unless extenuating" National Archives RG 407, Adjutant General's Office, Decimal File 726.1, War Department Circular 249.
86 "Bright Shield of Continence" *Reader's Digest* (August 1942).
87 "A man is going" National Archives RG 215 — Report 123 M-1, "VD Problems of White Enlisted Men in MTOUSA," prepared for Chief, Preventative Medicine Branch, MTOUSA by Research Branch 10 September 1945 — replies (hereinafter referred to as U.S. Army Sex Survey–W).
87 "I rejected the advice" Frank Richardson, *Mars without Venus,* p. 43.
88 "There was a colonel" Allan Sherman, op. cit., p. 81.
88 "The day I got my wing" Pete Grafton, *You, You and YOU!,* p. 126.
88 "Follow the red line" National Archives RG 247, Chaplain General, Decimal File 726.1, "Sex Morality Lecture" examples.
88 "I have been asked" Morris N. Kertzer, *With an H on My Dogtag,* p. 37.
89 "Sure I am just as tempted" U.S. Army Sex Survey–W.
89 "We go in search" W. Woodruff, *Vessel of Sadness,* p. 112.
89 "five million perfectly" John Steinbeck, *Once There Was a War,* p. 29.
89 "In his image of himself" Frederick Elkin, "The Soldier's Language," *American Journal of Sociology,* vol. 87 (March 1982).

Chapter 6: Jagged Glass

90 "Army life overseas"   U.S. Army Sex Survey–W.

90 "Fear of killing"   S. L. A. Marshall, *Men Against Fire*, pp. 50, 78.

91 "I remember myself"   John Horn Burns, op. cit., p. 21.

91 " 'When I come back' "   Dixon Wechter, op. cit., p. 483.

91 "In the war"   Aramis Hovespin, op. cit., p. 178.

92 "I have found fifty"   Jean Binder, op. cit., p. 151.

92 "You went to war"   Pete Grafton, op. cit., p. 100.

92 "While girls had a much"   Letter to the author.

93 "The typical soldier"   Nat Frankel, *Patton's Best*, pp. 76–77.

93 "After a while"   Aramis Hovespin, op. cit., p. 102.

94 "proximity of danger"   Myles Babcock, op. cit., p. 45.

94 "Whore of Death"   William Manchester, *Goodbye, Darkness*, p. 73.

95 "No social intercourse"   National Archives RG 331, Records of Allied Operational and Occupational Headquarters, Decimal File 250.1, SHAEF Policy Directive issued 12 September 1944.

95 "Ve haf vaited fife years"   Ibid., Report from Lt. Col. Gurfein, Chief of Intelligence, to SHAEF Psychological Warfare Division, 20 March 1945, and associated memos.

95 "Women were told"   Ibid.

95 "very serious consideration"   Ibid.

96 "Two things our soldiers"   *New York Herald-Tribune*, 15 May 1945.

96 "native females wandering"   National Archives, op. cit., RG 215, Report by Chief of Preventative Medicine, AFPAC.

96 "When VE-day finally"   Ibid., "A History of Preventative Medicine in the European Theater" — Part V, VD Control, by Col. John E. Gordon.

97 "The reason I haven't"   U.S. Sex Survey–W and "VD Problems of Negro Enlisted Men in MTOUSA" — Report 122 M2, 25 September 1945.

97 "Sex patterns of males"   Ibid.

98 "Until 9 months ago"   Ibid.

98 "There is a new set"   Ibid.

98 "This is the apparent"   Ibid.

98 "no evidence that"   Ibid.

99 "Why are officers"   Ibid.

99 "What's sauce for the goose"   Ibid.

99 "As for the officers"   Ibid.

99 "keep their price down"   Ibid.

100 "When 3 out of 4"   Ibid.

100 "However, the man"   Ibid.

Chapter 7: Comrades in Arms

101 "Sodomy is specifically"   National Archives RG 407, Records of the Adjutant General's Office, Decimal File 250.4, Confidential Memo to Assistant Chief of Staff, 4 June 1942.

101   "Sex was not really"   George Melly, *Rum, Bum and Concertina*, p. 175.
101   "Masturbation is the fashion"   "Aloha JICPOA."
101   "was perhaps the easiest"   Frank Richardson, op. cit., pp. 13–14.
102   "Formerly my wife"   Magnus Hirschfield, op. cit., p. 76.
102   "Don't talk to me"   *Oxford Dictionary of Quotations* (Third Edition, 1980), p. 151.
103   "nearly 40% of all males"   Alfred C. Kinsey et al., *Sexual Behavior in the Human Male*, p. 664.
103   "History paints in lurid"   Joel T. Boone, op. cit., p. 119.
104   "Sex on the *Dido*"   Melly, op. cit., p. 175.
105   "Many conscious homosexuals"   Charles Anderson, "On Certain Conscious and Unconscious Homosexual Responses to Warfare," *British Journal of Psychiatry*, vol. 22, pp. 161–174.
105   "Homosexuality is repellant"   Frederick Elkin, op. cit., p. 412.
105   "There is frequently"   Shelford Bidwell, *The Women's Royal Army Corps*.
106   "Being what they were"   Frank Richardson, op. cit., p. 37.
106   "For several obvious reasons"   Harry Pozner, "Sexual Disorders and Misconduct in Service Males," *Journal of the Royal Army Medical Corps*, vol. 103 (April 1957), pp. 51–52.
106   "This innocuous display"   Anne Somerhausen, *Written in Darkness*, p. 254.
107   "I had always considered"   Kenneth Harrison, *The Brave Japanese*, p. 136.
107   "Many of those"   L. H. Loeser, "The Sexual Psychopath in the Military Service," *American Journal of Psychiatry*, vol. 102 (July 1945), pp. 92–100.
107   "the frequency of men"   Harry Pozner, op. cit., p. 52.
108   "impression was also"   Ibid.
108   "achieved gratification"   Charles Anderson, op. cit., pp. 163–175.
108   "quietly invalided out"   Frank Richardson, op. cit., p. 37.
108   "chosen a way of life"   As quoted in G. F. Green, *A Skilled Hand*, pp. 107–111.
109   "A sergeant in our brigade"   Interview with the author.
109   "When the conversation"   Harry Pozner, op. cit., p. 62.
110   "soldiers ascertained"   National Archives RG 407, The Adjutant General's Office, File 250.4, Confidential G-1 Memo, 4 June 1942.
111   "I walked into this office"   Alan Berube, "Coming Out Under Fire," pp. 24–25.
111   "as a result of a probable"   U.S. Navy Department, "Survey of Development of Policy and Practice on Disposition of Personnel Involved in Homosexual Activity," 25 February 1957.
112   "willfully, knowingly"   National Archives RG 80, Confidential Files Sec Nav/CNO P11-2 Box 1762, Case Files, 1944.
112   "kissing and fondling"   Ibid.
113   "It is not believed"   Ibid., P11-2 Box 1362, Correspondence between HQ Eighth Naval District and JAG/Sec Navy, July 1944.
114   "ratings average"   L. H. Loeser, op. cit., p. 99.
114   "Some of us know"   A. L. Rowse, op. cit., p. 267.
115   "During the last war"   Douglas Plummer, *Queer People*, p. 27.
116   "In a few minutes"   Interview with the author.

116 "Famous Cocks" William Manchester, op. cit., pp. 99–100.
116 "In the Philippines" Letter to the author.
117 "We were treated" Ibid.
117 "an active homosexual" Letter to the author.
117 "signal proof" Charles Anderson, op. cit., pp. 172–173.
118 "Under light hypnosis" Ibid.
118 "I went into a three-day" Alan Berube, op. cit., pp. 28–29.
119 "No one asked me" Ibid.

Chapter 8: Sentimental Bullets

120 "I was reminding the boys" Vera Lynn, *Vocal Refrain*, p. 22.
120 "We want to give Hitler" *Variety*, 7 October 1942.
121 "You stay in the middle" As quoted in Richard R. Lingeman, *Don't You Know There's a War On*, p. 212.
121 "braving the angry skies" Ibid.
121 "bath voice" Vera Lynn, op. cit., p. 35.
121 "The words of her songs" Ibid.
122 "greeting-card song" Ibid., p. 42.
123 "during the war years" Ibid., p. 51.
123 "genuine respect" Ibid., p. 58.
123 "Certain belligerent MPs" Ibid.
124 "if Hitler was going" Ibid.
124 "this noisy exhibition" Ibid.
126 "It came out at a time" As quoted in Richard R. Lingeman, op. cit., p. 214.
126 "Underneath the lantern" As quoted in Derek Jewell (ed.), *El Alamein and the Desert War*.
126 "We're off to bomb Benghazi" Ibid.
127 "Their names could no longer" Ibid.
128 "But a BBC broadcast" Ibid.
128 "Look here, this is our song" Ibid.
128 "When we are marching" As quoted in *Stars & Stripes*, Sicily Edition, 31 March 1944.
129 "Our musical geniuses" Derek Jewell, op. cit.
130 "this little fella" As quoted in Tichi Wilkerson and Marcia Borie, *The Golden Age of the Hollywood Reporter*, p. 145.
130 "In a smoke-hazed aeroplane" Max Roberts, "The Dance Band Years" (liner notes), Saville Records, London, 1981.
132 "my pale pink dress" Vera Lynn, op. cit., p. 89.
132 "Munitions and movies" As quoted in Tichi Wilkerson and Marcia Borie, op. cit., p. 165.
132 "Carole Landis" Ibid., p. 164.
133 "I may have seemed" Ibid., p. 166.
133 "This leads me to" National Archives RG 247, Office of the Chief of Chaplains, Decimal File 250.1, "Morals and Conduct," Letter to Editor *Protestant Voice*, 27 March 1945.

133 "In seductive language" Ibid., Letter from Msgr. Arnold to Chief of Chaplains, 9 January 1945.

134 "We had two roosters" Ibid., 26 September 1944.

134 "of the large number" Ibid.

135 "I had so much romance" "Hi Yank — A Soldier Show's Blueprint Special," Music and Lyrics by Pvt. Frank Loesser et al. Issued by HQ, Army Service Forces Special Service Division, ASF.

135 "Actually there were" Nat Frankel, op. cit., pp. 161–162.

135 "at least two lilting" Masayo Duus, Tokyo Rose — Orphan of the Pacific, pp. 9–13.

136 "Tokyo Rose, ever" Ibid., p. 12.

137 "If the Secret Service" As quoted in Daniel Lerner, Sykewar: Psychological Warfare Against Germany, pp. 268–272.

138 "I am very dubious" Ibid.

Chapter 9: Ammunition for the Heart

140 "We're all in this fight" As quoted in Allen L. Woll, The Hollywood Musical Goes to War, p. 98.

140 "In trench or camp" "JANE Goes to War," p. 5.

142 "If I must lose him" As quoted in Marjorie Rosen, Popcorn Venus — Women, Movies and the American Dream, p. 192.

142 "This is not only" As quoted in Colin Shindler, Hollywood Goes to War, p. 46.

142 "the screen can be used" Ibid.

142 "An American will fight" As quoted in Shindler, op. cit., p. 65.

143 "Motion pictures are" As quoted in Joe Morella et al., The Films of World War II, p. 57.

143 "GIs like musical comedies" Ibid., p. 61.

144 "Let's have more movies" Ibid.

144 "I know what it is" As quoted in Tichi Wilkerson and Marcia Borie, op. cit., p. 148.

145 "We're all in this fight" As quoted in Allen L. Woll, op. cit., p. 98.

147 "Once they had so many" Ibid., p. 95.

150 "We ought to be mad" As quoted in Tichi Wilkerson and Marcia Borie, op. cit., p. 191.

151 "production out of Jane's" As quoted in Marjorie Rosen, op. cit., p. 213.

151 "What are the two" Ibid.

152 "You won't find one" As quoted in Time-Life Books, This Fabulous Century — 1940–1950, p. 122.

152 "Such pictures are" National Archives RG 247, Decimal Class 250.1, Memorandum 23 May 1945 from Luther D. Miller, Acting Chief of Chaplains, U.S.A.

152 "that should make any" Ibid.

153 "It is not one" Ibid.

153 "I would much rather" Yank magazine, 28 July 1944.

153 "Don't slam our pin-ups" Ibid.
153 "I have her picture" Ibid.
154 "One navigator had most" As quoted in Mark Gabor, *The Pin-up — A Modest History*, p. 77.
155 "I remember at the Admiralty" "JANE goes to War," p. 6.

Chapter 10: A Woman's Work Was Never Done

156 "Earlier I buttered" As quoted in Leila J. Rupp, *Mobilizing Women for War*, p. 15.
156 "It's no longer" As quoted in Raynes Minns, op. cit., p. 32.
156 "The burden of total war" H. M. D. Parker, *Manpower — A Study of Wartime Policy and Administration*, p. 111.
156 "The British girl" Women at War," *Picture Post*, 10 January 1942, p. 8.
158 "To be a good bus" Ibid., 15 November 1941, p. 19.
158 "Whether you'll like" Ibid.
160 "At first you think" Ibid., 10 January 1942, p. 16.
161 "I was sent" As quoted in Norman Longmate, *The Home Front*, p. 124.
161 "On the final assembly" *Picture Post*, 10 January 1942, p. 6.
162 "we shall have to call" *Hansard*, May 1940.
162 "to direct any person" Defence of Realm Regulation 58A PRO LAB 67/9.
162 "by presiding over" PRO LAB 26/59, 5 June 1940.
162 "Should we pay" PRO LAB 26/59, F. N. Tribe to Secretary.
163 "My machine is" As quoted in Raynes Minns, op. cit., p. 37.
163 "The release of" As quoted in Penny Summerfield, *Women Workers in the Second World War*, p. 33.
163 "There should be more" PRO LAB 67/9, Memo Minister of Supply.
164 "Today we are calling" As quoted in Raynes Minns, op. cit., p. 32.
164 "Did you know" Ibid.
165 "My husband's on night" As quoted in Penny Summerfield, op. cit., p. 38.
165 "I feel very guilty" Mass Observation Reports, *People in Production*, p. 176.
165 "If married women" As quoted in Penny Summerfield, op. cit., p. 41.
166 "It's no good" Mass Observation Reports, op. cit., p. 232.
166 "We have no objection" As quoted in Raynes Minns, op. cit., p. 39.
167 "As soon as my son" Letter to the author.
167 "In an industrial centre" *New Statesman*, 13 December 1941, p. 8.
168 "A married woman" PRO LAB 26/131, September 1942, Memo on Absenteeism.
168 "While winning the war" Mass Observation Reports, op. cit., p. 168.
168 "a whole family" *New Statesman*, 27 September 1941, p. 519.
169 "the paramount consideration" "Employment of Women," issued by Minister of Labor, 24 March 1941.
169 "Working in factories" As quoted in Raynes Minns, op. cit., p. 36.
170 "I'm only a wartime" Ibid., p. 37.

172 "The recruiting officer" Letter to the author.
172 "My first job" Ibid.
172 "If you think" Ibid.
172 "The life was quite" Ibid.
173 "When this silly war" Raynes Minns, op. cit., p. 80.
174 "Nothing that a woman" Memorandum "British Policies and Methods of Employing Women in Wartime," U.S. War Manpower Commission report to Women's Advisory Committee, National Archives RG 211 Box 161.
174 "This war effort" Ibid., p. 24.

Chapter 11: The Girls Behind the Guys Behind the Guns

175 "Whatever the degree" Katherine Archibald, *Wartime Shipyard*, p. 16.
175 "It is our inescapable" Josephine von Miklos, *I Took a War Job*, p. 188.
175 "age-old fight" December 1942 Minutes Women's Advisory Committee to War Manpower Commission National Archives RG 211 Box 161, p. 2.
176 "Women are working" Ibid., p. 4.
176 "The thing that interested" Ibid., p. 5.
177 "Give the women" Susan B. Anthony II, *Out of the Kitchen — Into the War*, p. 41.
177 "Poking with a flashlight" Josephine von Miklos, op. cit., p. 9.
177 "Working in munitions" Ibid.
178 "the war industries" National Archives RG 86, Women's Bureau — Mobilization Policies 1942, Box 153.
179 "In large and small" Ibid.
179 "Would you be willing" As quoted in Susan M. Hartmann, *The Home Front and Beyond*, p. 82.
179 "I never let my wife" As quoted in Karen Anderson, *Wartime Women: Sex Roles, Family Relations and the Status of Women During World War II*, p. 24.
180 "The Fortresses" Ibid., p. 28.
180 "We do feel that we" Ibid.
180 "Maybe they read" Josephine von Miklos, op. cit., p. 16.
181 "In the next twelve months" Ibid.
181 "First, women with" National Archives RG 86 Box 153, "Women's Work and the War."
181 "Staunchly have the women" As quoted in Mabel E. Deutsch and Virginia E. Purdy, eds., *Clio Was a Woman — Studies in the History of American Women*, p. 213.
182 "She's the keeper" National Archives RG 208 Box 587, RKO publicity brochure.
182 "In 1943 America" National Archives RG 86 Box 1533, 1943 publicity release.
182 "To win the war" Ibid.
182 "Women couldn't work" Archie Satterfield, *The Home Front — An Oral History*, p. 67.

183 "It wasn't heavy work" Ibid., p. 84.
183 "It was interesting" Roy Hoopes, *Americans Remember the Home Front —
An Oral Narrative*, p. 102.
183 "I worked on" Ibid.
184 "That American women" National Archives RG 86, Women's Bureau
Box 1533.
184 "Some of them want" As quoted in Karen Anderson, op. cit., p. 44.
185 "Rosie (brrr-rrrr) the riveter" As quoted in Alice Kessler-Harris, op.
cit., p. 276.
185 "The clamor was for big" Ibid.
185 "My first job" As quoted in Satterfield, op. cit.
185 "Maybe you think" As quoted in Karen Anderson, op. cit., p. 47.
186 "The truth of the matter" As quoted in Josephine von Miklos, op. cit.,
pp. 186–187.
186 "Sex attitudes made up" As quoted in Katherine Archibald, op. cit., p.
18.
187 "For once we had" Virginia Snow Wilkinson, "From Housewife to
Shipfitter," *Harper's Magazine*, March 1943, p. 335.
187 "They're just like" As quoted in Josephine von Miklos, op. cit., p. 190.
188 "In the shipyards" As quoted in Katherine Archibald, op. cit., p. 19.
189 "We like to feel" Advertisements in *Life* magazine, 9 November 1942.
189 "Now at day's end" *Life* magazine, 6 July 1942.
189 "throwing a monkey wrench" As quoted in Leila J. Rupp, op. cit., p.
155.
189 "ABSENTEEISM" National Archives RG 86, Women's Bureau Box
1533.
190 "This Soldier May Die" Ibid.
190 "Whether we like it" Ibid.
190 "It's no slap-dash" Ibid.
190 "They're here to make" As quoted in *Survey Graphic*, March 1943, p.
19.
191 "I used to earn $15" As quoted in Roy Hoopes, op. cit., p. 92.

Chapter 12: The Girls They Left Behind

192 "Hasty war marriages" As quoted in S. M. Ferguson and H. Fitzgerald, eds., *Studies in the Social Services*, p. 99.
192 "From Buffalo to Wichita" Agnes E. Meyer, *Journey Through Chaos*, p.
60.
192 "In wartime there is" Francis E. Merril, *Social Problems on the Home Front*,
p. 103.
192 "They were wonderful days" Letter to the author.
193 "War, however, is" Willard Waller, *The Veteran Comes Back*, p. 139.
193 "about half the increase" *Ladies' Home Journal*, 7 March 1942.
193 "And what boy can help" Ibid.
194 "It was a very emotional" As quoted in Archie Satterfield, op. cit., p.
180.

194 "We were both emotionally" As quoted in Willard Waller, op. cit., p. 136.

194 "When the troops came" As quoted in Archie Satterfield, op. cit., p. 161.

196 "We met often" Letter to the author.

196 "When the sirens went off" Letter to the author.

197 "We must learn to wait" As quoted in Richard R. Lingeman, op. cit., p. 94.

198 "One day someone" As quoted in Willard Waller, op. cit., p. 137.

198 "I think that as well" Letter to the author.

198 "He was sent to Italy" As quoted in Agnes E. Meyer, op. cit., p. 65.

199 "So at this time" As quoted in Benjamin C. Bowker, *Out of Uniform*, p. 147.

199 "The time has come" As quoted in U.S. Army Weekly Editors, *The Best of YANK*, p. 173.

199 "Yours is the classic" Ibid.

199 "Two weeks before" Ibid., p. 174.

200 "For most soldiers" Benjamin C. Bowker, op. cit., p. 172.

201 "Separation was intolerable" Letter to the author.

201 "Men came home" Barbara Cartland, op. cit., p. 147.

201 "It is not very easy" Ibid., p. 222.

202 "Some were adolescent" As quoted in S. M. Ferguson and H. Fitzgerald, op. cit., p. 95.

203 "It is somewhat surprising" As quoted in Francis E. Merril, op. cit., p. 104.

204 "Total war is the most" Ibid., p. 2.

205 "Millions of families" Ibid.

206 "All that seems to be" As quoted in S. M. Ferguson and H. Fitzgerald, op. cit., p. 97.

206 "To girls brought up" Ibid.

207 "because it's my patriotic" National Archives RG 215, Social Protection Agency Reports.

207 "sexual delinquency" "Sex Delinquency Among Girls," *Journal of Social Hygiene*, November 1943, p. 493.

207 "I've only gone with" *Newsweek* magazine, 6 March 1944, p. 88.

207 "Goodtime girls" National Archives RG 215, Report 1943.

207 "From one end" *Washington Post*, March–May 1943.

208 "Many of them under" Agnes E. Meyer, op. cit., p. 65.

209 "War situations may" National Archives RG 215, Report of the Chief of the Children's Bureau, U.S. Department of Labor, 22 May 1944.

Chapter 13: The Girls They Met "Over There"

210 "The type of woman" *Yank* magazine, May 1944.

210 "Lust, bargaining" Willard Waller, op. cit., p. 134.

211 "Every man and boy" Charles Winnick and Paul M. Kinsie, *The Lively Commerce — Prostitution in the United States*, p. 258.

211 "You men in the army"   National Archives RG 215, Report 1943.

213 "The oldtime prostitute"   *American Medical Journal,* February 1942.

214 "Whereas before Pearl Harbor"   *Time* magazine, 20 March 1942.

214 "They say the young chippies"   Ibid.

214 "We've got the finest beach"   Ibid.

214 "When they closed down"   As quoted in Archie Satterfield, op. cit., pp. 105–106.

215 "the females in question"   National Archives RG 250, U.S. Army Office of Adjutant General, Decimal File 726.1, Report of Colonel Eugene Miller USA & Captain Thomas E. van Metre USN, March 1942.

217 *"One . . . Two"*   As quoted in William Bradford Huie, *Hotel Mamie Stover,* p. 9.

217 "I think it's immoral"   Ibid., p. 10.

217 "Never had so many"   Ibid.

219 "One day I escorted"   Roxane Pitt, *The Courage of Fear,* p. 76.

219 "Among other ranks"   Harry Pozner, "The Problems of Sex in the Services," *The Practitioner,* vol. 172 (April 1954), p. 437.

221 "The queen of Karaya Road"   *Newsweek* magazine, 11 September 1944.

221 "Give Us the Tools"   Letter to the author.

222 "Do you see that sunset?"   National Archives RG 247, U.S. Army Chaplaincy, Decimal File 726.1, "Morality Lectures," June 1943.

223 "operating under the VERBAL"   Ibid.

223 "Army life overseas"   National Archives RG 112, Box 1266, MTO Sex Survey.

224 "Prostitution is almost universal"   Ibid.

224 "Even when they aren't in love"   Ibid.

224 "Women of all classes"   Ibid.

224 "The purpose of the visit"   Ibid.

225 "undetermined number of brothels"   Ibid.

225 "From reports that have"   As quoted in Norman Lewis, *Naples 1944,* pp. 94–95.

225 "Women of all classes"   National Archives RG 112, Records of Surgeon General's Office, Report on Mediterranean Theatre Operations, Box 1266.

226 "On the back of the jacket"   John Horn Burns, op. cit., p. 284.

226 "To us GIs"   Ibid., p. 304.

227 "When ya walk"   Ibid.

227 "27 percent pay nothing"   Ibid.

227 "There are plenty"   National Archives RG 112, Box 1266, MTO Sex Survey Questionnaire.

228 "Should a soldier"   Ibid.

Chapter 14: Oversexed, Overpaid, and Over Here!

229 "Americans were 'cheeky' "   Letter to the author.

229 "The British consider sex"   National Archives RG 112, ETOUSA Medical Officers Reports.

229 "Suddenly the GIs" As quoted in Norman Longmate, *The GIs—The Americans in Britain 1942–5,* p. 85.
230 "We were half starved" Letter to the author.
231 "The first time" As quoted in Ralph G. Martin, op. cit., p. 28.
231 "Their main aim" Letter to the author.
232 "camp-followers secreted" Ibid.
232 "Along came a jeep" Ibid.
232 "Almost every evening" Ibid.
233 "The girls were there" As quoted in Norman Longmate, op. cit., p. 225.
233 "One night, as Ambassador" National Archives RG 215, ETOUSA Medical Officers Reports.
233 "There is absolutely" National Archives RG 247, Chaplain General Confidential File, 726.1, Letters.
234 "Most of my friends" Letter to the author.
234 "found one of our men" Ibid.
235 "make friendly representations" As quoted in Norman Longmate, op. cit., p. 150.
235 "We find the coloured" Ibid., p. 123.
235 "Some British women" Ibid.
235 "It was the white women" Barbara Cartland, op. cit., p. 150.
236 "A new aspect of sex" As quoted in Norman Longmate, op. cit., p. 271.
236 "But we were not" Letter to the author.
237 "American men and boys" As quoted in Norman Longmate, op. cit., p. 261.
237 "By and large" Letter to the author.
238 "The soldiers used to" Ibid.
238 *"They tell us we"* As quoted in Norman Longmate, op. cit., p. 254.
238 *"With Yankee girls"* Ibid., p. 255.
239 "It was rather fun" As quoted in Thomas R. St. George, *C/O Postmaster,* p. 116.
240 "full of soldiers" Allen Stuart, op. cit., p. 71.
240 "I'm sure they helped" Letter to the author.
240 "There does not exist" National Archives RG 215, Surgeon General's Office, Decimal File 726.1, History of Preventative Medicine ETOUSA, p. 5.
241 "British sensibilities" Ibid.
242 "It is hard to realize" Ibid.

Chapter 15: Yielding to the Conquerors

244 "The average soldier" Nat Frankel, op. cit., p. 75.
244 "It seems to me that" National Archives RG 247, Chaplain General Confidential File 726.1, June 1944.
244 "You will go in there" Ibid.
245 "run for, and indirectly by" National Archives RG 112, ETO Medical Reports.

245 "Approximately 60 per cent" "Aggressive and Erotic Tendencies: Military Life," *American Journal of Sociology*, vol. 51 (March 1946).

245 "We went in there" Letter to the author.

246 "firm conviction that" National Archives RG 247, Chaplain General Confidential File 726.1, September 1944.

246 "After my last Mass" Ibid.

247 "German officers had" Ibid.

247 "for the express purpose" ETO Medical Reports, op. cit.

247 "had all the better aspects" *Newsweek* magazine, 11 September 1944.

248 "the natural objective of" ETO Medical Reports, op. cit.

248 "French girls are easy" Aramis Hovespin, op. cit., p. 114.

248 "A warmth and pleasurable" Letter to the author.

249 "Nazism has so poisoned" As quoted in Saul K. Padover, op. cit., p. 60.

250 "The essential kindness" National Archives RG 331, SHAEF HQ File 250.1, Report on Civilian Relations, May 1945.

250 "Women were told" Ibid.

251 "Despite living in cellars" Ibid.

251 "We cannot expect the GI" Ibid.

251 "In this economic setup" Ibid.

251 "Have six years" *The Spectator*, 3 August 1945, p. 108.

251 "vast social, ideological" Overseas Press Club of America, *Deadline Delayed*, p. 71.

252 "In the old days" *Yank* magazine, 5 May 1945.

252 "obviously not expected" National Archives RG 331, SHAEF HQ File 250.1, June 1945.

252 "Women are always" Robert H. Welker, op. cit., p. 230.

252 "5,000 women entertainers" *Newsweek* magazine, 12 November 1945.

253 "20 Yen—" Ibid.

253 "MPs kept the lines" Ibid.

254 "We have won" National Archives RG 247, Chaplain General Confidential File 726.1, June 1945.

254 "It was held" Letter to the author.

255 "My first impression" Interviewee on BBC Television's "GI Brides," May 1984.

255 "owned a fleet" Letter to the author.

256 "It was getting dark" Interviewee on BBC Television's "GI Brides," May 1984.

256 "Like many young girls" Letter to the author.

256 "My husband says" *Ladies' Home Journal*, May 1946.

Chapter 16: The Seeds of Sexual Revolution

257 "World War II" Letter to the author.

257 "Like you, Mrs. America" Advertisement in *Saturday Evening Post*, May 1943.

257 "Was the permissive society" Letter to the author.

258 "We have known terror" Mary Seaton, in Stephan Shimanski and Henry Treece, op. cit., p. 261.
259 "People are not conscious" *The Times* (London), 13 July 1945.
259 "the increase in divorce" *The Spectator*, 20 July 1945.
259 "accelerated changes already" "Forum of the Air" transcript, 29 September 1945.
260 "the moral life of America" *Ladies' Home Journal*, 4 April 1944.
262 "let him know" As quoted in Susan M. Hartmann, op. cit., p. 526.
262 "We may as well" Benjamin C. Bowker, op. cit., p. 148.
262 "When my husband finally" Letter to the author.
263 "The time has come" As quoted in Alice Kessler-Harris, *Out to Work — A History of Wage-Earning Women in the U.S.*, p. 224.
264 "Some just love" Ibid.
265 "to cheapen the industry" As quoted in Penny Summerfield, op. cit., p. 158.
266 "If they hadn't let us" Ibid., p. 166.
266 "they found this business" Ibid.
266 "Rolls-Royce workers" Ibid., p. 172.
267 "When a girl" Ibid.
268 "Women still enjoy" National Archives RG 211, Women's Advisory Committee, Box 162, Surveys.
268 "I'd stay if they want me" Ibid.
268 "Rose Carson" Ibid.
269 "The most general opinion" Mass Observation Reports, *The Journey Home* (London: John Murray, 1944), p. 64.
269 "It will become" As quoted in "Bevin's Belles" in *Survey Midmonthly*, July 1942, p. 434.
269 "Women have established" National Archives RG 211 Box 161, British bulletins.
269 "The American people" National Archives RG 211, Women's Bureau, Box 164, Speeches of Margaret A. Hickey.
270 "Surely we will not" Ibid.
270 "Americans may no longer" *Time* magazine, 7 February 1945.
270 "There are two things" National Archives RG 86, Women's Bureau, Box 1545, brochure.
271 "Women are not all alike" Ibid.
271 "When the men came back" Betty Friedan, *The Feminine Mystique*, p. 175.
271 "She does a man's work" *McCall's* magazine, August 1943.
272 "looked and dressed" As quoted in Susan M. Hartmann, op. cit., p. 203.

Bibliography

A. Books

Allen, Frederick Lewis. *The Big Change — America Transforms Itself 1900–1950*. New York: Harper & Row, 1952.

Alsop, Guilema Fell, and McBride, Mary F. *Arms and the Girl: A Guide to Personal Adjustment at War Work and War Marriage*. New York: Vanguard Press, 1943.

Anderson, Karen. *Wartime Women: Sex Roles, Family Relations and the Status of Women During World War II*. Westport: Greenwood Press, 1976.

Anthony, Susan B., II. *Out of the Kitchen — Into the War*. New York: Stephen Daye, 1943.

Archibald, Katherine. *Wartime Shipyard*. Berkeley: University of California, 1947.

Ayling, Keith. *Calling All Women*. New York: Harper Bros., 1943.

Babcock, Myles. *A Guy Who Knows*. Bemidji, Minnesota: Myles Babcock, 1946.

Baetjer, Anna M. *Women in Industry: Their Health and Efficiency*. Philadelphia: Saunders, 1946.

Baker, Laura N. *Women in War Industry: The Complete Guide*. New York: E. P. Dutton, 1943.

Balfour, Michael. *Propaganda in World War II*. London: Routledge and Kegan Paul, 1979.

Banning, Margaret Culkin. *Women in Defense*. New York: Duell, Sloan & Pearce, 1942.

Baxandall, Rosalyn. *America's Working Women — A Documentary History*. New York: Vantage Books, 1976.

Beck, C. L. *Fighter Pilot*. California: privately published, 1946.

Bendit, P. and L. *Living Together Again*. London: Gramol, 1946.

Berkin, Carol R., and Lovett, Clara M. (eds.). *Women, War and Revolution*. New York: Holmes and Meier, 1980.

Berkin, Carol R., and Norton, Mary B. (eds.). *Women of America — A History*. Boston: Houghton Mifflin, 1979.

Bidwell, Shelford. *The Women's Royal Army Corps*. London: Leo Cooper, 1977.

Binder, Jean Patterson. *One Crowded Hour*. New York: William Frederick Press, 1946.

Bleuel, Hans P. *Sex and Society in Nazi Germany*. Philadelphia: Lippincott, 1973.

Bloch, I. *The Sexual Life of Our Time*. New York: Falstaff Publishers, 1937.

Blum, John Morton. *V Was for Victory: Politics and American Culture During World War II*. New York: Harcourt Brace Jovanovich, 1976.

Bowker, Benjamin C. *Out of Uniform*. New York: W. W. Norton, 1945.

Bowman, Constance. *Slacks and Callouses*. New York: Longmans, Green, 1944.

Braybon, G. *Women Workers in the First World War: The British Experience*. London: Croon, Helm, 1981.

Briggs, Susan. *Keep Smiling Through*. London: Weidenfeld & Nicholson, 1975.

Bryn Mawr College. *Women During the War and After*. Philadelphia: Curtis Publishing, 1945.

Bullock, Alan. *The Life and Times of Ernest Bevin*. Vol. II: *Minister of Labour 1941–1945*. London: Heinemann, 1981.

Bullough, V. L. *A History of Prostitution*. New York: Universe Books, 1964.

———. *Sexual Variance in Society and History*. Chicago: University of Chicago Press, 1976.

Burns, John Horn. *The Gallery*. New York: Harper Bros., 1947.

Burstein, Herbert. *Women in War: A Complete Guide to Service in the Armed Forces and War Industries*. New York: Service Publishing, 1943.

Burton, E. *What of the Women? A Study of Women in Wartime*. London: Frederick Muller, 1941.

Calder, Angus. *The People's War*. London: Jonathan Cape, 1969.

Caplow, Theodore, et al. *Middletown Families — Fifty Years of Change and Continuity*. Minneapolis: University of Minnesota Press, 1982.

Cartland, Barbara. *The Years of Opportunity*. London: Hutchinson, 1948.

Cassin-Scott, Jack. *Women at War*. London: Osprey Publishing, 1980.

Causley, Charles. *Hands to Dance and Skylark*. London: Robson Book, 1979.

Central Statistical Office. *Statistical Digest of the War*. London: HMSO, 1951.

Chafe, William Henry. *The American Woman: Her Changing Social, Economic and Political Role, 1920–1970*. London: Oxford University Press, 1972.

Churchill, Winston S. *The World in Crisis*. Vol. 1. London: Cassell & Co., 1923.

Cillespie, D. M. *The Psychological Effects of War*. London: Chapman Hall, 1944.

Clawson, Augusta. *Shipyard Diary of a Woman Welder*. New York: Penguin, 1944.

Colett, Wadge D. *Women in Uniform*. London: Sampson & Low, 1946.

Cox, M. D. *British Women at War*. London: John Murray, 1941.

Crew, F. A. E. (ed.). *The Army Medical Services: Campaigns*. 5 vols. London: HMSO, 1955–6.

Darwin, B. *War on the Line — The Story of the Southern Railway in Wartime*. London: Southern Railway Co., 1946.

Davies, Christie. *Permissive Britain — Social Change in the Sixties and Seventies*. London: Pitman, 1975.

Davies, R. *Women and Work*. London: Arrow, 1975.

Delmer, Sefton. *Black Boomerang*. New York: Viking Press, 1962.

Deutrich, Mabel E., and Purdy, Virginia C. *And Clio Was a Woman: Studies in the History of American Women*. Washington, D.C.: Howard University Press, 1980.

Dos Passos, John. *The State of the Nation*. Boston: Houghton Mifflin, 1944.

Duus, Masayo. *Tokyo Rose — Orphan of the Pacific*. Tokyo: Kodansha International, 1983.

Dworkin, Andrea. *Pornography — Men Possessing Women*. New York: Perigee-Putnam's, 1979.

Ellis, John. *The Sharp End of World War — The Fighting Man of World War II*. London: David and Charles, 1980.

Enloe, Cynthia. *Does Khaki Become You? The Militarization of Women's Lives*. Boston: South End Press, 1983.

Fabry, Joseph. *Swing Shift — Building the Liberty Ships*. San Francisco: Strawberry Hill Press, 1982.

Ferguson, S. M., and Fitzgerald, H. (eds.). *Studies in the Social Services.* Civil History Series. London: HMSO, 1954.

Fischer, H. C., and Dubois, E. *Sexual Life During the World War.* London: Francis Aldor Publishers, 1937.

Flynn, Elizabeth Gurley. *Women in the War.* New York: Workers Library Publications, 1942.

Forster, Anneliese. *Wooden Monkeys.* Chicago: Academy Press, 1961.

Forty, George. *Afrika Korps — The Long Road Back.* London: Ian Allan, 1966.

Frankel, Nat, with Smith, Larry. *Patton's Best.* New York: Hawthorn Books, 1960.

Franklin Institute. *Women in War Work.* Philadelphia: Curtis Publishing, 1943.

Freud, Sigmund (A. A. Brill & A. B. Kuttner, trans.). *Reflections on War and Death.* New York: W. W. Norton, 1950.

Friedan, Betty. *The Feminine Mystique.* New York: Dell, 1963.

Fyfe, Hamilton. *Britain's Wartime Revolution.* London, 1944.

Gabor, Mark. *The Pin-up — A Modest History.* New York: Universe Books, 1972.

Gardner, Brian. *The Terrible Rain — The War Poets 1939–45.* London: Eyre Methuen, 1966.

Garthaus, Ils. *The Way We Lived.* Sydney, Australia, 1975.

Geis, Francis. *Joan of Arc.* New York: Harper & Row, 1981.

Gerken, Mable R. *Ladies in Pants.* New York: Exposition Press, 1949.

Giles, Nell. *Punch in Susie! A Woman's War Factory Diary.* New York: Harper Bros., 1943.

Ginter, Maria. *Life in Both Hands.* London: Hodder & Stoughton, 1960.

Gittins, D. *Fair Sex, Family Size and Structure 1900–1939.* London: Hutchinson, 1982.

Goodman, Jack. *While You Were Gone: A Report on Wartime Life in the United States.* New York: Simon & Schuster, 1974.

Goulden, Joseph C. *The Best Years 1945–1950.* New York: Atheneum, 1976.

Grafton, Pete. *You, You and YOU!* London: Pluto Press, 1981.

Graves, C. *Women in Green: The Story of Women's Voluntary Service.* London: Heinemann, 1949.

Green, G. F. *A Skilled Hand.* London: Macmillan, 1980.

Greer, Germaine. *The Female Eunuch.* New York: McGraw-Hill, 1971.

———. *Sex & Destiny.* New York: Harper & Row, 1984.

Gregory, Chester. *Women in Defense Work in World War II*. New York: Exposition, 1974.

Hale, Edwin R., and Turner, John Frayn. *The Yanks Are Coming*. Kent: Midas Books, 1983.

Harris, J. *William Beveridge: A Biography*. London: Oxford University Press, 1977.

Harrison, Kenneth. *The Brave Japanese*. London: Rigby Ltd, 1958.

Hartmann, Susan M. *The Home Front and Beyond*. Boston: Twayne Publishers, 1982.

Haslett, C. *Munitions Girl: A Handbook for Women of the Industrial Army*. London: English University Press, 1942.

Heger, Heinz. *The Men with the Pink Triangle*. Boston: Alyson Publications, 1980.

Henrey, Robert. *The Incredible City — London in Wartime*. London: J. M. Dent, 1944.

Higham, Charles. *Trading With the Enemy*. New York: Dell, 1983.

Hinshaw, David. *The Home Front*. New York: G. P. Putnam, 1943.

Hirschfeld, Magnus. *The Sexual History of the World War*. New York: Panurge Press, 1934.

Hodson, J. L. *The Home Front*. London: Gollancz, 1944.

Hoehling, A. A. *Home Front, U.S.A.* New York: Thomas Y. Crowell, 1966.

Holm, Jeanne. *Women in the Military — An Unfinished Revolution*. Novato, California: Presidio Press, 1982.

Hoopes, Roy. *Americans Remember the Home Front — An Oral Narrative*. New York: Hawthorn Books, 1973.

Horne, Alistair. *To Lose a Battle: France 1940*. London: Penguin, 1982.

Hovespin, Aramis. *Your Son and Mine*. New York: Duell, Sloan & Pearce, 1944.

Huie, William Bradford. *Hotel Mamie Stover*. New York: Signet, 1963.

———. *From Omaha to Okinawa — The Story of the Seabees*. New York: E. P. Dutton, 1945.

Hull, David Stewart. *Film in the Third Reich*. New York: Berkley, 1969.

Hymowitz, Carol, and Weissman, Michaele. *A History of Women in America*. New York: Bantam, 1978.

Jewell, Derek (ed.). *El Alamein and the Desert War*. London: Sphere/Sunday Times, 1967.

Jones, James. *WWII*. New York: Ballantine Books, 1975.

Jones, Peter G. *War and the Novelist*. Columbia: University of Missouri, 1976.

Joseph, S. *If Their Mothers Only Knew: An Official Account of Life in the Women's Land Army.* London: Faber, 1945.

Ka-Tzetnik 135633. *House of Dolls.* London: Granada, 1973.

Katchadourian, Herant A., and Lunde, Donald T. *Fundamentals of Human Sexuality.* New York: Holt, Rinehart and Winston, 1975.

Kee, Robert. *We'll Meet Again — Photographs of Daily Life During World War Two.* London: J. M. Dent & Sons, 1984.

Keil, Sally Van Wegegen. *Those Wonderful Women in Their Flying Machines: The Unknown Heroines of World War II.* New York: Rawson, Wade, 1979.

Kertzer, Morris N. *With an H on My Dogtag.* New York: Random House, 1947.

Kessler-Harris, Alice. *Out to Work — A History of Wage-Earning Women in the U.S.* Oxford: Oxford University Press, 1962.

Kinsey, Alfred C., et al. *Sexual Behavior in the Human Female.* Philadelphia: Saunders, 1953.

———. *Sexual Behavior in the Human Male.* Philadelphia: Saunders, 1948.

Klein, V. *Britain's Married Women Workers.* London: Routledge and Kegan Paul, 1965.

Klink, Gertrud Scholtz. *Einsatz der Frau in der Nation.* Berlin, 1937.

Lapin, Eva. *Mothers in Overalls.* New York: Workers Library, 1943.

Leed, Eric J. *No Man's Land — Combat & Identity in World War I.* Cambridge: Cambridge University Press, 1979.

Leizer, Erwin. *The Nazi Cinema.* London, 1974.

Lerner, David. *Sykewar: Psychological Warfare Against Germany.* Cambridge: M.I.T. Press, 1971.

Lewis, Norman. *Naples 1944.* London: Eland Books, 1978.

Lingeman, Richard R. *Don't You Know There's a War On.* New York: G. P. Putnam, 1965.

Lingenfelter, Mary Rebecca. *Wartime Jobs for Girls.* New York: Harcourt Brace, 1943.

London Feminist History Group. *The Sexual Dynamics of History.* London: Pluto Press, 1983.

Longmate, Norman. *The GIs — The Americans in Britain 1942–5.* London: Hutchinson, 1975.

———. *The Home Front, An Anthology.* London: Chatto & Windus, 1981.

———. *How We Lived Then: A History of Everyday Life During the Second World War.* London: Arrow, 1973.

Lynd, Robert and Helen Merrell. *Middletown in Transition — A Study in Cultural Conflicts*. New York: Harcourt Brace & World, 1937.

———. *Middletown — A Study in Modern American Culture*. New York: Harcourt Brace & World, 1929.

Lynn, Vera. *Vocal Refrain*. London: Heinemann, 1976.

MacCallum, N. *Journey with a Pistol*. London: Gollancz, 1959.

Macmillan, Richard. *Mediterranean Assignment*. New York: Doubleday, 1943.

MacNalty, A. S., and Mellor, W. F. (eds.). *Medical Services in War*. London: HMSO, 1968.

Malkin, Richard. *Marriage, Morals and War*. New York: Arden, 1943.

Manchel, Frank. *Women on the Hollywood Screen*. New York: Franklin Watts, 1977.

Manchester, William. *Goodbye, Darkness*. Boston: Little, Brown, 1980.

Marshall, S. L. A. *Men Against Fire*. Washington, D.C.: Department of the Army, 1947.

Martin, Ralph G. (ed.). *The GI War*. Boston: Little, Brown, 1967.

Marwick, Arthur. *Britain in the Century of Total War: War, Peace and Social Change, 1900–1967*. London: Macmillan, 1968.

———. *The Home Front — The British and the Second World War*. London: Thames and Hudson, 1976.

———. *War and Social Change in the Twentieth Century*. London: Macmillan, 1974.

Mass Observation Reports. *People in Production*. London: John Murray, 1942.

———. *War Factory*. London: Gollancz, 1943.

Mauldin, Bill. *Back Home*. New York: William Sloane Associates, 1947.

———. *Up Front*. New York: Bantam Books, 1983 (1945).

McCrary, John R., and Scherman, David E. *First of the Many — A Journal of Action with the Men of the Eighth Air Force*. London: Robson Books, 1984 (1944).

Mead, James M. *Tell It to the Folks Back Home*. New York: Appleton-Century, 1944.

Mead, Margaret. *And Keep Your Powder Dry*. New York: Morrow-Quill, 1942.

———. *Male and Female*. New York: William Morrow, 1967 (1949).

Melly, George. *Rum, Bum and Concertina*. London: Weidenfeld & Nicholson, 1977.

Merril, Francis E. *Social Problems on the Home Front*. New York: Harper Bros., 1947.

Meyer, Agnes E. *Journey Through Chaos*. New York: Harcourt Brace, 1944.

Miklos, Josephine von. *I Took a War Job*. New York: Simon & Schuster, 1943.

Millett, Kate. *Sexual Politics*. New York: Doubleday, 1969.

Milward, A. S. *War, Economy and Society 1939–1945*. London: Allen Lane, 1977.

Ministry of Health. *Report on the State of the Public Health During Six Years of War: Report of the Chief Medical Officer*. London: HMSO, 1946.

Minney, R. J. *I Shall Fear No Evil — The Story of Dr Alina Brewda*. London: William Kimber, 1962.

Minns, Raynes. *Bombers & Mash — The Domestic Front 1939–1945*. London: Virago, 1980.

Mitchell, Juliet. *A Woman's Estate*. New York: Pantheon Books, 1971.

Moore, John Hammond. *Over-Sexed, Over-Paid and Over Here!* Queensland: University of Queensland Press, 1981.

Morella, Joe, et al. *The Films of World War II*. Secaucus: Citadel Press, 1973.

Mosley, Leonard. *The Druid*. New York: Berkley Books, 1981.

Myles, Bruce. *The Night Witches — The Untold Story of Soviet Women in Combat*. Novato, California: Presidio Press, 1981.

Nelson, Donald M. *Arsenal of Democracy*. New York: Harcourt Brace, 1946.

New Yorker (eds.) *The* New Yorker *Book of War Pieces*. New York: Reynal & Hitchcock, 1947.

Nicholson, Jenny. *Kiss the Girls Goodbye*. London: Hutchinson, 1944.

Oechsner, Frederick, et al. *This is the Enemy*. Boston: Little, Brown, 1942.

Overseas Press Club of America. *Deadline Delayed*. New York: E. P. Dutton, 1947.

Padover, Saul K. *Psychologist in Germany — The Story of an American Intelligence Officer*. London: Phoenix House, 1946.

Page, Martin. *The Songs and Ballads of World War II*. London: Granada, 1975.

Parker, H. H. D. *Manpower — A Study of Wartime Policy and Administration*. London: HMSO, 1957.

Parliament. *Report of Parliamentary Committee on Amenities and Welfare Conditions in the Three Women's Services*. HMSO CMMD 6384, August 1942.

———. *Statistics Relating to the War Effort of the United Kingdom*. London: HMSO, 1945.

Parry, Albert. *What Women Can Do to Win the War*. Chicago: Consolidated Book Publishers, 1942.

Pawalowicz, Sala, with Klose, Kevin. *I Will Survive*. New York: W. W. Norton, 1963.

Pelling, H. *Britain and the Second World War*. London: Collins, 1970.

Pendleton, Ann (Trask, Mary Beatty). *Hit the Rivet, Sister!*. New York: Howell, Soskin Publishers, 1943.

Perrett, Geoffrey. *Days of Sadness, Years of Triumph: The American People 1939–1945*. New York: Coward, McCann & Geoghan, 1973.

Pitt, Roxane. *The Courage of Fear*. London: Jarrolds, 1958.

Plummer, Douglas. *Queer People*. London: W. H. Allen, 1963.

Polenberg, Richard. *America at War: The Home Front*. Englewood Cliffs: Prentice-Hall, 1968.

———. *War and Society: The U.S., 1941–1945*. Philadelphia: Lippincott, 1972.

Priestly, J. B. *British Women Go to War*. London: Collins, 1944.

Pruller, Wilhelm. *Diary of a German Soldier*. New York: Coward-McCann, 1966.

Rhodes, Anthony. *Propaganda: The Art of Persuasion: World War II*. New York: Chelsea House, 1976.

Richardson, Frank. *Mars Without Venus*. Edinburgh: Blackwood, 1981.

Robinson, Victor (ed.). *Morals in Wartime*. New York: Publishers Foundation, 1943.

Rogan, Helen. *Mixed Company — Women in the Modern Army*. Boston: Beacon Press, 1981.

Rosaldo, Michelle Zimbalist, and Lamphere, Louise. *Woman, Culture and Society*. Stanford: Stanford University Press, 1974.

Rosen, Marjorie. *Popcorn Venus — Women, Movies and the American Dream*. London: Peter Owen, 1975.

Rowse, A. L. *Homosexuals in History*. New York: Macmillan, 1977.

Rupp, Leila J. *Mobilizing Women for War*. Princeton: Princeton University, 1978.

Ryan, Cornelius. *The Final Battle*. New York: Simon & Schuster, 1966.

Ryan, Mary P. *Womanhood in America: From Colonial Times to the Present*. New York: New Viewpoints, 1975.

Sackville-West, V. *The Women's Land Army*. London: Michael Joseph, 1944.

Sandburg, Carl. *Home Front Memoir*. New York: Harcourt Brace, 1943.

Satterfield, Archie. *The Home Front—An Oral History*. Chicago: Playboy Press, 1976.

Scannell, Vernon (ed.). *Not Without Glory*. London: Woburn Press, 1976.

Schimanski, Stefan, and Treece, Henry (eds.). *Leaves in the Storm — A Book of Diaries*. London: Lindsay Drummond, 1947.

Schindler, Colin. *Hollywood Goes to War*. London: Routledge and Keegan Paul, 1979.

Schwarz, William J. *War and the Mind of Germany*. Frankfurt: Peter Lang, 1963.

Scott, P. *British Women in War*. London: Hutchinson, 1940.

Seidler, Franz W. *Blitzmaedschen — Die Geschichte der Helferinnen der Deutschen Wehrmacht im Zweiten Weltkrieg*. Hamburg: Wehr & Wiseen, 1968.

———. *Prostitution, Homosexualitat, Selbstverstummelung*. Neckarmund: Kurt Vowinkel, 1977.

Sherman, Allan. *The Rape of the Ape*. Chicago: Playboy Press, 1973.

Smart, Charles Allen. *The Long Watch*. Cleveland: World, 1967.

Smuts, Robert. *Women and Work in America*. New York: Columbia University Press, 1959.

Snitow, Ann (ed.). *Powers of Desire — The Politics of Sexuality*. New York: Monthly Review Press, 1983.

Snyder, Louis L. (ed.). *Masterpieces of War Reporting — Great Moments of World War II*. New York: Julian Messner, 1964.

Somerhausen, Ann. *Written in Darkness*. New York: Knopf, 1946.

St. George, Thomas R. *C/O Postmaster*. New York: Crowell, 1946.

Stearn, James (trans.). *A Woman in Berlin*. New York: Harcourt Brace.

Stein, Ralph. *The Pin-up — From 1852 to Today*. New York: Crescent Books, 1984.

Steinbeck, John. *Once There Was a War*. London: Corgi, 1961 (1943).

Stephenson, Jill. *Women in Nazi Society*. New York: Barnes & Noble, 1975.

Stouffel, Samuel A., et al. *The American Soldier*. New York: John Wiley, 1949.

———. *The American Soldier*. 2 vols. Princeton: Princeton University Press, 1949.

Straubel, James H. *Air Force Diary*. New York: Simon & Schuster, 1947.

Summerfield, Penny. *Women Workers in the Second World War*. Kent: Croom Helm, 1984.

Tannahill, Reay. *Sex in History*. New York: Stein and Day, 1982.

Taylor, Marjorie A. *The Language of World War II*. New York: H. W. Wilson, 1948.

Time-Life Books. *This Fabulous Century — 1940–1950*. New York: Time-Life Books, 1969.

———. *Time Capsule-1941-1942-1943-1944-1945*. New York: Time-Life Books, 1967–8.

Titmus, R. M. *Problems of Social Policy.* London: HMSO, 1950.

Tobias, Sheila, and Anderson, L. *What Really Happened to Rosie the Riveter? — Demobilization and the Female Labor Force.* Modular Publications, 1973.

Treadwell, Mattie. *The U.S. Army in World War II — The Women's Army Corps.* Washington, D.C.: Office of Chief of Military History, U.S. Army, 1954.

Tripp, C. A. *The Homosexual Matrix.* New York: McGraw-Hill, 1975.

U.S. Army Weekly Editors. *The Best of YANK.* New York: E. P. Dutton, 1947.

————. *YANK.* New York: Greenwich House, 1984.

U.S. War Department. *What the Soldier Thinks.* 2 vols. Princeton: Princeton University Press, 1954.

Vinde, Victor. *America at War.* London: Hutchinson, 1944.

Wahle, Anne. *Ordeal by Fire.* New York: World Publishing, 1965.

Wakeman, Frederick. *Shore Leave.* New York: Farrar & Rhinehart, 1944.

Waller, Willard. *The Veteran Comes Back.* New York: Dryden Press, 1944.

Wechter, Dixon. *When Johnny Comes Marching Home.* Westport: Greenwood Press, 1945.

Weeks, Jeffrey. *Sex, Politics and Society — The Regulation of Sexuality since 1800.* London: Longman, 1981.

Welker, Robert H. *A Different Drummer.* Boston: Beacon Press, 1958.

Wendel, Else. *Hausfrau at War: A German Woman's Account of Life in Hitler's Reich.* London: Odhams Press, 1957.

Wilder, Margaret Buell. *Since You Went Away.* New York: McGraw-Hill, 1943.

Wilkerson, Tichi, and Borie, Marcia. *The Golden Age of the Hollywood Reporter.* New York: Coward-McCann, 1984.

Williams-Ellis, Anable. *Women in War Factories.* London: Gollancz, 1946.

Wilson, E. *Only Halfway to Paradise: Women in Postwar Britain 1945–1968.* London: Travistock, 1980.

Wilson, Marion F. *The Story of Willow Run.* Ann Arbor: University of Michigan Press, 1956.

Winnick, Charles C., and Kinsie, Paul M. *The Lively Commerce — Prostitution in the United States.* Chicago: Quadrangle Books, 1971.

Woll, Allen L. *The Hollywood Musical Goes to War.* Chicago: Nelson Hall, 1983.

Wolsey, Serge J. *Call House Madam.* New York: Berkley Davis, 1955.

Wood, Leland Foster, and Mullen, John W. (eds.). *What the American Family Faces.* Chicago: Eugene Hugh Publishers, 1943.

Woodruff, W. *Vessel of Sadness*. London: Chatto & Windus, 1967.

Woolfit, Susan. *Idle Women*. London: Ernest Benn, 1947.

Young, Wayland. *Eros Denied — Sex in Western Society*. New York: Grove Press, 1964.

B. JOURNALS AND MAGAZINES

"Afraid to Love?" *Colliers* (14 Sept. 1946).

"All-Out War on Vice" *Newsweek* (29 Sept. 1941).

"Aloha JICPOA — A Songbook." Honolulu, 1941.

"Anal Military Sex." *Journal of General Psychology*, vol. 34 (Jan. 1946).

Anderson, Charles. "On Certain Conscious and Unconscious Homosexual Responses to Warfare." *British Journal of Psychiatry*, vol. 22.

"Are Morals Out of Date?" *Ladies' Home Journal*, vol. 61 (Oct. 1944).

"Army Nurses." *American Journal of Nursing*, vol. 43 (Dec. 1943).

"Australian War Brides." *Newsweek* (1 May 1944).

Berube, Alan. "Coming Out Under Fire — Lesbians and Homosexuals in World War II." *Mother Jones* (Feb.–Mar. 1983).

Beulah, Amidon. "Arms and the Woman." *Survey Graphic* (May 1942).

Boone, Joel T. "The Sexual Aspects of Military Personnel." *American Journal of Social Hygiene*, vol. 27 (Mar. 1941).

British Medical Association. "Homosexuality and Prostitution." London: British Medical Association, 1955.

"British Women at War." *Life* (4 Aug. 1941).

Bromley, Dorothy Dunbar. "Women on the Home Front." *Harper's* (July 1941).

"Brothel Girls." *Newsweek* (11 Feb. 1946).

Brotz, Howard, and Wilson, Everet. "Characteristics of Military Society." *American Journal of Sociology*, vol. 51 (Mar. 1946).

"Can We Win the War on the Home Front?" *Catholic World*, vol. 158 (Feb. 1944).

Clark, Robert A. "Aggressiveness and Military Training." *American Journal of Sociology*, vol. 51 (Mar. 1946).

Davies, Christie. "Sexual Taboos and Social Boundaries." *American Journal of Sociology*, vol. 87 (Mar. 1982).

"Does War Brutalize Men?" *Ladies' Home Journal* (Nov. 1943).

"Do Women Want to Leave the Job?" *Ladies' Home Journal* (June 1944).

"Do You Want to Win a War Job, Girls?" *McCalls* (Aug. 1943).

Elkin, Frederick. "The Soldier's Language." *American Journal of Sociology,* vol. 51 (Mar. 1946).

Elkin, Henry. "Aggressive and Erotic Tendencies in Army Life." *American Journal of Sociology,* vol. 51 (Mar. 1946).

"Extra-Marital Relations in Wartime." *American Sociology Review,* vol. 3 (June 1945).

"The Family in World War II." *Annals of the American Academy of Political and Social Science* (1942).

"Females in Factories." *Time* (17 July 1944).

"GI Babies." *Time* (4 Oct. 1943).

"GI Jane." *Newsweek* (29 Oct. 1945).

Glaser, Daniel. "The Sentiments of American Soldiers Abroad toward Europeans." *American Journal of Sociology,* vol. 51 (Mar. 1946).

Grabill, Wilson H. "Effect of the War on the Birth Rate and Postwar Fertility Prospects." *American Journal of Sociology,* vol. 50 (Jan. 1945).

"Hats Off to the Girls in the Factories." *Ladies' Home Journal* (Oct. 1942).

"He Slew the VD Dragon." *Reader's Digest* (Sept. 1946).

Hitches, Arthur Parker. "How the Army Protects Soldiers from Syphilis and Gonorrhea." *Journal of Social Hygiene,* vol. 27 (Mar. 1941).

Hoey, Jane M. "The Family in Wartime." *Family,* vol. 24 (Apr. 1943).

Hollingshead, August B. "Adjustment to Military Life." *American Journal of Sociology,* vol. 51 (Mar. 1946).

House of Commons. "Report of Committee on Amenities and Welfare Conditions in the Three Armed Services." HMSO CMMD 6384 (Aug. 1942).

"How to Shoot a Rifle." *U.S. Infantry Journal* (Mar. 1941).

"How to Torture a Returning Serviceman." *Ladies' Home Journal* (Aug. 1944).

Huppert, Thurle. "Bevin Belles." *Survey Midmonthly,* vol 78 (July 1942).

"I'm So Proud of My Wife's War Job." *McCalls* (Sept. 1943).

"Informal Social Organization in the Army." *American Journal of Sociology,* vol. 51 (Mar. 1946).

Johnson, F. Ernest. "The Impact of War on Religion in America." *American Journal of Sociology,* vol. 48 (July 1942–May 1943).

King, Beatrice. "Soviet Women at War." *Anglo-Soviet Journal* (June 1942).

Kinsie, Paul M. "The Prostitution Racket Today." *Journal of Social Hygiene*, vol. 28 (Apr. 1942).

"Life Without Father." *Ladies' Home Journal* (Mar. 1944).

Loeser, L. H. "The Sexual Psychopath in Military Service." *American Journal of Psychiatry*, vol. 102 (July 1945).

MacAffee Horton, Mildred. "Women in the United States Navy." *American Journal of Sociology*, vol. 51 (July 1945–May 1946).

McCallum, Malcolm R. "The Study of the Delinquent in the Army." *American Journal of Sociology*, vol. 51 (Mar. 1946).

McDonagh, Edward. "The Discharged Serviceman and His Family." *American Journal of Sociology*, vol. 51 (Mar. 1946).

McDonagh, Edward and Louise. "War Anxieties of Soldiers and Their Wives." *Social Forces*, vol. 24 (Oct. 1945–May 1946).

"The Making of the Infantryman." *American Journal of Sociology*, vol. 51 (Mar. 1946).

"Marriages at War." *Ladies' Home Journal* (Mar. 1942).

"May Act Emergency." *Survey Midmonthly*, vol. 79 (Mar. 1943).

Menninger, William C. "Psychiatry and the War." *Atlantic Monthly* (Nov. 1945).

"Now It's Woman's Work." *Ladies' Home Journal* (May 1942).

"Nurses at Anzio." *American Journal of Nursing*, vol. 44 (Apr. 1944).

"The Nurses' Contribution to American Victory." *American Journal of Nursing*, vol. 45 (Sept. 1945).

Parker, Dorothy. "Are We Women or Are We Mice?" *Reader's Digest* (July 1943).

Pearce, J. D. W. "Problems of Sex in the Services." *The Practitioner*, vol. 172 (Apr. 1954).

Pozner, Harry. "Sexual Disorders and Misconduct in Service Males." *Journal of the Royal Army Medical Corps*, vol. 103 (Apr. 1957).

"Promiscuity and VD." *Ladies' Home Journal* (Aug. 1945).

"Prostitutes in India." *Newsweek* (11 Sept. 1944).

"Psychology of the Fighting Man." *U.S. Infantry Journal* (Jan.–May 1945).

Ratcliffe, T. A. "Psychiatric and Allied Aspects of the Problem of Venereal Disease in the Army." *Journal of the Royal Army Medical Corps*, vol. 93 (1947).

"Redlight for Redlights." *Time* (27 Apr. 1942).

"Report to Mother." *Time* (4 Oct. 1943).

Roosevelt, Eleanor. "American Women in the War." *Reader's Digest* (Jan. 1944).

————. "Defense and Girls." *Ladies' Home Journal* (May 1941).

Rose, Arnold. "The Social Structure of the Army." *American Journal of Sociology*, vol. 51 (Mar. 1946).

"Sex Is a Nazi Weapon." *Reader's Digest* (Oct. 1942).

"Sexual Behavior of Adolescents in World War II." *Annals of the American Academy of Political and Social Sciences*, 1942.

"The Sexual Psychopath and the Military." *American Journal of Psychiatry*, vol. 102 (July 1945).

"Society and Total War." *American Social Review*, vol. 8 (Oct. 1943).

Stephenson, C. S. "Venereal Disease Education in the U.S. Navy." *Journal of Social Hygiene*, vol. 28 (Feb. 1942).

"Trouble on Street Corners." *Reader's Digest* (May 1943).

"VD from Anonymous Amateurs." *Time* (29 Mar. 1943).

"VD Balance Sheet." *Time* (6 Sept. 1946).

"VD in London." *Newsweek* (14 June 1944).

"Victory Girls." *Newsweek* (6 Mar. 1944).

Wanger, Walter. "The Role of Movies in Morale." *American Journal of Sociology*, vol. 47 (July 1941–May 1942).

"The Wartime Delinquent in the United Kingdom." National Probational Association of New York, vol. 96 (1943).

"War Widow." *Ladies' Home Journal* (Jan. 1945).

"What Is Your Dream Girl Like?" *Ladies' Home Journal* (Mar. 1942).

Weatherly, Eugene T. "Local Control of Prostitution in Wartime." *Journal of Social Hygiene*, vol. 28 (Aug. 1942).

Weinberg, S. Kirkson. "The Combat Neuroses." *American Journal of Sociology*, vol. 51 (Mar. 1946).

"When the Boys Get Home." *Time* (6 Sept. 1942).

"Will GI Joe Be Changed?" *Ladies' Home Journal* (Jan. 1945).

Whyte, William Foote. "A Slum Sex Code." *American Journal of Sociology*, vol. 49 (July 1943–May 1944).

Williams, D. "The Gunner Girls." *The Spectator* (24 Apr. 1942).

"Woman's Responsibility." *Reader's Digest* (July 1942).

"A Woman's Work Is Never Done." *New Statesman* (Sept. 1941).

"Women and Army Morale." *Ladies' Home Journal* (Sept. 1941).

"Women at War." *Life* (5 June 1944).

"Women at War" Series. *Picture Post* (1942–1943).

"Women in Dangerous Service." *New Statesman* (6 July 1942).

"Women in Industry." *New Statesman* (13 Dec. 1941).

"Women War Workers." *Life* (4 Jan. 1943).

"The World Will Belong to the Women." *New York Times Magazine* (14 Mar. 1943).

"Yoshiwara Destroyed." *Time* (4 Feb. 1946).

B & To
18